T0355727

Teaching about Religions

# Teaching about Religions

## A DEMOCRATIC APPROACH
## FOR PUBLIC SCHOOLS

*Emile Lester*

THE UNIVERSITY OF MICHIGAN PRESS

ANN ARBOR

First paperback edition 2013
Copyright © by the University of Michigan 2011
All rights reserved

Published in the United States of America by
The University of Michigan Press
Printed and bound by CPI Group (UK) Ltd, Croydon, CR0 4YY


2016   2015   2014   2013     5   4   3   2

*A CIP catalog record for this book is available from the British Library.*

Library of Congress Cataloging-in-Publication Data

Lester, Emile.
    Teaching about religions : a democratic approach for public
schools / Emile Lester.
        p.      cm.
    Includes bibliographical references (p.      ) and index.
    ISBN 978-0-472-11764-2 (cloth : alk. paper) —
    ISBN 978-0-472-02674-6 (ebook)
    1. Religions—Study and teaching—United States.   2. Religion in
the public schools—United States.   I. Title.
    BL41.L47     2011
    200.71'073—dc22                                      2010047500


ISBN 978-0-472-03526-7 (pbk. : alk. paper)

*To my wife, Kelly, with love*

# Contents

# Acknowledgments

In more ways than one, the Modesto City School District made this book possible. The incredible dedication, diligence, and hard work that Modesto's school administrators, teachers, and community leaders showed in enacting a world religions course encouraged a dedication on my part to record their triumph.

My debt to Modesto teachers Connie Hernandez, Mary Kappas, Sherry McIntyre, Curtis Speltz, Amado Meraz, Mike Johnson, and Eddie Godinez is also more specific and practical. They helped administer the surveys, encouraged students to take them seriously, ensured they were returned, and engaged in the often Sisyphean task of securing permission forms from students. Teachers and administrators frankly shared their insights about the course with me and recommended questions to include on the survey. How they managed to do all this amid their demanding schedules is a constant source of wonder to me. Given the great debt I owe to the goodwill and altruism of each and every teacher, I am hesitant to further single out any teachers in particular. Still, I would be remiss if I did not express a special sense of gratitude for the efforts of Yvonne Taylor and Jonathan Couchman.

Modesto administrators Linda Erickson and Jenny Sweeney helped to coordinate my schedule of school visits and student interviews, and I am grateful to James Enochs for granting me permission to conduct my research and for providing his insights on Modesto's course. School board members Gary Lopez, Cindy Marks, and Connie Chin helped me understand the course's origins.

While teachers and administrators enabled my understanding of the world religions course and its origins, religious leaders and community members provided crucial details about Modesto's religious landscape. I am grateful for the information and insights provided by Ida Bowers, Sam

Oppenheim, Father John Magoulias, Father Joseph Illo, Parmanand Tiwari, Mohammed Said, Pastor Russ Matteson, Pastor Wendy Warner, Pastor Paul Zeek, Rabbi Paul Gordon, and Amy White.

I owe numerous debts, both large and small, to Charles Haynes. His pioneering work on religion and public schools provides a model of socially engaged scholarship. His altruism, almost legendary among many who work on First Amendment issues, continues to astonish me. I am grateful to him and the First Amendment Center for, among other things, helping Patrick Roberts and me secure permission to conduct research in Modesto, putting me in touch with numerous invaluable contacts in the religion and education field, and helping to spread awareness of the research results. One of Charles's great contributions to the religion and education field is to have helped create a civil space where those with different views can deliberate and, more than occasionally, find common ground. The views of this book may often depart from Charles's own views, but I hope they provide a contribution to the discussion he helped conceive. Two other pioneers in the religion and education field, Marcia Beauchamp and Jim Antenore, were frequent sources of insight.

Fellow academics, including George Klosko, Colin Bird, Jim Dwyer, Paul Manna, Erik Owens, and Charles Mathewes, reviewed various sections of the manuscript and provided essential advice and insights. The manuscript benefited as well from the comments of the anonymous reviewers for the University of Michigan Press.

Melody Herr, my editor at University of Michigan Press, provided vital guidance and encouragement that helped me frame and summarize my arguments in a concise and direct manner, and she made sure that the political theorist in me did not get carried away too often into the realm of abstraction. Student assistants Paul Tindall and Jeanne McDonnell helped with major and minor research tasks, proofread the manuscript, and provided advice suggesting an intellectual sophistication far beyond their years.

I have saved the largest debts for last. When I initially sought a research partner for Modesto's course, I was hoping to find a skilled numbers cruncher and an expert in the methodology of political science research. In Patrick Roberts, I was extremely fortunate to find someone who possessed these qualities and much more. Patrick possesses an enviable intellectual breadth matched by an engaging prose style. He provided astute advice on empirical and theoretical political matters alike and pushed me to become a better writer. I will let readers judge the content and style of this book, but I urge them to remember that both would be much worse without Patrick's advice.

Finally, my wife, Kelly, is the most amazing person I know. Her love and support make the good days great and the bad days bearable. I have a tendency to spend too much time wandering in the clouds. Kelly helps keep me grounded and focused on what I have to do today, while my son, Elijah, inspires dreams of a better tomorrow.

Some of the material in this book appeared in "World Religions in Modesto: Findings from a Curricular Innovation," *Religion and Education* 35 (2002), and in the following works coauthored by Patrick Roberts: "How Teaching World Religions Brought a Truce to the Culture Wars in Modesto California," *British Journal of Religious Education* 31 (2009); "Talking about God in Modesto," *American Interest* 3 (May–June 2008); "The Distinctive Paradox of Religious Tolerance: Active Tolerance as a Mean Between Passive Tolerance and Recognition," *Public Affairs Quarterly* 20 (2006); and *Learning about World Religions in Public Schools: The Impact on Student Attitudes and Community Acceptance in Modesto, Calif.* (Nashville, TN: First Amendment Center, 2006). I am deeply grateful to the editors and publishers of the journals and the First Amendment Center for their permission to reprint material from these works.

# *Introduction*

Over four years had passed since the Hindu temple where he worshiped had been the victim of vandalism, but Parmanand Tiwari, a respected leader in the Hindu community in Modesto, California, vividly recalled the details of the event in our phone conversation. In the days and months following 9/11, any hint of foreignness turned out to be a liability for many religious minorities around the country. Vandals in Modesto—a city that residents describe routinely as part of the California Bible Belt but that is also home to a large and growing number of immigrants belonging to many faiths—took little time to consider the differences between Muslims and Hindus as they inflicted significant property damage on the temple.

My own trip to Modesto's Hindu temple took me from my hotel at the city's center past ever more remote subdivisions to an exurban fringe where residences blend into farmland. A dairy farm's silos cast shadows nearly reaching across the street to the temple's entrance. The temple's location struck me as a metaphor for the community's cultural standing on the edge of the mainstream. But if the temple's location was an attempt to avoid attention, the desire for an oasis was not successful on the day of my visit. On the grass right outside of the temple's decorated iron gates lay a grotesque sacrifice to America's worse angels. A dead baby calf held a placard between its hoofs containing a derogatory crack too moronic and despicable to bear repetition. The culprits apparently understood just enough about Hinduism to realize that desecrating a cow would cause particular offense.

The religion reporter for Modesto's daily newspaper, Amy White, had assured me previously that acts of overt religious discrimination in Modesto were relatively rare, and this accorded with what I heard from other sources. But I was also uncomfortable chalking up the dead baby calf on the very day of my visit to simple coincidence. Were Modesto's religious minorities wary about reporting all acts of vandalism to the media because this would only attract more attention and make them the fodder for additional attacks? Even if vandalism was indeed rare, Amy also reminded me of the more hidden costs of intolerance. Because they were wary of visibility, Hindu, Muslim, and Sikh leaders had shunned a public role in a 9/11 memorial event intended in part as a show of solidarity between faiths. The social science tools at my disposal could not measure fully the passing comments and looks that made Modesto's Hindus, Sikhs, Muslims, Buddhists, Jews, and yet more religious minorities feel less than full members of their own community.

But when I returned to my hotel room the night of my visit to the Hindu temple, I also thought about my good friend Jerry. In my first year as a college professor at the College of William and Mary, I offered a seminar entitled "Religion and American Democracy." My views at the time were strongly secularist, and the course's approach emphasized the importance of neutrality in a democratic education. Recognition of sectarian beliefs, such as teaching about intelligent design, had no place in the public school curriculum, I argued, because it would violate the rights of secularists and vulnerable religious minorities.

Jerry was a student in that class. He had been an army chaplain for over 20 years and liked to refer to himself as a "fundie." In our class conversations, he not only challenged my position on specific church-state policies but objected to the neutrality approach I emphasized. An attempt to create a public school curriculum excluding all discussion of sectarian beliefs, he argued, would only succeed in creating a bland curriculum. Despite its alleged neutrality, it would be unfair to those who held robust beliefs related to religion and central to their belief systems, like those on human origins. Many conservative Christians like himself felt they had adapted their beliefs to satisfy democratic norms but still could not get a fair hearing from major public institutions like schools. The other 14 students in the seminar—none from conservative Christian backgrounds—were often persuaded by Jerry's arguments, which were presented invariably in a gracious manner.

At the course's conclusion, Jerry and I continued our discussions over coffee almost every month. I learned more about his beliefs and came to know Jerry's family. His pleas on behalf of teaching intelligent design were civil yet impassioned. He was genuinely anxious not only about the moral and religious implications of the evolution-only curriculum his children learned in public schools but that they were not being taught the scientific truth. He spent hours going over the science textbooks his children studied and discussing flaws in Darwin's argument with them.

Public schools should serve two crucial democratic functions when it comes to religion. To ensure a more inclusive American democracy in the future, they should teach students that a robust respect for religious free-dom involves the right of all believers—especially those newest to Amer-ica's religious landscape—not only to practice their beliefs but to express their religious identities, views, and values in public without inhibition. But the public school curriculum—what it includes and what it lacks—also sends a potent symbolic message to communities in the present. Public schools send a powerful democratic message when the curriculum models full inclusion and when they provide each group with a sense of ownership over the curriculum. But they fail to be truly public when any significant group feels its values and views are simply ignored.

Public schools, to be sure, are not solely or primarily responsible for the feelings of religious exclusion many Americans feel. Still, they are in a unique position to address them. At a time when Americans of different re-ligious, ethnic, and ideological backgrounds increasingly live apart (Bishop 2008) and get their news from different and polarized sources (Sunstein 2007), public schools are one of the few remaining places where Americans from different backgrounds gather together and learn about views other than their own. Implementing the right type of public education about re-ligion can promote more democratic behavior toward religion among fu-ture citizens and can send a powerful symbolic message about democratic inclusion to people of all different faiths and none. *To be fully inclusive of re-ligion, American public schools should promote robust tolerance for those of all faiths and none, and provide a special recognition of conservative Christian beliefs. Schools must encourage consensus about the civil rights of each and every per-spective about religion and allow ample room for faiths to express their conflicts about politics and eternal salvation.*

But the preceding stories highlight that public schools are currently meeting neither of these goals. The trepidation Muslims and Hindus felt about participating in Modesto's 9/11 memorial is hardly compatible with the right to robust religious free expression for all. Public schools have expanded their treatment of religion and minority religions over the last quarter century. Still, this treatment is too cursory and unalloyed with the promotion of religious liberty to ensure a flourishing respect for it at a time when religious diversity is expanding. The exclusion Parmanand Tiwari and members of religious minorities like him feel did not begin in public schools, but public schools have done precious little to combat it. The beliefs of conservative Christians like Jerry may differ greatly from those of Parmanand Tiwari, but the sense of exclusion from the mainstream is similar. The symbolic message that public schools send conservative Christians by ignoring their views is an important cause of this exclusion.

## THE TRIUMPH OF THE EXTREMISTS

Perhaps challenging public schools to help America fulfill its democratic commitments to religious liberty is asking too much. Many Americans—more crucially, most public school administrators and teachers—believe that accommodating religious minorities and conservative Christians at the same time would be too controversial or impossible practically. Several years ago, I asked an adviser on social studies curriculum in the Richmond, Virginia, area if his public school district would consider adding world religion or Bible courses to the elective curriculum. "Why would we want to trouble with all that?" he responded. To him and those who share his views, stories like Parmanand Tiwari's and Jerry's are less causes for action than reasons for inaction, as they suggest what appear to be the deep gulfs dividing Americans about what religious freedom and inclusion mean.

To be fair, holding this belief is quite reasonable. A mainstream media increasingly fractured along partisan lines and religiously based interest groups on the right and left revel in stories of religious and cultural conflict. Civil conversations between moderates attract few readers and viewers, but controversies generate advertising revenue. Groups such as the Family Research Council and People for the American Way can drum up greater financial contributions by convincing members that their core values are under siege.

Synergy between these two forces often results in perfect media storms. Not only do the media focus on the most sensational stories, but they invite the most partisan and polarizing voices to comment on these stories. Shouting among extremists, after all, produces better ratings than civil conversations between moderates. The most prominent headlines in recent years about religion and schools have focused on controversies and the most strident views on these controversies. Teaching about evolution and its alternatives has sparked controversy in Kansas; Texas; Dover, Pennsylvania; and Lebec, California. A challenge to the recitation of the phrase "under God" in the Pledge of Allegiance provoked a firestorm nationally and in California. Residents of Odessa, Texas, battled over the teaching of a controversial elective course on the Bible. Meanwhile, moderate voices and civil cease-fires are ignored. Our best may not lack conviction, but they too often lack the access extremists have.

Public schools, this narrative of conflict tells us, must choose between accommodating secularists[1] and non-Christian minorities who want greater tolerance or accommodating conservative Christians who want special recognition of their beliefs, because these groups are implacable foes. In fact, what this narrative really does is convince schools to accommodate neither, because a robust teaching about religion in any form would only deepen our cultural divide. Like the Richmond social studies adviser I interviewed, school administrators are understandably reluctant to bring controversy on themselves.

To those fed a constant diet of stories about controversies, this book's central claim that a fully democratic and inclusive public education about religion could heal our divisions over religion may come off as almost laughably naive. Democratic inclusion of religion in schools may appear a worthy goal, but it does not fit with the facts on the ground. Schools, according to this view, can teach either consensus around robust tolerance for civil rights or conflicts about politics and salvation, but they cannot do both. The American experiment may prove that Jean-Jacques Rousseau (1987, 220) was wrong to conclude that "it is impossible" for a believer "to live in peace with those one believes to be damned." But given America's division over religion, it is impossible to *teach* students to live in peace with everyone and that some believe others are damned. The current inadequate treatment of religion may be neither fully democratic nor as neutral as alleged, but it is the least of all evils.

But is this dire story right, or is this a case where blaming the messenger—the mainstream media—is actually fair? To see if schools can fulfill the democratic mission this book charges them with, we must return to the stories of Parmanand Tiwari, Jerry, and Modesto and see if they contradict the lessons about our religious disputes that are proclaimed so insistently by the mainstream media and the culture warriors who comprise its frequent collaborators.

## DEFYING THE CONVENTIONAL WISDOM

Parmanand Tiwari's and Jerry's stories could, to be sure, provide rich fuel for the familiar narrative of religious conflict. The Hindu temple's vandals in 2001 were never identified. The vandals could have been motivated by religious extremism or could simply have been mindless miscreants engaged in a thoroughly despicable prank. Still, some secularists have not been shy about blaming instances of vandalism like this on extremists of the religious right who preach hate. Meanwhile, the religious right has used stories like Jerry's to rail against allegedly godless public schools dominated by secular humanists.

If I had held the same views as I did when I first started teaching the "Religion and American Democracy" seminar, I would probably have drawn these conclusions. But the second time I taught the seminar, I invited Charles Haynes, a senior scholar at the First Amendment Center in Washington, D.C., to speak to my students. Charles has spent almost a quarter century defying the conventional wisdom by working in the trenches of our religious and cultural conflicts to achieve fair and reasonable cease-fires. Aided by First Amendment legal expert and Baptist minister Oliver Thomas, Charles has mediated disputes in some of the most divided communities about some of the most culturally and religiously divisive issues.[2] He works from the faith that for all their disagreement, most Americans share a connection to America's democratic ideals and will realize this when they talk to, rather than past, each other. Charles admits freely that some of his reconciliation efforts have fallen short of their goals and that his pleas for common ground and common sense occasionally fall on deaf ears. But he has also defied conventional wisdom about public schools by successfully mediating school district disputes and enacting consensus policies in states like Utah and Alabama. Inspired by Charles's example of locating common ground, my discussions with Parmanand Tiwari and Jerry and my investigation of the religious climate in Modesto looked beyond their potential value as fodder for a culture war. This approach yielded a more complex and hopeful portrait than the media's narrative of religious conflict allows.

After relating the details of the 2001 vandalism, for instance, Tiwari proceeded to tell me about how the Modesto community responded. Newspaper reports of vandalism were followed by numerous letters to the temple expressing regret about the incident and friendship for Hindus in Modesto. Many letters included cash and checks to help repair the damage. Tiwari concluded our phone conversation by telling me how the community's response reminded him why America "can be a great country."

Jerry may have stressed to his children what he believed their textbooks missed about evolution, but he has never contemplated removing his children from public schools. He draws a sharp line between teaching about intelligent design and the teaching of literal biblical creationism, which he deems too sectarian for discussion in the public school curriculum. He believes that a world religions course teaching respect for other faiths would be a welcome addition to the public school curriculum.

Unlike the strong-voiced extremists who have quit on common institutions and exploit controversies—often manufactured—to encourage others to do the same, Parmanand Tiwari and Jerry represent the less prominent majority of Americans who combine strong religious beliefs with an equally strong commitment to basic democratic values. Despite their struggles, Parmanand Tiwari and Jerry were not driven by bitterness into the arms of radicalism or separatism. Neither had lost hope in the promise of American democracy. Both shared a faith in public schools. This faith was not a blind trust in the status quo but a hope for things not yet seen.

To be sure, the differences in their preferred policies are significant and should not be overlooked. Tiwari, like many members of non-Christian minorities, wants a curriculum favoring robust tolerance, while conservative Christians like Jerry favor some form of special recognition of their beliefs. But there is a common strand even in their apparent differences. Both Parmanand Tiwari and Jerry are united by a sense that they do not enjoy full participation and respect in the American center and that their faiths are the victims of misunderstanding. They believe that current school policies reflect this exclusion and misinterpretation.

If Parmanand Tiwari's and Jerry's stories suggest that the conventional wisdom about Americans' differences over religion is often wrong when it comes to individuals, the story of Modesto teaches the same lesson about communities. In the late 1990s, religious divisions in Modesto produced controversy about an attempt to promote respect for homosexuality in Modesto's public schools. Out of this conflict and in part through Charles's mediation, however, grew a consensus about the need for schools to ensure the religious liberty of all students. In 2000, Modesto became the first public school district in the nation to require all high school students to take an extended and independent course in world religions. Research that Patrick Roberts and I conducted about the course shows that it brought students from diverse religious backgrounds closer together. The course may not have prevented the vandalism that Tiwari described or I witnessed, but the research suggests that similar incidents are likely to be rarer in the future.

Even more remarkable is that the course's implementation received support from all of Modesto's religious communities. Tiwari described the course as a "wonderful idea," and the pastor of a major evangelical megachurch told me he was pleased his daughter would be taking the course and learning respect for other religious traditions. Just as crucially, Modesto's diverse communities largely agreed on the need to teach consensus and conflict. Modesto's conservatives may have stressed recognition of religion and religious differences in schools more, but liberals thought it was a good idea, too. Liberals may have wanted tolerance more, but conservatives valued civil rights and student safety. The course has not been the subject of a single lawsuit or significant opposition from the community.

## TEACHING CONSENSUS AND CONFLICT

By portraying conservative Christians, secularists, and religious minorities as implacable foes, the conventional narrative about our religious differences has conditioned Americans to think of curriculum disputes as a zero-sum game. For religious minorities and secularists to win, conservative Christians must lose, and vice versa. Increased tolerance for religious minorities cannot coexist with a special recognition of sectarian beliefs, such as a curricular discussion of intelligent design. Teaching both consensus about tolerance and conflict about contentious political issues and salvation is a contradiction in terms.

This narrative, to be sure, is not pure illusion spun out of thin air. It may be full of sound and fury, but it signifies something. The division of Americans into religious conservatives, on the one hand, and secularists and religious minorities, on the other, does have some justification. The differences between these groups produce genuine and occasionally deep disagreements over the proper role of religion in politics and the place for religion in the public square.

But the stories of Modesto, the vandalism at its Hindu temple, and Jerry refute the excessive pessimism of the conventional wisdom by demonstrating that democratic commitments can coexist alongside strong sectarian beliefs. These stories are far from unique. For instance, the most in-depth and nuanced research available on the political beliefs of evangelical Christians—such as Christian Smith's national survey (2000) and Alan Wolfe's interviews (2003)—shows that most evangelicals have a solid commitment to democratic values of fairness and tolerance. Although they may have different priorities concerning the public school curriculum, religious minorities and conservative Christians are far from inevitable enemies.

If these groups are not inevitable enemies, the public school curriculum need not be a zero-sum game.[3] The commitment to civility by most on both sides of our religious divide and shared beliefs—an alienation from the current public school curriculum, yet a continued commitment to the ideal of fair public schools—are resources that public schools can draw on to accommodate the interests of both sides *at the same time.* The acceptance of Modesto's world religion course—by religious minorities because it promotes robust tolerance and by conservative Christians because it recognizes religion—provides crucial confirmation that the school curriculum can be a positive-sum game. It also inspires this book's contention that the adoption of required world religions courses at the high school level must be at the center of a democratic education about religion.[4]

But schools should not stop there. Many Americans assume that world religions courses accommodate some conservative Christian interests, but their inevitable bias toward relativism, syncretism, and ecumenism is inimical to conservative Christian views about the mutual exclusivity of religious truth claims. The rights to disagree with other religions and even to believe that other believers will suffer damnation are critical to religious freedom, and even the least intrusive of world religion courses imperil these rights. Recognizing this crucial but commonly ignored truth is necessary for reconciling the teaching of consensus and conflict in theory. Many Americans assume that teaching religious tolerance is synonymous with teaching religious liberty, implying that the teaching of conflict and conservative Christian views teaches the opposite of liberty. But expressing profound disagreement with other religions when accompanied by a respect for religious civil rights is not a species of religious tyranny but an essential part of religious liberty. *To teach religious consensus and conflict is not to teach liberty and its opposite but to teach the two sides of the same religious liberty coin.* A truly inclusive education about religion must balance required world religion courses with carefully constructed and balanced elective courses on intelligent design and the Bible that involve special recognition of crucial conservative Christian beliefs.

Reconciling the teaching of conflict and consensus in theory is, of course, not the same as reconciling them in practice. The interests and hopes they share does not, of course, mean that conservative Christians will ever support world religions courses as strongly as non-Christian minorities do or that non-Christian minorities will ever support an elective course concerning intelligent design as strongly as conservative Christians do. But realizing that both approaches are based on a shared desire for greater inclusion in the American center, religious minorities can and should accept elective courses involving special recognition of Christian beliefs as long as these courses are sufficiently balanced, and conservative Christians can and should accept required world religions course as long as they do not impose ecumenism. Even if they do not back each part of the package with equal devotion, they can realize that a curriculum devoted to both robust tolerance and special recognition, to teaching both consensus and conflict, is just overall.

Transforming the school curriculum might do more than lead all sides in our religious divide to merely acknowledge the legitimacy of each others' concerns. The current view of curricular attention as a scarce resource that the sides in our religious divide must compete for engenders ill will and hostility. But when both sides are secure that victory by others does not imply their own loss, generosity is likely to triumph over hostility. Once conservative Christians realize that tolerance of religious minorities does not mean they must abandon their own religious commitments or their rightful place in the curriculum, they are more likely to extend respect toward religious minorities and the nonreligious, as conservative Christians in Modesto did. Having their more moderate concerns met, they are likely to forgo more extreme, divisive, and illegitimate demands for teaching conflict, like discussions of intelligent design in the required curriculum. The best research on evangelical views suggests that giving evangelicals a half mile will not inspire the taking of a mile but, rather, the giving of a half mile in return.

As these points suggest, the benefits of transforming education about religion into a positive-sum game are likely to extend beyond schoolhouse doors and have a large effect on the health of American democracy. The current failure of public schools to provide an inclusive education about religion empowers extremists. Right-wing extremists, for instance, seize on the exclusion of conservative Christian concerns as evidence of a secular humanist conspiracy and to recruit many with otherwise moderate dispositions and beliefs into their ranks. By exploiting this exclusion to call for the introduction of unabashedly sectarian, divisive, and impractical changes to the school curriculum, however, they only ensure that no action is taken. So the cycle goes. The laws of physics may dictate that perpetual motion machines are impossible, but our conflicts over religion seem to constitute an unfortunate exception.

Public schools are in a unique position to reverse this vicious cycle and empower the civil majorities on all sides of our religious divide against the extremists who currently dominate. By providing reasonable accommodation of conservative Christians in the public school curriculum, schools can rid right-wing extremists of their talking points and expose as dangerous nonsense the claim that the public school curriculum reflects a secular humanist plot against religion. By stressing robust tolerance for those of minority faiths and no faith at all, they can help prevent alienation and inspire inclusion of all views about religion. But this is not the only benefit to secularists and the nonreligious of the curricular changes this book recommends. Secularists and the nonreligious are concerned rightly about the proliferation of sectarian arguments in political discourse. By discouraging the use of purely sectarian arguments and encouraging secularists to take seriously the more moderate and nonsectarian claims that believers use in

political discourse, the democratic education about religion this book recommends can produce a more inclusive and democratic dialogue about
politics. By doing so, schools can help to create a more consensual politics
even as they provide ample room for political conflict related to religion.

Making the treatment of religion more democratic will establish public
schools as crucial and unique public institutions that recognize diverse beliefs and believers rather than largely ignoring diversity out of fear of controversy, as public schools currently do. On a more far-reaching and symbolic level, public schools that are more democratic can play a crucial role
in ensuring the triumph of civility and moderation over the manufactured
prominence of rigid ideologues and extremists. The goal of these changes is
not to preclude conflict or impose uniformity. Religious diversity and differences over values related to religion are crucial for a robust democratic
discourse. But democratic discourse also suffers when uncivil views are exaggerated, especially when more measured views are more widely held. It
is time for schools to hinder, rather than help, this exaggeration.

Given the prominence of extremist voices, this book understands the
powerful resistance that transforming public school curriculum concerning
religion is likely to meet. Moreover, for all they share, the consensus among
moderates on all sides is more inchoate than realized. Shared principles
must be made more elaborate and concrete. Specific, carefully constructed
and nuanced policies must be developed that demonstrate to secularists,
religious minorities, and conservative Christians how their central concerns will be met in practice.

As vital as humility is to the approach this book takes, Parmanand Tiwari's and Jerry's stories, Modesto's example, and the frequent successes of
Charles Haynes's reconciliation efforts suggest that leavening caution with
hope is not utopian and that history need not be destiny. More crucially,
given the way American society and schools currently fail to honor religious liberty, America's core democratic commitments demand that
schools try to honor the wary faith most Americans have in them. This
book is thus dedicated to vulnerable religious minorities like Parmanand
Tiwari who hold out hope in the ultimate inclusiveness of America, conservative Christians like Jerry who plea for the inclusion of those with robust and often countercultural beliefs, and mediators like Charles who are
striving to create public schools that are truly public and where Americans
of all religious backgrounds and none feel included. They have not quit on

the American dream of full inclusion for all religions, and public schools should not continue to quit on them.

## WHAT POLITICAL SCIENCE AND PHILOSOPHY HAVE TO OFFER

A number of distinguished and valuable works on religion and public education have been published over the last 15 years. Although none make the distinctive claim that public schools should both teach tolerance and provide special recognition of conservative Christian beliefs, several of these works have addressed the civic benefits of a more robust teaching about religion. This book is an attempt to build on the work of these eminent scholars.[5] Its aim is less to oppose than to supplement, by bringing the resources of political science to bear on an already flourishing discussion.

For all their considerable virtues, there are two crucial oversights in previous works on religion and public schools. First, the literature lacks a robust elaboration and defense of the democratic ideals public schools should be serving when they teach about religion. Without such a discussion, we cannot appreciate the central role that teaching about religion in the right way can play in bringing America closer to fulfilling its central democratic commitments. But public schools will also fall short of fulfilling their democratic commitments if implementing policies consistent with them is deemed impractical. Second, the literature lacks robust empirical evidence suggesting that the major groups in our cultural conflicts might accept curricular reforms regarding religion.[6] Without such evidence, the conventional wisdom that greater discussion of religion will breed controversy will continue to prevail. This book aims to address both oversights.[7]

The first two chapters use the resources of political philosophy to identify two guiding democratic principles for treating religion in democratic public schools. They spell out the terms of consensus that Americans should and often do share about the proper treatment of religion by public institutions. Chapter 1 focuses on the model of tolerance appropriate for religion in democratic societies and ours in particular. The model of tolerance proposed—active tolerance—is a mean between the two models of tolerance prevalent in the political science literature: passive tolerance and tolerance as recognition. Unlike passive tolerance, active tolerance stresses that citizens have an obligation to take positive action to make religious minorities feel included in American society in public and semipublic arenas. Active tolerance, however, is careful to avoid encouraging citizens to explore the objective validity of other religions. Its aim is to enhance respect for the civil status of religious minorities rather than to increase appreciation for these minorities' beliefs themselves.

While chapter 1 addresses the accommodation of vulnerable religious minorities, chapter 2 focuses on the disputes over religion in the public square that are at the heart of the conflict between secularists and conservative Christians. The increasing tendency of many evangelicals to eschew purely sectarian arguments makes possible a reasonable accommodation of secularist and conservative Christian views on religion and politics. Central to this compromise, chapter 2 proposes, is the principle of good faith. Good faith requires that when religious believers make a sincere and substantial effort to balance sectarian claims with secular logical and empirical claims, other citizens have an obligation to take these arguments at face value and engage with them. Good faith, unlike secularism, does not require religious believers to check their beliefs at the door to democratic politics. But it also reminds believers that participants in American politics act more democratically when they strive to present more universally appealing arguments for their positions.

While the first two chapters identify the democratic principles that should guide curricular treatment of religion, the next three focus on implementing them in practice. Chapter 3 draws on the original research Patrick Roberts and I conducted on Modesto's required world religions course—the first large-scale empirical examination of a course about religion in American public schools—to argue that all school districts around the nation should implement similar required world religions courses. Our surveys and interviews found that Modesto's course significantly increased students' knowledge about religion and passive and active tolerance toward religion and that it even exceeded our expectations by encouraging greater respect for First Amendment rights in general. Confirming chapter 1's claim that democracies can promote robust tolerance without illegitimately imposing acceptance of other religions' truth claims, students who began the course with strong religious beliefs generally retained their strong beliefs even as their religious tolerance increased.

Of all the controversies surrounding religion and public schools in recent years, the one over teaching about evolution and intelligent design (ID) has been the most intense. While many secularist critics have argued that ID has no place in the school curriculum at all, chapter 4 argues that such critics overlook both the sincerity of many conservative Christians' beliefs in ID and the fact that many conservative Christians have made a good-faith transition from advocating the teaching of literal creationism to the more nonsectarian ID. ID is still sectarian enough that examining it in required biology courses would violate active tolerance. But public schools have an obligation to reciprocate conservative Christian good faith by offering a one-semester elective course that takes ID seriously as a scientific theory, as long as the course also includes critiques of ID as a scientific theory and examines ways in which Darwinian science and religion might be reconciled.

Elective Bible courses have experienced something of a renaissance in recent years, and Stephen Prothero (2007) has argued for implementing required Bible courses to improve biblical literacy. While his argument is elegant and eloquent, chapter 5 in the present study claims not only that a required course would send an alienating message to religious minorities but that the aim of Prothero's Bible course makes it unsuitable for the elective curriculum as well. Prothero's goal of having schools provide incontrovertible facts about the Bible may appear neutral in theory but is likely to prove unfriendly in practice to unpopular and countercultural beliefs, including those of conservative Christians. Chapter 5 instead advocates a one-semester elective course focusing on different faith commitments and views of the Bible and on the moral dimensions of conflicting Jewish and Christian beliefs in America today. Instead of viewing robust religious disagreements as a civic problem, the course's intent is to recognize that, more often than not, these disagreements benefit democracy by making room for countercultural beliefs that just might be prophetic.

As this book's conclusion argues, reminders of the value of political conflicts rooted in religion and even of some of their more extreme expressions are particularly useful at this moment in American history. Barack Obama's election in 2008 unleashed much speculation on the left that conflicts over religion and culture are winding down. Obama's emphasis on civility clearly struck a chord among a significant number of voters. Still, the zero-sum nature of many policy disputes related to religion leaves little room for common ground. More crucially, attempting to create consensus and end conflict in the present by excluding cultural and religious concerns from political discourse, which some liberals support, is contrary to the democratic value of inclusion and would likely provoke a backlash in the future, as did the vital center politics of the 1950s and early 1960s.

The curricular recommendations in this book, the conclusion argues, are particularly fitted to our political moment. Since the public school curriculum is concerned with exposing students to different views rather than choosing between them, it is largely exempt from the zero-sum nature of disputes on issues like gay marriage and abortion. Schools are one of the few places in American society where the interests of each major group in our religious disputes can be accommodated. At the same time, teaching students that religious views are relevant to politics but must be expressed civilly will help to create a future where the democratic values of respect and inclusion can coexist. Hopes that the conflicts over religion and culture will end in the near future are inaccurate, and beliefs that these conflicts should end are misplaced, but removing the excessive vitriol that has plagued political discourse over the last 40 years is a realistic goal. Teaching about religion in a democratic way can help us reach it.

# CHAPTER 1

## The Distinctive Paradox of Religious Tolerance

Abraham Lincoln's second inaugural address is perhaps the most subtle declaration of America's most subtle political thinker. Having urged Northern soldiers to stay faithful to the spirit of America's founding ideals and fight to extend equality to all men in the Gettysburg Address, Lincoln strikes a more conciliatory tone in the second inaugural. He famously urges "malice towards none" and "charity towards all." This conciliation should not be confused with agnosticism at odds with the Gettysburg's moral assurance. The inaugural describes slavery as an "offense" that may have provoked God to give the North and South "this terrible war." But Lincoln cannot bring himself to condemn Southerners absolutely for the *source* of their beliefs. In a speech full of courageous challenges to Northerners eager to hear self-righteous affirmations of their cause, perhaps the most challenging reminder is the following:

> Both read the same Bible and pray to the same God, and each invokes His aid against the other. It may seem strange that any men should dare to ask a just God's assistance in wringing their bread from the sweat of other men's faces, but let us judge not, that we be not judged.

Lincoln condemns the outcomes of Southerners' beliefs but treads lightly when discussing the beliefs themselves. Lincoln seems to suggest that even religious beliefs used to justify the most heinous positions deserve some form of respect. Resistant to the simplistic formulations of the war endorsed by the North and the South, Lincoln resists a simplistic solution to the problem of religious tolerance. We have a special obligation to fight against injustice but a strong opposing obligation to respect religious beliefs when they ground such injustice. Assassinated little more than a month after the second inaugural, Lincoln never had the chance to expand on his provocative statements about religious tolerance or to explain how the paradox he identified could be resolved in practice. This is a great shame, because the middle ground Lincoln refers to remains elusive.

Lincoln's challenge is profoundly consequential for this book. If our society is to educate students effectively for religious tolerance, we must determine what type of tolerance religious beliefs are entitled to in a democracy like ours. Lincoln's second inaugural reminds us that this is a far more delicate matter than it might at first seem. But the two prevailing definitions of tolerance in the academic literature are too narrow to capture the subtle middle ground on religious tolerance that Lincoln identifies. Empirical researchers emphasize a passive form of tolerance that is too tepid to address the real and serious injustice of religious intolerance. But the alleged cure that several prominent political philosophers propose is so robust that it disregards the right to religious disagreement and may spur almost as much injustice as the injustice it sets out to remedy.

Several scholars have recognized the enigmatic nature of tolerance. Since, by definition, tolerance requires us to accept what we do not like, Bernard Williams (1996) has described it as a "paradoxical" virtue, and Hans Oberdiek (2001) has questioned if genuine tolerance is even possible. But none of these scholars have recognized, as Lincoln did, that if this is true of tolerance in general, it is even truer of religious tolerance. They assume too glibly that all forms of tolerance are created equal.

This chapter begins from the premise that Lincoln captured something profound about the distinctive dilemma that the promotion of religious tolerance poses, something that subsequent scholars have missed. Religious tolerance is distinctive because not only the targets of religious intolerance but intolerant religious beliefs themselves are entitled to special consideration. Lincoln's flash of insight, of course, requires much elaboration, and the reasoning he does use is outdated. Christian humility may have sufficed in Lincoln's day to explain why all Americans should provide special consideration to religiously intolerant beliefs, but this explanation is inadequate in the more religiously diverse America of our day. The strength of many Americans' religious beliefs and the centrality of these beliefs to many Americans' identities, this chapter argues, imposes an obligation on Americans today to cultivate a robust form of tolerance regarding religion, and it simultaneously places strong limits on how American society should attempt to erase religious intolerance.

The concept of active tolerance introduced in this chapter is intended as a mean between the extremes of passive tolerance and recognition. Passive tolerance is too weak to ensure adequate protection to religious believers, and the requirements of recognition are too strenuous for many religious believers to accept. Unlike passive tolerance, active tolerance recognizes the need of citizens to take action in private and public spheres to make religious minorities and those who hold minority views on religion feel accepted.[1] But contrary to the recognition position, active tolerance aims to cultivate this behavior through the acknowledgment of the subjective value that religious minorities attribute to their beliefs, rather than through respect for the objective legitimacy of these beliefs.

While one goal of this book is to better understand religious tolerance, its more immediate aim is to determine how schools can improve religious tolerance in practice. The chapter's final section speculates about how public schools should balance the need to promote tolerance with the need to protect some forms of religious intolerance. The burden of robust tolerance, this chapter argues, weighs heavily and disproportionately on conservative Christians.[2] For this problem, this chapter eventually proposes a curricular remedy that is bound to surprise many readers, in light of the chapter's prior rejection of the recognition of religious beliefs in public schools.

## WHY IS RELIGION SPECIAL?

Empirical evidence and theoretical arguments attest to the centrality of religion in many contemporary Americans' identities. In a 2004 Gallup poll, 9 out of 10 of those surveyed said that they believed in God.[3] Fifty-five percent reported that religion is "very important to their lives," while an additional 29 percent described religion as "fairly important"—numbers consistent with previous iterations of the survey. Although fewer Americans are highly involved in religious worship, a substantial number—in contrast to other liberal democracies—avidly attend religious services at their chosen place of worship.

Religion is not only a crucial aspect of many Americans' identities; it is also the matrix that holds their identity together and shapes other crucial aspects of their identities. Many theologians follow Paul Tillich (1958) in describing beliefs about religion as "ultimate" concerns that have a strong influence on important life decisions and other subordinate beliefs that individuals hold. Liberal political theorists concur by classifying religious beliefs as comprehensive. A belief is comprehensive, according to John Rawls (1993, 13), when

> it includes conceptions of what is of value in human life, and ideals of personal character, as well as ideals of friendship and of familial and associational relationships, and much else that is to inform our conduct, and in the limit to our life as a whole. A conception is fully comprehensive if it covers all recognized values and virtues within one rather precisely articulated system.

In light of Rawls's criteria, religious perspectives are not only comprehensive perspectives; they are the most paradigmatic examples of fully comprehensive views. A person's views on religion often shape attitudes toward romantic relationships, professional pursuits, artistic endeavors, and much more. Even secularists or atheists depend on religion, since their identities are defined in opposition to religious faith and culture (Buckley 1987).[4]

Why does religion's centrality to many Americans' identities mean that citizens ought to strive vigorously to be religiously tolerant? Liberal democratic societies are distinguished by their heightened respect for the dignity of every citizen. Respecting each person's dignity requires a considerate treatment of central aspects of their identities. To borrow from W. E. B. DuBois's reflection on race in *The Souls of Black Folk* (2004), religious insults often produce a painful double consciousness. Because of the centrality of religion to identity, insults are unlikely to change religious beliefs, but they can cause many believers to feel ambivalent about their beliefs and can even cause some to treat their beliefs as a badge of inferiority.

Religion's status as a comprehensive belief also suggests the need for heightened respect. Since many people's religious beliefs are essential to their most precious aspirations and views on life's meaning, beliefs not only inform the choices they make but provide them with a sense of why their life is worth living and their plans are worth carrying out. Liberal democratic societies are particularly concerned with enabling us to choose our aspirations on our own and ensuring that we have the self-esteem necessary to feel that our life plans are worth carrying out (Rawls 1993, 77). Believers who regularly encounter discrimination or whose religious beliefs are ignored in the public sphere to a far greater extent than mainstream beliefs may be led to doubt the value of their aspirations and view of life's meaning and may lack the self-esteem to carry out their plans.

Slights about central aspects of a person's identity also produce a sense of alienation from the community. Liberal democratic societies are distinguished by their inclusiveness, recognizing members as citizens and equally valued political participants. To foster inclusion and participation, they strive to make citizens of various backgrounds feel welcome and comfortable. Citizens who experience insults about such a central aspect of their identity as their religion or whose religion is severely ignored relative to mainstream beliefs are especially likely to feel that the community does not accept people like them. They may question if it is possible to reconcile their religious identity with their membership in American society.

But emphasizing religious believers' heightened sensitivity to explain why democratic citizens should be religiously tolerant might still seem to beg the question. Tolerance can be defined according to standard criteria or subjectively by the alleged victim of intolerance. For instance, a Christian who asks a male Sikh coworker why he wears a turban may commit an intolerant act even though he does not intend to insult. Especially if Sikhs are a minority in the office, the Sikh may take this question as alienating, because it singles him out as different from his coworkers. Can we determine objectively if the Christian's question is intolerant or whether the Sikh is being overly sensitive in this case? Instead of striving to reduce religious intolerance, perhaps our society's main focus should be on reducing religious believers' excessive sensitivity to slights (Weissberg 1998, 77).

One reason to prefer greater tolerance to lesser sensitivity in the case of religion is that many religious believers feel that their beliefs are immutable or nonnegotiable. Beliefs or characteristics that are or are felt to be outside of a person's discretion are entitled to heightened respect. Unlike other important aspects of a person's identity, such as race and gender, however, a person's religion is not physically immutable. Only a handful of religious groups in America today, such as the Amish, Sikhs, and Hasidic Jews, are required to demonstrate their religions physically through distinctive dress or physical attributes. It is also not clear that religion is intellectually immutable. Many religions allow for rational discussion, conversion, and evangelism. To support his thesis about the individualistic approach Americans tend to take toward religion, Robert Bellah (1986, 228) cited a 1978 Gallup poll in which 80 percent of Americans agreed that "an individual should arrive at his or her own religious beliefs independent of any churches or synagogues."

To understand why it is possible for people to change their religions while simultaneously feeling their religious beliefs to be immutable, we must consider how converts typically reason. One prevalent reason for conversion is a person's introduction to particularly compelling arguments that the person's current belief system is deficient and that another belief system is more fulfilling. When this occurs, people explain their conversion in nonvoluntary terms. A Baptist who is persuaded by argument to convert to Catholicism will reason, "Given the compelling evidence in favor of Catholicism I've discovered through study and reflection, I have no other choice but to abandon Baptism and convert to Catholicism." Another prevalent reason for conversion is the experience of a sudden revelation or direct communication from a divine being, like the one Saul had on the road to Damascus. In these cases, converts reason, "Since God commands me to change my religion, I have no choice but to change it." In both cases, even though converts are in some sense choosing their new beliefs, they still feel their religious beliefs to be immutable, because they have changed their beliefs for reasons they believe to be outside of their control. The same types of reasoning occur when individuals and religious groups discuss and change aspects of their religions without leaving their denomination.[5]

The distinctive way in which religion is immutable has important consequences for tolerance. In his fascinating recent book, Yale University law professor Kenji Yoshino focuses on the phenomenon of covering. Yoshino (2006, 18) quotes Erving Goffman's claim that covering exists when "persons who are ready to admit possession of a stigma . . . may nonetheless make a great effort to keep the stigma from looming large." He proceeds to provide compelling evidence about the mainstream pressure on homosexuals, racial minorities, and women to downplay their identities at work and in the public square.

The extent of covering may be most acute in the case of religion. Since religious identity in America today is often not physically obvious, religious believers are more capable of concealing their religious identities than other minorities. In fact, when unrelated to ethnicity, religion can be so easily concealed that many religious minorities not only downplay their identities but continue today to try to "pass" by not identifying themselves publicly with their religion in any way. That religious people sometimes conceal their religious identities should by no means, of course, be taken as evidence that such concealment is satisfactory to them. Almost all religious believers who engage in concealment do so because it is the lesser of two evils.[6] In extreme cases, such as with the Marrano Jews in Spain who remained faithful to their religion in private while publicly professing Catholicism to satisfy inquisitors during the Inquisition, religious groups have no choice but to conceal for the sake of survival. In America today, concealment occurs more often in uncomfortable, rather than dangerous, environments. A lone Muslim American man at a workplace composed of Christians may choose to conceal or downplay his religious identity because he feels the revelation of his religion may trigger insults and conflict. Even when they are open about their religious identity, members of minority religions may conceal the degree of their religious commitment to avoid comments or insults from peers. Religious believers who conceal their beliefs feel doubly pained by a sense of betrayal of their faith and by the inability to protest when peers make hurtful comments about their religious beliefs.

In our discussions with religious minorities in Modesto, California, Patrick Roberts and I found evidence of both covering and passing. Many religious minorities we spoke with experienced little overt discrimination but shunned participation in high-profile public events because they did not want to accentuate their prominence and distinctiveness. Passing was also evident. A teacher who was an atheist asked that we not identify him by name as an atheist in our published reports about Modesto's course. Rabbi Paul Gordon of Modesto's Congregation Beth Shalom said that several students in his congregation received invitations to participate in after-hours pizza parties thrown by Christian student groups. The students did not know how to respond, because they did not want to reveal their religion to their friends and risk more strained relationships.

It would be wrong, then, to assume that an environment in which discriminatory policies or overt slurs and insults are absent qualifies as tolerant or that America is a religiously tolerant nation merely because a significant majority of Americans refuse to support discriminatory laws. Such an environment may be the result of dominant religious groups not feeling the need to discriminate publicly or insult vulnerable and smaller religious groups, because they can simply assume their dominance and do not feel threatened by the presence of these groups. In these situations, religious minorities cannot be certain if a robust expression of their religious identity and views would be welcome or at least not mocked. They may conceal their beliefs to prevent discriminatory policies or insults.

The post-9/11 environment has led to even more prevalent conceal-ment than usual, especially among Muslims.[7] Numerous tolerance studies suggest that threat perception is one of the factors most strongly related to intolerant beliefs (Marcus 1995; Feldman and Stenner 1997; Duckitt and Fisher 2003; Sniderman, Brody, and Tetlock 1991).[8] Groups seen as threat-ening, this research indicates, are more likely to be disliked and experience intolerance. People who perceive a threat, especially to the "American way of life," are less likely to hold abstract democratic principles supportive of liberty. Even when they hold these abstract principles, they are less likely, in times of heightened perceived threat, to apply these principles to groups they feel threatened by. The onus on a liberal democracy to promote toler-ance is particularly strong when groups that share nominal characteristics with the groups or nations the democracy is at war with constitute a signif-icant population within the given democratic society. Religious tolerance becomes all the more important in a climate of increased anxiety when re-ligious differences are at the heart of foreign and domestic policy issues.

Young people in the United States today are clearly growing up in a cul-ture of anxiety and under conditions that are fostering greater intolerance. An ABC News poll found that from January 2002 to September 2003, the number of Americans who thought that Islam encourages violence rose from 14 to 34 percent, while the number of Americans who had an unfa-vorable view of Islam rose from 24 to 34 percent.[9] A 2006 *Washington Post*–ABC News poll found that 58 percent of Americans believed "that Is-lam has more violent followers than any other religion."[10] The 2004 Amer-ican National Election Study ranked the favorability of Americans toward 31 social groups on a "feeling thermometer" of 0 to 100, where 0 equals least favorable and 100 equals most favorable. Only 38.6 percent of Ameri-cans gave Muslims a thermometer rating of over 50, ranking them 29 out of the 31 groups (Bartels 2008, 136).[11]

This shift in attitudes has had real and disturbing behavioral consequences. The Council on American-Islamic Relations, an Islamic civil rights group, released a finding in 2004 showing a 15 percent increase in incidents of violence, discrimination, and harassment of Muslims in America since 2002 (Council on American-Islamic Relations 2004). Anti-Muslim sentiment is at least partly responsible for the prison abuse scandals at Guantánamo Bay and Abu Ghraib and the neglect of civilian welfare in Iraq that have outraged countless Muslims in America. One American soldier who returned from Iraq described how a top officer urged his platoon to "kill some ragheads and burn some turbans" and how his fellow soldiers threw glass bottles at Iraqi civilians from Humvees while uttering anti-Arab epithets (Herbert 2005). Although not excusable, the extreme stress of the battlefield makes abusive behavior by members of the military understandable. No such excuse is available to the many political leaders who have sanctioned or failed to denounce this behavior and have passed the overly broad Patriot Act, leading to the routine harassment of Muslim Americans by law enforcement officials. The exploitation by a significant number of politicians of the controversy over the proposed Islamic center near Ground Zero in August 2010 provides a particularly crude and transparent example of the manipulation of anti-Muslim animus for political gain (Robinson 2010; Greewald 2010; Chait 2010). This official behavior and most Americans' at least tacit acceptance of it has had a profoundly alienating effect for many Muslims.[12]

Even these disturbing numbers might not reflect the true extent of discrimination against Muslims. Since the conclusion of the civil rights movement, scholars of racial intolerance have noticed an increase in covert or "symbolic" racism that masks itself as cultural or political critique (Kinder and Sears 1981, 416; Kinder and Sanders 1997). Like symbolic racism, religious intolerance could flourish through a combination of hostile affect toward religious groups and support for traditional liberal or conservative values. Surveys measuring religiously intolerant opinions or behavior may fail to capture the true extent of religious intolerance by ignoring symbolic intolerance. The frequent depiction of Arabs in the media as Saudi Arabian oil sheikhs or Palestinian rock throwers at least implicitly suggests that Arabs respectively do not behave according to the Protestant work ethic and are a threat to law and order.[13] The reciprocal relationship between religious and cultural prejudice means that the fight against intolerance must be fought on two fronts. Our society must address cultural as well as religious stereotypes.

Although our survey in Modesto found relatively low levels of explicit anti-Muslim prejudice among students even before the world religions course, the research provided anecdotal evidence of the possible presence of symbolic intolerance. In a discussion I had with a class of Modesto students about the inclusion of the phrase "under God" in the Pledge of Allegiance, the majority of students strongly insisted that all students stand during the pledge, and several argued that students who, on conscience, refused to stand should "leave the country."[14] These students' opinions indicated that insufficient patriotism could be used as covert grounds for discriminating against nonmainstream religious groups that feel uncomfortable pledging allegiance to a conception of God different from their own or linking allegiance to God with allegiance to state.

Other forms of symbolic intolerance against a wide range of religious groups may be at work as well. America has a long and unfortunate history of symbolic intolerance toward Catholics and Jews.[15] Many anti-Catholic bigots of the late nineteenth and early twentieth centuries routinely hid their religious animus by claiming that the alleged clannishness of the Irish, Italians, and Poles was inconsistent with the Protestant work ethic and self-reliance or by complaining that Catholics could not make good citizens because of their ultimate allegiance to the pope. Anti-Semitism has often been concealed beneath the claim that Jews hold leftist or radical opinions out of step with mainstream American political beliefs and are concentrated in intellectual professions and pursuits. Liberals could discriminate against conservative religious believers in a similar way by pledging support for free exercise of religion while justifying intolerance on the grounds that evangelicals or Orthodox Jews are not supportive of traditional American values of autonomy, openness, and free expression.[16] Tolerance scholars should also pay attention to the discrepancy between the level of discrimination religious minorities and the religious majority perceive in America today. Kinder and Sears (1981) contend that denying the existence of pervasive discrimination when it clearly exists can itself be a form of symbolic intolerance and can be used to claim that minorities illegitimately blame their failures on others.

## PASSIVE AND ACTIVE TOLERANCE

The distinctive nature of religion, we have found, requires a heightened form of tolerance. The distinctive nature of the times in which we live makes the cultivation of this tolerance particularly urgent. Unfortunately, the importance and urgency of religious tolerance are not reflected in the empirical political science literature on the subject. Instead, this literature defines tolerance as a passive virtue requiring individuals to refrain from taking discriminatory or hurtful action. In a classic statement of this position, John Sullivan, George Marcus, and James Piereson (1982, 2) explain that tolerance is the "willingness to 'put up with' those things that one rejects . . . Politically it implies a willingness to permit the expression of ideas or interests one opposes." This literature treats people as sufficiently tolerant when they express support for basic civil liberties and as intolerant when they support government policies that infringe on the important rights of particular groups.[17] The previous section suggests that tolerance regarding religion must involve a more active component. Active tolerance, broadly defined, involves the willingness of individuals to act on behalf of others who are discriminated against in public policy or law or who are the targets of slights and insults. To be actively tolerant, for instance, individuals not only must refrain from preventing Muslim groups from holding rallies in public parks but must actively protest if their local government enacts such a ban. The current climate of suspicion surrounding Muslims makes it essential that Americans avoid not only sins of commission but sins of omission, by taking action to protect imperiled religious minorities.

Above all, active tolerance regarding religion requires the establishment of an environment where believers are able to feel comfortable expressing their religious identity. Creating such an environment not only will prevent painful and inauthentic concealments of religion but will further the cause of liberal democracy. The ability of individuals to interact with people they disagree with is integral to the flourishing of a liberal democratic society. We cannot learn to get along with those we disagree with if we are not aware that others disagree with us. For such an environment to exist, members of dominant religious groups must provide members of small and vulnerable religious groups some sign that expression of their religious identities is acceptable. One way this can happen is if the members of dominant groups take political action to protect the rights of minority groups. Such action by individuals, as opposed to government officials, will work to counter the sense of alienation and insecurity that religious minorities are likely to feel as a result of their minority status. Religious minorities are likely to feel truly welcome and included in their communities when their neighbors and coworkers rally to their side in difficult situations.[18]

Many prominent empirical researchers of tolerance pay exclusive attention to the legal and political treatment of minorities (Sullivan, Marcus, and Piereson 1982; McClosky and Brill 1983). They concern themselves solely with discriminatory public policies, forgetting that even if egalitarian laws and policies prevail, taunts and slights in such private arenas as the workplace, school, or one's neighborhood can have an alienating effect on religious minorities. Active tolerance strives to provide religious minorities with a sense of inclusion in the private as well as the public sphere. Instilling religious minorities with the comfort necessary to express their identity requires not only forbearance in the political sphere but active steps to make religious minorities feel welcome in smaller public and private arenas, such as schools, workplaces, businesses, and neighborhoods.

Another essential way to make religious minorities comfortable in expressing their beliefs is for dominant religious groups to cultivate some understanding of their beliefs. A person's religion, as we have seen, is more than an aspect of that person's identity. For many, a religion is a comprehensive belief system that organizes the individual's activities and thoughts, commands adherents to engage in certain behaviors, and prohibits them from engaging in others. Since a person's religion is relevant to a wider range of activities and beliefs, religious tolerance consists, in many cases, in understanding the various implications of religion rather than ignoring it. To be tolerant of religion, Americans must know something about the practices that religions enjoin. This matters in both large and small cases. Without an understanding of the dietary restrictions religions impose, for instance, a person may place a coworker or neighbor in an awkward situation by offering a prohibited food or by failing to provide adequate alternatives to a prohibited meal.[19] On a more explicitly political level, knowledge about religions will enable Americans to understand the logic of religious minorities who request exemptions from military service or from compulsory public school curriculum material that they find objectionable. When dominant religious groups display understanding of the practices of minority religions, minority religions are more likely to be willing to share and express their beliefs.

Kenji Yoshino's approach to remedying discrimination provides a useful contrast to the active tolerance approach. Like major empirical researchers of tolerance, Yoshino (2006, 167–83) primarily focuses on combating intolerance through legal means. Unlike these researchers, however, Yoshino believes that combating intolerance requires an active approach. He proposes a new civil rights paradigm in constitutional interpretation to accommodate the protection of robust expressions of identity. But as Yoshino himself acknowledges (193), legal remedies are an awkward and often counterproductive way to provide minorities with a robust ability to free expression. They only secure forbearance from discrimination under the threat of coercion, which the targets of possible coercion are likely to resent. Yoshino concludes that covering is often "better redressed through appeals to our individual faculties of conscience and compassion" (24).

This solution is too minimalist. The choice Yoshino offers between legal coercion and complete trust in individuals to change their behavior is too limiting. Active tolerance, by contrast, places positive obligations on citizens to act to protect and understand religious minorities. For these reasons, education, rather than legal coercion, is its preferred tool, and the focus in the remainder of this book is on education rather than the law. Securing active tolerance in schools—assuming that an acceptable way of promoting it in schools can be found—would preempt many of the legal controversies over covering Yoshino identifies. Sharing and taking inspiration from Yoshino's thoughts about the essential problem of tolerance in American society, this chapter's focus on understanding and education provides the type of more robust solution to the current deficits of tolerance in America today that Yoshino himself claims to be seeking.

Active tolerance is a high bar, though. Given the reluctance of many Americans to participate in public affairs in general, perhaps it is unrealistic to expect a significant number of Americans to engage in actively tolerant behavior regarding religion. There are, however, different degrees of active tolerance. The most obvious examples of actions or behavior intended to combat discrimination would be citizens taking political action, such as protesting a discriminatory policy against religious minorities by signing a petition, writing a letter to a local newspaper, or organizing a protest march. Undoubtedly, these types of public behavior are bound to have a profoundly heartening effect for religious minorities, and our society should strive to encourage them as long as doing so does not indoctrinate citizens or disrespect their rights to freedom of conscience.

At the same time, even small gestures can have significance for members of alienated religious minorities. In a 2005 op-ed letter to the *New York Times*, Fatina Abdrabboh, a Muslim American student at Harvard's Kennedy School who wears a hijab, began by discussing the increasing alienation she felt as a result of the U.S. government's recent treatment of Muslims at home and abroad and the hostile stares her headdress had drawn. A recent experience at a local gym, however, brightened her outlook. While exercising on the treadmill, she inadvertently dropped her keys. When she looked up, her keys were handed to her by former vice president Al Gore, who happened to be exercising in the same gym. She concludes,

> It was nothing more than a kind gesture, but at that moment Mr. Gore's act represented all that I yearned for—acceptance and acknowledgement. There in front of me, he stood for a part of America that has not made itself well known to 10 million Arab and Muslim-Americans, many of whom are becoming increasingly withdrawn and reclusive because of the everyday hostility they feel. (Abdrabboh 2005)

Like Parmanand Tiwari, who took heart from the many small contributions mailed to him after vandalism marred his Hindu temple in Modesto, Ms. Abdrabboh claims that Mr. Gore's gesture provided the sense of inclusion and comfort with expressing identity that active tolerance is intended to achieve. Her story echoes the sentiments of several religious minority students in Modesto I talked with who were heartened when classmates defended them against religious taunts used by other students in classes and schoolyards.

These anecdotes not only remind us that small actions can have profound consequences; they also suggest that active tolerance is grounded in realistic expectations. Even if it is unrealistic to expect most citizens to engage in large-scale social protest or if such protest is too strenuous for citizens with full-time jobs and family obligations, the smaller gestures that feed a sense of inclusion are within reach of all citizens, and expecting a significant number of Americans to perform them is reasonable. The goals of active tolerance will not always be as easily achieved as they are in Ms. Abdrabboh's case, but small gestures can have an impact. The anecdotes also usefully remind us that private actions can have just as much significance as political actions.

Even if active tolerance is realistic, passive tolerance scholars may question whether cultivating active tolerance among the general population is necessary. After all, Americans have always demonstrated seemingly acceptable levels of passive tolerance, and the lack of active tolerance has not seemed to affect the stability of the American political system. Perhaps passive tolerance is a sufficient guarantee of the rights of religious minorities, with active tolerance being simply a luxury.

The flawed assumption at the heart of this claim, however, is that the implications of intolerance—the suppression of rights and liberties through law and social movements—turn on the conduct of elites. Community leaders, lawyers, newspaper publishers, and public officials are presumably more amenable to democratic values, and there may even be something about the experience of being a leader that functions as a civics or tolerance course, exposing elites to problems that force them to confront the distinction between belief and behavior and to question the link between the perception of threat and tolerance. The ability of elites to temper intolerant attitudes when making policy is of only small comfort, though. Even if elites are more tolerant in general (Sullivan et al. 1993; Gibson 1988), the political incentives for inciting intolerance or for restricting basic civil rights and liberties become, at some point, too great to resist. Many legislators during the cold war, for instance, found it politically profitable to play on public fears of Communists, just as legislators today have exploited fears toward Muslims, perhaps most notably in the debate over the proposed Islamic center near Ground Zero.[20] Finally, even if we could depend on elites to secure tolerant policies and laws for religious minorities, this would still leave religious minorities vulnerable to alienating slights and insults by ordinary citizens in the private realm.

Instead of relying on the experience of being a leader to override the political incentives for appealing to intolerance, a democratic society must prepare its citizens to resist appeals to prejudice. This capacity for resistance is particularly important in the war being currently waged against al-Qaeda and fundamentalist Muslim terrorists. A stated goal of these groups is to create a wider rift between Muslims and non-Muslims, in both American society and the world at large, by encouraging non-Muslims to see all Muslims as sympathetic to the terrorists' means and ends and by enacting discriminatory policies. These actions will trigger an increased sense of alienation and an extremist turn among Muslims. It is crucial that Americans refuse to play into the hands of these groups and continue to make sensible distinctions between moderate Muslims in their own and other nations and those who use Islam for terror.

### ACTIVE TOLERANCE VERSUS RECOGNITION

Perhaps the fundamental problem with active tolerance is not that it is too strenuous but that it is not strenuous enough. In his book *Multiculturalism and "the Politics of Recognition,"* Charles Taylor claims that equal respect for other cultures involves some recognition of the values and beliefs that these cultures hold dear. Taylor (1992, 66) rejects the idea that liberal democracies should instruct citizens to treat "all human cultures that have animated whole societies over some considerable stretch of time" as having equal or even considerable value. He does argue, however, that citizens should treat as a "starting hypothesis" the "presumption" that all cultures are of equal value and thus entitled to equal respect. Citizens must make a good-faith and open-minded effort to explore the objective value of other cultures. Active tolerance calls for an increase in understanding and knowledge about other cultures and for a change in behavior based on this awareness. Recognition involves an internal change in perspective that not only consists of learning about what people do or believe in other cultures but requires, in Hans-Georg Gadamer's phrase, a "fusion of horizons" (Taylor 1992, 66–67). We must be open to changing the standards and norms we use to evaluate cultures and to considering the way in which the premises we currently use to evaluate cultures may be tainted by ethnocentric bias.[21]

Although recognition theorists usually focus on race, gender, and sexual orientation, the discussion in the previous two sections would seem to suggest that the centrality of religion to identity means that it, too, should be accorded recognition. If religious believers are only accorded active tolerance, we are failing to respect the rights to which they are entitled. But the very same features that make religion distinctive and justify a heightened form of religious tolerance also entitle religiously *intolerant* beliefs to a special consideration that the promotion of recognition violates.

Neglect of this point is also evident in Kenji Yoshino's response to the problem of covering. Yoshino (2006, 167–83) supports a novel and aggressive legal approach in antidiscrimination law to secure a robust right of free expression for minorities. Citizens must go out of their way, Yoshino argues, to make vulnerable minorities comfortable in expressing their identity to the fullest in various public arenas, such as workplaces and schools. While such an approach has great merit and is largely unproblematic in terms of combating discrimination based on race, gender, or sexual orientation, Yoshino fails to realize that this approach is more problematic when applied to religion. Like recognition theorists, Yoshino overlooks the differences between religion and other essential aspects of a person's identity and ignores that religiously intolerant views may have a moral value that other types of intolerant beliefs lack. Overly aggressive attempts to encourage robust religious free expression or to combat religious discrimination are likely to interfere themselves with religious beliefs and free expression. The goal Yoshino wishes to realize is honorable and compatible with the goal of active tolerance, but religion's special status means democratic societies must take great care in how they strive to achieve this goal.

This can be made clearer through a contrast of actual school policies of teaching for racial tolerance and a hypothetically analogous example of teaching for religious tolerance. Imagine that your local school district already has a policy in place to promote racial and ethnic tolerance through a course that all students are required to take.[22] The goal of this policy is to teach students that people of all races and ethnicities are equal not only in terms of their rights but also in terms of their intellectual and moral potential. The school board and administrators decide, however, that it is necessary but not sufficient to teach abstract formulations of tolerance; they decide to teach students about various members of different races and ethnicities who have achieved positions of influence and power in mainstream America. Since race and ethnicity are central to many individuals' identities, individuals should have the ability to express their racial and ethnic identity and to have the importance of their identity acknowledged by mainstream culture, and the only way this can happen is if students learn to take pride in their racial and ethnic history and heritage. The promotion of racial and ethnic pride is especially important because, in the past, mainstream American culture has often suppressed the expression of racial and ethnic identity and denigrated the culture and history of minority races and ethnicities. To achieve this promotional result, the district decides to implement a multicultural education encouraging students to accept that the practices and beliefs of a variety of racial and ethnic groups are legitimate. To enable African Americans to take pride in their heritage and encourage other students to acknowledge that the ancestors of African Americans belonged to flourishing cultures before their forcible incorporation into American society, teachers ask students to consider the merits of African art, music, distinct family organizations, and attitudes to the relation between humans and nature. Students are taught that while some practices in these cultures might be harmful, these perspectives might also have some advantages that are lacking in mainstream American culture.

Now imagine that the school board decides to implement a similar compulsory course intended to encourage religious tolerance. Textbooks could show people of different religions fulfilling the same public functions: a Sikh with a headdress serving as a judge or teacher, a Buddhist as president, and so on. Most readers would probably not find this approach problematic. It is not disrespectful and does no violence to religious belief. Problems are likely to arise, however, if the district takes a more explicitly multicultural approach to religion. The specter of relativism arises if the curriculum encourages students to treat the beliefs and practices of other religious groups as legitimate ways of worshiping the divine and if it teaches students to compare and contrast the advantages and disadvantages of each religious tradition. Before long, students may follow Walt Whitman in

> Lithographing Kronos and Zeus his son, and Hercules his grandson,
> Buying drafts of Osiris and Isis and Belus and Brahma and Adonai,
> In my portfolio placing Manito loose, and Allah on a leaf, and the crucifix engraved.

Relativism, syncretism, and ecumenism are, of course, legitimate religious options.[23] Many have found profound meaning by adopting them, and schools should certainly avoid discouraging them. At the same time, their promotion by schools violates democratic neutrality and violates the religious liberty of conservative Christians in particular. A similar danger accompanies teaching that all religions preach the same basic views about morality. To be sure, this point has been made by influential Christian apologists, such as C. S. Lewis in his *Abolition of Man*. In less skillful hands, however, it can reduce religion to the Decalogue and the Golden Rule and ignore the role of practice, sacraments, and sacred space and time that form the core of many Christian and non-Christian forms of religion.

Most readers will likely respond against the religious tolerance curriculum with a visceral reaction that is absent in the case of the aggressive racial tolerance curriculum. Multicultural education regarding race and ethnicity is, of course, controversial, but the main objections are political. Conservatives like Dinesh D'Souza (2002) claim that in order for the United States to be an effective player on the world stage, citizens must have confidence in the superiority of mainstream American beliefs and practices. Even some liberals, such as Arthur Schlesinger Jr. (1992), warn that excessive emphasis on the differences between Americans will produce a Balkanization of American society. But many will feel that religious multicultural education violates the personal rights of students in a way that education for racial and ethnic tolerance does not. What explains these different reactions to two apparently identical curriculum policies? Is the distinction legitimate? Or are our instincts wrong, and is there merely a greater conventional taboo against racial prejudice in our society than against religious prejudice, a taboo that, on reflection, lacks a rational basis?

The most persuasive distinction between these two curriculum policies involves the differences between the nature of beliefs critical of races and those critical of religions. Beliefs critical of religions seem to possess some merit that is lacking in the case of racially intolerant beliefs. A society risks eliminating potentially valuable perspectives when it encourages students to accept the legitimacy of religious beliefs and practices beside their own. This is not to categorically assert that racist beliefs lack normative value. The very fact that racists hold these beliefs strongly is normatively significant to some (albeit very weak) extent, because encouraging them to change their beliefs would cause them some degree of psychological suffering.

But the amount of pain caused by changing or muting racist beliefs should not be sufficient to guarantee protection for those beliefs. Even if racist beliefs possess some normative significance, they fail to meet the threshold of moral significance required for protection in a liberal democratic society. The approach here is similar to the compelling interest test that the Supreme Court has used in First Amendment and equal protection cases. In cases involving especially important rights claims, such as the right to free exercise of religion, the Supreme Court requires the government to meet a heightened threshold to override these rights claims by demonstrating that its actions are based on a compelling interest. The promotion of racial and religious tolerance in our society and the corresponding rights to be free of racial and religious discrimination are especially important. To override these claims by protecting racially and religiously intolerant beliefs requires showing that racially and religiously intolerant beliefs possess not only some merit but a special degree of merit. Religiously intolerant beliefs are morally significant to a much greater degree than racially intolerant beliefs, and this moral significance entitles them to a greater degree of protection from state interference.

One possible basis for the legitimacy of the distinction has to do with the social value of devoutly religious views. Theorists from Tocqueville (2000) to Robert Booth Fowler (1989) have cogently argued that religion can be a sanctuary from the capitalist ethos. In America, where rampant consumerism reigns, religion can remind people that there is something outside the self and material values. The presence of robust religious worldviews can reinforce individual autonomy—a value dear to liberal political theorists—by encouraging believers to examine liberal society critically and by presenting alternative ways of life. The absence of robust religious perspectives and communities can lead to a flat and homogenous social landscape. Religions have often served as an equally effective tool for challenging questionable majoritarian norms and policies. They often hold that there is a higher, natural law that can be used as a standard to evaluate the laws and policies states enact. The belief in natural law mobilized resistance to slavery among abolitionists and to segregation laws during the civil rights movements.

These examples remind us that religious intolerance is often valuable because a main purpose of religious beliefs is their *intolerance of unjust and evil beliefs and practices.* An overly vigorous attempt to erase religious intolerance may have the perverse effect of eliminating legitimate religious objections to evil. "Metaphysical relativism," Jay Newman (1982, 59) writes, "is likely to lead a man to do too much tolerating; it would seem to promote moral weakness, apathy, and passivity rather than genuine tolerance, tolerance of what ought to be tolerated." Although the curriculum policy for religious tolerance will erode socially dangerous views based on religion, it is problematic because it might simultaneously erode robust religious perspectives that have real social value.

Racially intolerant views, by contrast, do not seem to possess any socially redeeming characteristics; they are unmitigated obstacles to a society's welfare. Proponents of racist beliefs might respond that the elimination of these views would also flatten and homogenize American society. But such an argument relies on the premises that diversity is valuable for diversity's sake and that all forms of diversity are equally valuable. A rich cultural landscape depends not on the availability of all possible beliefs but only on a significant diversity of beliefs. If, for instance, a sufficient variety of religious, national, and ethnic views are already present and flourishing in a liberal democratic culture, there is no need to ensure that worthless racially intolerant beliefs and communities flourish as well.[24]

Even more important than the social harm that would be caused by the religious tolerance curriculum previously outlined, however, is the harm to individual conscience. The basis for this harm is that the truth claims of different religions are often mutually exclusive, while beliefs about racial and ethnic identity are less likely to be so. Almost all Americans do not believe that the achievements and positive attributes of one race are negated or diminished by accepting the achievements and positive attributes of other races. But many Americans do believe that the respect for the truth of other religions negates the truth of their religion. The mutual exclusivity of religious beliefs is most clear in the case of monotheistic religions and perhaps most true of Christianity. Many Christians—particularly fundamentalists and those believers James Davidson Hunter describes as "orthodox"—believe that to reconcile themselves to the belief that there are many ways to be saved denies the central role that accepting Christ plays in salvation.[25] The Qur'an does state explicitly that Jews and Christians are eligible for salvation because they have received a true, if partial, revelation. A Muslim man would betray his faith, however, if he were to accept the view of Jews and Christians that Muhammad is not a true prophet. Even the most ecumenical of faiths view other religious beliefs as incompatible with their own. The henotheistic belief that it is possible to worship one deity without denying the worship of other deities is central to Hinduism. But it is exactly this belief in henotheism that renders Hindus unable to accept the legitimacy of monotheistic religions' truth claims that there is only one God and that the worship of several deities is idolatrous.

The distinction between race and religion on the grounds of mutual exclusivity does not merely rest on the fact that more Americans are more likely to view religious beliefs as mutually exclusive. Even if citizens held mutually exclusive views about race and ethnicity in equal numbers, race and religion would still be distinct because the consequences of accepting alternative truth claims for religious believers are greater than the consequences racists endure when they are encouraged or required to accept the value of other races' beliefs and practices. Intolerant religious believers and racists alike may face temporal consequences for embracing the value of alternative beliefs, such as the loss of community, family, and friends. Many religious believers, however, hold that there are eternal consequences for accepting the legitimacy of other religions' truth claims. Many Christian parents feel that by being encouraged to accept the legitimacy of belief systems that deny Christ's divinity, their children risk betraying God and earning damnation. Orthodox Muslim parents will feel similarly about an education that encourages children to accept the legitimacy of beliefs that deny the centrality of Muhammad's revelation and behavior to human experience. For many orthodox and fundamentalist believers, changing beliefs or holding that there is more than one path to salvation is not even necessary to risk damnation. Merely entertaining doubt and skepticism about one's religion for any considerable period may produce this result (Stolzenberg 1993, 594). Many Christians construe as support for this conclusion Jesus's "greatest" commandment at Matthew 22:37 to "Love the lord with all your heart and all your soul, and with all your mind." The connection between religious beliefs, central aspirations, and self-esteem means that encouraging doubt and skepticism about religious beliefs may undermine many believers' central aspirations and their self-esteem about the value of their activities.

The intellectual belief in mutually exclusive religious truth has profound this-worldly as well as otherworldly consequences. Friendships and marriages traverse racial, professional, and political lines, but these connections become difficult between members of different religions if those religions are taken seriously. Believers, to be sure, can have friends of different faith traditions, but if faith is fundamental to their identity, there is often only so far a believer can go before reaching a fundamental disagreement with someone of a different faith. Intermarriage and even dating outside of the faith is of particular concern for many religions because it leads to controversy over the religious education of children produced in mixed marriages. Many religious communities hold that an upbringing exposing a child to two different views of religious truth is likely to dilute the child's commitment to the truth claims of each religion. Abstaining from close relationships with members of other religions is highly evident among religious fundamentalists and in separatist communities, such as the Amish community, which go so far as to engage in shunning of those who have left the faith. More important, this practice is also engaged in by religious groups that are orthodox or traditional and who engage in mainstream American society to a large extent and constitute a significant portion of America's population in communities around the nation (Marty and Appleby 1991; J. D. Hunter 1991). Democratic states must be wary of encouraging the acceptance of alternative beliefs where many believers feel this acceptance will have such profound mundane and eternal consequences.

Secularists and more progressive religious believers may wonder, why should all democratic citizens care if religious believers hold that there are eternal consequences for accepting alternative religious beliefs? Aren't beliefs about eternal consequences grounded only in subjective opinion? The mutual exclusivity of religious beliefs seems vulnerable to the same type of critique. Still, even if we were to grant that the irreconcilability of religious beliefs and the belief in eternal consequences are only subjectively held and have no objective basis, democratic states must show them special respect because their believers hold them so strongly.

Consider a hypothetically analogous situation. Imagine that the majority of American voters are single and concerned about overpopulation and the costs they and society bear for supporting schools. This majority decides to enact a legal regulation in America identical to China's one-child policy. To protest this policy, parents desiring more than one child could make an objectively verifiable argument and attempt to provide empirical evidence demonstrating that children who grow up with siblings tend to be more successful and happy than only children. But what if such evidence was not available or if the preponderance of evidence supported opposite conclusions? Would there still be grounds for validating our visceral belief that such a policy is inconsistent with basic democratic norms?

The more basic problems with this policy are that it would interfere significantly with a central aspiration of would-be parents and would cause would-be parents to feel that their decisions were not fully their own. Parents often feel driven by biological and moral imperatives in their decisions about having children. Not only *can* single people imagine sympathetically the value of having children, but they *ought* to engage in this sympathetic imagination and accept the special protection given to procreative decisions. Similarly, to justify special protection for religious beliefs, it is not necessary that all people be certain that religious truth claims are in fact irreconcilable and that there are eternal consequences for betraying one's faith. It is sufficient that religious believers believe that truth claims are irreconcilable and that there will be eternal consequences for betraying their faith.

If recognizing the legitimacy of other religions' truth claims often involves a negation of the believer's own truth claims and causes religious believers to feel they are betraying their faith, the state's encouragement of this recognition is clearly problematic. The multicultural education for religious intolerance previously outlined would involve a violation of democratic norms of state neutrality in several ways. On a general level, it runs the risk of placing excessive emphasis on the similarities between religion and discouraging students from realizing the way in which their religious traditions believe that religious truth claims are mutually exclusive. More specifically, it would at least implicitly bias students toward a pluralistic or henotheistic conception of religious truth inconsistent with monotheistic religious traditions. Even if such an education did not achieve its intended effect of having students accept the legitimacy of a variety of religious views, it might violate neutrality by encouraging students to hold a more skeptical view of the religious traditions they come from. The encouragement of skepticism would most strongly conflict with the views of James Davison Hunter's orthodox believers and evangelical and fundamentalist Christians in particular. Many members of these groups stress that even temporarily entertaining doubts about the truth of one's religion could interfere with salvation, which requires a wholehearted commitment to the faith's central doctrines and leaves no room for skepticism.

The special nature of religious beliefs critical of other religions means that democratic states must be considerably more careful regarding *how* they promote religious tolerance than they are in promoting other important forms of tolerance. A multicultural education for recognition may be appropriate for race and ethnicity, but it is inappropriate for religion. Charles Taylor's recognition argument implies a strong relationship between external behavior that makes minority groups comfortable and internal beliefs about the objective value of these groups' beliefs. Recognition requires not only tolerant behavior but the reduction or elimination of aversion for the target group's beliefs and views that other groups hold false or meaningless beliefs. Aversion involves internal attitudes and beliefs regarding alternative belief systems or characteristics different than one's own. Minority groups will only feel respected when state-sponsored education and other state legislation recognize the objective value of their beliefs. Ordinary citizens will only feel sufficiently motivated to act in ways consistent with respect for minorities when they acknowledge or at least explore in good faith the objective value of their beliefs.

These claims are empirically questionable. Theological aversion toward other religions does not necessarily entail civilly intolerant views that members of these religions should be deprived of equal political rights and treatment. This amalgam is exemplified in Voltaire's classic statement "I disapprove of what you say, but I will defend to the death your right to say it." A Muslim may reject Jewish beliefs on theological grounds and still hold that Jews are entitled to equal political rights. Similarly, there may be other ways to motivate citizens to make minorities feel comfortable and respected besides having them explore the objective validity of minority beliefs, values, and practices. Minorities may feel comfortable expressing their views and participating in politics even if the objective validity of their beliefs is not widely held. These empirical doubts are of little concern in the case of race and ethnicity. Even if widespread recognition of the validity of minority views is not undeniably necessary to make racial or ethnic minorities feel comfortable, it is still a good idea for the state to encourage this openness, because the relationship between denying objective value to minority beliefs and practices and intolerant behavior may well exist, and this state action does not infringe on the legitimate claims of racists.

Attempts to encourage recognition, reduce aversion, and change internal attitudes about the objective value of religious beliefs are more problematic because religious aversion is connected to the freedom of conscience and is more worthy of protection than is prejudice toward physical characteristics. The state does have a clear obligation to eliminate aversion when it leads citizens to infringe on the basic rights and liberties of those with whom they disagree, but it should refrain from doing so otherwise. If Charles Taylor's beliefs about the relationship between the reduction of prejudice and tolerant behavior are correct, society is faced inescapably with a tragic choice between promoting recognition and the reduction of religiously intolerant behavior, on the one hand, and the protection of legitimate religiously tolerant beliefs, on the other.

The importance of both promoting religiously tolerant behavior and protecting beliefs critical of religion requires political leaders and tolerance scholars alike to question this inevitability and to explore if promotion and protection can coexist.[26] To do both, it is crucial to secure respect for religious minorities through a change in behavior and actions toward religious minorities. As I will suggest, this does not require perfect neutrality regarding religious aversion and internal beliefs but, rather, involves bringing about an increase in respect through a less intrusive change in beliefs than recognition. The following section explores ways in which the state might attempt to promote civically tolerant behavior without illegitimately interfering with religiously intolerant beliefs.

## CIVIL AND THEOLOGICAL TOLERANCE

### Providing Accurate Information

The previous section suggests that the state interferes with religious beliefs when it meddles with believers' value judgments about other religions. The problem with tolerance as recognition is that it encourages believers to change the value they attribute to other groups' beliefs. But this does not, of course, mean that the government must forbear from attempting to change how students think about other religions. Providing accurate information about other religions, for instance, need not encourage citizens to change the value they attribute to other groups' beliefs. Teaching students that many Muslims interpret the concept of jihad in spiritual and not martial terms is at least theoretically distinct from teaching students that they should value Islam as a legitimate belief system.[27] Research suggests that Americans become more tolerant as they gain knowledge about a group. To take one example, Americans in the late 1980s became more willing to give rights to homosexuals as they learned more about how AIDS is and is not transmitted (Sniderman, Brody, and Tetlock 1991, 31–57).

But if providing accurate information is distinct in theory from encouraging a change in perceptions, the two are often connected in practice. Consider an example reflecting this connection from our research about Modesto's world religions course. Several Modesto teachers provided handouts to their students showing that a version of the Golden Rule could be found in the sacred texts of seven major religious traditions. As one piece of information among many, this handout is unobjectionable. But when unaccompanied by a balancing discussion of the substantial differences between the moral perspectives of these religions, which we found was occasionally the case, this information is likely to have the illegitimate effect of encouraging students strongly to hold more positive views of other religious traditions.

A democratic state must carefully consider what information it distributes to its members. In determining what type of information to provide about other religions, the state must keep in mind that the goal of providing information is to promote civic tolerance of other religions and inclusion of minority religions in public life. The provision of information should be narrowly tailored to achieve this purpose. As we saw in the second section of this chapter, one way to do this is to ensure that information provided about the beliefs and practices of religion will allow citizens to avoid unintentional slights of religious beliefs. This serves the active tolerance goal of enabling religious minorities to feel a sense of comfort and belonging. There are three additional forms of information that are particularly crucial to achieving the goals of active and civic tolerance.

Most important, the state should concentrate on eliminating dangerous misperceptions that are particularly likely to trigger civically intolerant behavior. We have seen that a common aspect of symbolic intolerance is the tendency to link all members of a group to its most extremist members, or those who espouse the most extreme version of the group's beliefs. The many Americans who say in surveys that they believe Islam to be an inherently violent religion apparently connect all or most Muslims to the extreme acts of those who commit terrorism in the name of Islam. Those who make this mistake are likely to see all Muslims as a threat to civil order and to support laws restrictive of Muslims' civil rights.[28] The state has an obligation to inform citizens that most Muslims and almost all Muslim Americans object to the means and ends of terrorists. Then, citizens can come to tolerate groups who do not pose a real threat, while those citizens can still harbor legitimate suspicion toward groups that do pose a danger to the democratic order. A more indirect way of questioning the connection between most Muslims and terrorists is to remind students of the great national and ethnic diversity of Muslims. Stereotypical assumptions that all Muslims are Arabs from the Middle East exaggerate the association between the Islam and the form of Islamic fundamentalism some Muslims in the Middle East practice. Schools should question the perception that most Muslims support violent extremism, but they could also stress to students that a majority of the world's Muslims do not live in the Middle East.

Another way that education in a democratic state could dispel the association of religious minorities with their extremist elements is to expose students to examples of prominent religious minorities who occupy powerful and respected positions in mainstream American culture. The state must be careful, however, that it does not choose only examples of religious minorities who have lost all the distinctive features of their cultures and religions. Reminiscent of the much-maligned "melting-pot" approach to immigration, this approach might suggest that mainstream acceptance can only come at the sacrifice of distinctive cultural and religious attributes. The state should stress that it is possible for religious minorities to thrive in mainstream culture while maintaining at least some of these attributes.

A final element of symbolic intolerance, mentioned in the first section of this chapter, is the tendency to deny the existence of discrimination when it exists. The state has an obligation to make citizens aware not only of discrimination against religious minorities in public policy or law but of discrimination against religious minorities in semipublic and private spheres. Such awareness is essential for active tolerance because Americans will obviously not work to counteract intolerance they are not aware exists. Although active tolerance is not overly strenuous, it is more strenuous than passive tolerance and requires a greater degree of motivation. Americans standing up in support of rights for targets of discrimination are likely to experience criticism from those supporting discriminatory policies, who may include coworkers, classmates, neighbors, and even relatives and friends. The most effective way to motivate people to engage in actively tolerant behavior is to encourage a sense of outrage at injustice. The knowledge of discrimination can spark this outrage.

## The Subjective Value versus the Objective Value of Religious Beliefs

Providing Americans with more accurate knowledge of other religious traditions will not, of course, automatically lead to more civic tolerance in all cases. Greater exposure to and knowledge of other religions might even increase aversion of some to other religions by encouraging them to dwell on differences between religions. Some Christian students initially unaware that Muslims treat the New Testament as a legitimate source of revelation but one superseded by the Qur'an's revelations may, on learning this, only grow more averse to Islam for what they perceive as religious condescension. Moreover, the state should, by and large, respect aversion based on accurate information, lest it encourage religiously conservative believers to change their views about the mutual exclusivity of religious claims. Respecting religiously intolerant opinions means the state ought, for instance, to respect the opinion of a Christian who rejects Islam because of an inability to accept that Muhammad was a true prophet or that Muhammad's prophecy overrides Jesus's revelation. Still, the state does not have an obligation to remain completely passive in the face of aversion based on accurate information, even if it does not directly and immediately lead to civilly intolerant behavior.

The most effective and legitimate way to discourage this aversion is to distinguish appreciation of the subjective and objective values of other beliefs by encouraging theologically intolerant citizens to take the approach of objecting to the "sin" but not the "sinner." A multicultural education for recognition is problematic because it encourages citizens to explore the *objective* value of alternative religious beliefs. But encouraging citizens to understand the *subjective* value that people of various religions find in their beliefs does not involve a violation of religiously intolerant beliefs, at least in theory. Encouraging Orthodox Jews or fundamentalist Christians to accept that Muhammad is or may be a legitimate prophet of God is mutually exclusive with their core beliefs, but encouraging them to realize the strength of Muslims' belief in Muhammad's legitimacy as a prophet and the consequences of this for Islamic beliefs and practices is not.

Holding robust religious beliefs is not only consistent with appreciation of the subjective value of other religions; it may often deepen this appreciation. "Genuine religious toleration is achieved," writes former archbishop of Canterbury George Carey (2000, 52), "when people hold their religion as so important, so absolute, that to part from it is to die, and yet at the same time realize from their absolute centre of being that another person's values and beliefs are just as important and just as real." Although Carey's statement exaggerates the importance of robust belief to religious tolerance, it does raise a compelling point. Who would better understand the anguish caused by religious discrimination than people who place their religious beliefs at the core of their identities? There seems to be no better way to motivate citizens who hold robust commitments to their own belief systems to engage in the occasionally demanding work of actively tolerant behavior than to link their commitment with the commitments religious minorities have. Combining the subjective appreciation of deep believers with a reminder that religious intolerance is a real problem—not only in their country, but often in their community—can help transform tolerant beliefs into tolerant action.

Still, the state must take care in how it encourages citizens to identify with the subjective value other believers attribute to their beliefs. While encouraging sympathetic imagination for other believers is legitimate, the state should strictly avoid promoting empathy. Sympathetic imagination involves learning to appreciate a person's situation from the outside. A Hindu man who understands how a Christian feels when Christ's role in salvation is criticized because he imagines what it would be like if a Christian criticized his henotheism is engaged in sympathetic imagination. Since a sympathetic person is able to feel compassion while managing to maintain some distance from the object of compassion, promoting sympathetic imagination is more consistent with protecting believers' freedom of conscience. Empathy involves an emotional and intellectual identification with another person through an attempt to fully understand what it is like to be another person "from the inside" and involves a more total, even if temporary, divestment of one's own identity than sympathy. A Christian woman engages in empathy when she tries to comprehend why Muslims believe that Muhammad is God's final prophet through an extended study of the Qur'an and the works of Muslim philosophers, attempting to grasp these texts' meanings and value as Muslims themselves do.[29] Besides empirical questions about whether empathy is really necessary for tolerance, encouraging empathy directly conflicts with the freedom of conscience of many re-ligious believers, particularly of conservative and fundamentalist believers.

Schools must also be careful to avoid reducing religious differences to mere cultural prejudices. At times, the prejudiced bury religious aversions beneath a cultural veneer, but there are also times when religious prejudice is preferred because it is more socially acceptable. Gordon Allport noted this phenomenon over 50 years ago. After explaining that "piety is the mask" and "the inner force is tribal instinct" (Allport 1950, 36), he argued that "piety may thus be a convenient mask for prejudices which intrinsically have nothing to do with religion" (42). Perhaps the more compelling expla-nation for the persistent specious rumors among some conservative parti-sans during the 2008 presidential campaign that Barack Obama is a practic-ing Muslim is that such religious prejudice is more publicly acceptable than racial prejudice (Kristof 2008). Similarly, raw prejudice against homosexuals is increasingly unacceptable in American society, but using religion as a jus-tification for such prejudice makes it appear more acceptable.

Using religion to mask cultural prejudice no doubt exists in our society, but there are strong reasons that schools should err on the side of accepting religious explanations rather than exposing them as cultural prejudices. Despite the use of religion to rationalize cultural prejudice, much religious disagreement or criticism of cultural practices is rooted in faith and theol-ogy. To call into question all instances where religion criticizes cultural prej-udices as inauthentic would call much of faith itself into question, particu-larly in the cases of religions, like evangelical Christianity, that critique mainstream culture. Like promoting recognition, such unmasking would have the impermissible effect of undermining religious beliefs. Besides, schools may be able to promote the civil rights of the targets of these beliefs without calling into question the authenticity of the beliefs' religious justi-fication. The best way for schools to combat intolerance of the civil rights of gays is to stress to students that they have a democratic obligation to pro-tect the civil rights of gays even if they feel aversion toward this group.

Just because we can distinguish between ways to promote civil toler-ance without simultaneously promoting theological tolerance in theory, however, does not mean that attempts to accomplish both goals will be suc-cessful in practice. Moral concerns and empirical questions remain. One set of questions involves the strength of the relationship between an increase in knowledge and decline in intolerance. Promoting active tolerance without recognition relies on the related claims that increased understanding and the acceptance of the subjective value of beliefs is sufficient to make religious minorities feel respected and comfortable enough to participate in the public sphere. Perhaps this is insufficient, with full-fledged recognition of the objective value of beliefs being necessary. Does more knowledge about the Islamic world, for instance, increase tolerance toward Muslims? Another set of questions involves the distinction between the acceptance of the subjective and objective values of other religious beliefs. Although acceptance of the subjective importance and objective validity of religious beliefs is distinguishable in theory, it may not be so in practice. Perhaps Christians introduced to arguments about how strongly Buddhists or Muslims feel about their beliefs will inevitably proceed to examine whether these beliefs may have some objective validity or even some direct relevance to their own lives and religious practices.

Constructing effective survey questions to measure recognition of subjective and objective validity and the effect of increased knowledge and understanding is one way to address these concerns. Although previous tolerance scholars have not done this, the research on the effects of Modesto's course in chapter 3 speaks to these questions. But examining this research at this point would put the cart ahead of the horse. To determine if public schools can promote active tolerance but not recognition, we must start with a concrete treatment of specific curriculum policies. The following section provides such a treatment, and readers are likely to be surprised by its conclusions.

## WON'T PROMOTING ACTIVE TOLERANCE DEEPEN RELIGIOUS CONFLICTS?

### Required World Religions Courses: The Civic and Liberal Educational Approaches Compared

The real religious conflicts in the United States and, even more, the imagined religious conflicts the mainstream media harps on have left many American public school officials anxious. In an environment where saying anything could lead to recriminations and even lawsuits, silence about religion was the golden rule that governed much curriculum. Too harshly judging the overly careful decisions of administrators whose jobs were on the line would be captious. But ignoring the civic consequences of their omissions would be unwise.

Perhaps those who lose the most from this silence, this chapter suggests, are religious minorities. The growing numbers of non-Christians in the United States are not the only ones affected, though. A large majority of Americans are Christians, but Christianity is a minority religion in at least some communities. In many more communities, particular versions of Christianity, like evangelicalism, are minority beliefs. Other scholars have noted several strong reasons for greater teaching about religion in the curriculum, such as improving religious literacy (Prothero 2007; Nord 1995). But the promotion of active tolerance, the strongest democratic reason of all for teaching more about religion, has gone unnoticed. The lack of religious literacy is a grave disservice to students' awareness of the world around them, but a dearth of active tolerance can deprive Americans of their rights. "But it does me no injury for my neighbor to say there are twenty gods or no god," Thomas Jefferson (1993, 254) famously argued in defense of religious liberty, adding, "It neither picks my pocket nor breaks my leg." As progressive as Jefferson's position was in his day, American democracy can no longer be content with passive acceptance. Today, it is the *failure* of Americans to go out of their way to include religious minorities that is most likely to end up in Jefferson's broken legs and picked pockets, metaphorically and sometimes literally.

The pioneering work of a small but growing group of activists and scholars (Nord and Haynes 1998; Wexler 2002; Douglass 2000) has encouraged a growing, though still small, group of courageous public school administrators and teachers to reverse this trend. Many public schools now realize that silence about one of humanity's central activities is in no one's interest. The most welcome change has been an enhanced "natural inclusion" of religion in existing compulsory curriculum courses, like social studies, history, and English classes.[30]

As significant as this accomplishment is, active tolerance is too important of a goal to be left to natural inclusion. Since religion is one of many topics in the courses where it is naturally included, students too often receive only a cursory introduction to the basic beliefs of the world's major religions. Even when they receive extended information about religion, the information may not be particularly relevant to the promotion of active tolerance. Discussions of religion in history and social studies courses dwell almost exclusively on the role of religion in history and largely ignore the powerful way that religion shapes contemporary societies and lives. The treatment of religion in literature courses is interested only peripherally, if at all, with the practical aspects and rituals of major world religions. Indeed, since literature courses focus on Western literature and its influences, these courses usually pay more attention to the Jewish and Christian sacred texts than to those of other major world religions.

Not treating religion as a discrete subject matter in the curriculum prevents students from considering the distinctive attributes of religious beliefs. Unless elevated to the status of an independent subject matter in the curriculum, students are unlikely to appreciate the special importance that religion plays in the lives of religious minorities and the deep hurt caused by religious intolerance or the exceptional importance of religious tolerance to the flourishing of our democratic deliberation. The willingness to defend religious minorities actively requires that students have a sense of sympathy for groups vulnerable to persecution and a strong sense of objection to the injustice of religious intolerance. Protesting injustice is not easy. It takes a significant degree of motivation, for instance, to write a letter to a politician on behalf of a group being discriminated against. The opponents of intolerance need a strong motivation in order to resist negative peer pressure.

Sympathy for persecuted religious groups and outrage for the injustice of religious tolerance can supply this motivation. But they, in turn, depend on a robust knowledge of religion and its central subjective value for many people's lives. To appreciate fully, for instance, why repeatedly attempting to persuade Hindus to convert to Christianity is offensive, students must understand the tremendous value that Hindus find in adhering to their religion. Treated as one of many topics, the discussion of religion is too cursory to provide an inspiration for students to engage in not only the many small gestures but especially the occasional large actions that active tolerance requires.

Even if natural inclusion did provide students with sufficient motivation for active tolerance, it will not instruct them on how to avoid offending members of other religions. Appropriate skills and knowledge are as important for active religious tolerance as are correct motivations. Comments not intended to be intolerant may still be so if they touch on a particularly sensitive aspect of a person's belief system. To avoid making comments that alienate religious believers, students must be familiar with the basic tenets of major religious points of view. Scattered references to religion in history and English classes will not encourage students to engage in the extended reflection and discussion of religion, in and out of class, that they need to negotiate the religious differences they will encounter as adults.

A society like ours in need of both active tolerance and citizens educated for democratic participation can do no other than require students in its public schools to take an independent, extended course on world religions. The course must be required, because among the students most likely to opt out—religious conservatives—are those most in need of the skills for active tolerance. Many public schools have elective courses in world religions, but Modesto, California, has the only school district in the country to require all students to take a world religions course. The discussion of religion must be extended—consisting of one or two semesters of instruction—to provide students with the information, inspiration, and skills necessary for active tolerance. Only an extended teaching of religion will provide students with sufficient information about current beliefs and practices of major world religions so that they can avoid inadvertent slights. Only an in-depth presentation of religious views will enable students to recognize the sometimes subtle distinctions between them that will prevent the lumping together of mainstream and extremist believers. But information alone cannot provide the inspiration for the sometimes arduous work of active tolerance. World religions course should be framed by a civic narrative that reminds students explicitly of their active tolerance duties and of the centrality of active religious tolerance to American democracy. The Modesto required course included such a civic framework, and the research discussed in chapter 3 suggests that this approach led to a significant increase in students' tolerance.

Still, the news from our Modesto research is not without cause for concern. Modesto's teachers and administrators at times took the promotion of tolerance too far. Emphasis on the similarities of religion were not coupled with a balancing discussion of major differences. Rabbi Paul Gordon expressed concern that some teachers were passing on a "warm and fuzzy" view of religion that tended to blur the lines between faiths. The teachers' behavior did not rise to the level of legally actionable complaints, but democratic education must adhere to a standard higher than the law. Besides some evidence to the contrary from our interviews, our large-scale surveys found no substantial evidence that the course pushed students to take more syncretistic and ecumenist stances on religion.[31] But, as chapter 3 discusses in more detail, Modesto's course had a positive but limited effect on *active* tolerance, despite its significant effect on *passive* tolerance. The abbreviated length of Modesto's required course—half a semester—is the most likely explanation for this shortfall in active tolerance. Public schools need to implement a one-semester world religions course—or, if feasible, a two-semester course—to ensure active tolerance. But this added length would almost certainly increase the course's syncretistic and ecumenist push. Even if schools could take steps that Modesto did not take to temper these effects of world religions courses, such attempts would likely be self-defeating, because they might eliminate active tolerance as well.

If a more extended course were to increase at least anecdotes of recognition, syncretism, and ecumenism, it would threaten the growing, still fragile consensus over schools that exists between secularists, religious minorities, and religious conservatives, a consensus this book is devoted to strengthening. Modesto's large population of evangelical Christians and conservative Catholics, our research found, have not registered significant public or legal challenges to Modesto's course since its outset. But Modesto's religious conservatives may have found a one- or two-semester course more intrusive, especially if it was the only discussion of religion in the required or elective curriculum. Even if Modesto's religious conservatives would accept the course, religious conservatives elsewhere may be more reluctant to accept an extended course. Modesto's evangelicals, for instance, often observe that the city is part of the California Bible Belt, but more than one Modesto resident cautioned against exaggerating the resemblance of Modesto's evangelicals to evangelicals of the southeastern Bible Belt states.

Besides, mere acceptance of a required world religions course by religious conservatives is not the goal of a democratic education about religion and would, indeed, be counterproductive. The promotion of active tolerance requires not just the absence of aversion to it but a modicum of enthusiasm. Americans are simply not likely to take even the small steps to include religious minorities if they do not, on some level, buy into the importance of promoting active tolerance. If the implementation of a world religions course were seen as forced on or even as simply extraneous to religious conservative interests, the course could not serve the goal of promoting active tolerance and might even discourage it. Democracies are neither wise nor moral when they rely on unilateral altruism. The legitimacy of and the motivation to meet democratic goals should instead depend on reciprocity.

But a special concern with the course's effect on conservative Christians goes beyond the practical and political. Conservative Christians are most likely to believe that their beliefs are imperiled by a required world religions course because their beliefs *are* most imperiled by such courses.[32] A required world religions course for active tolerance poses the greatest challenge for the most exclusive religions. The beliefs of monotheistic religions tend to be more exclusive than those of other faiths, and this is probably truer of Christianity than of other monotheistic faiths. Conservative Christians—evangelical and fundamentalist Protestants, conservative Catholics, and conservative Orthodox believers—see the truth of their faith as more exclusive with recognizing the truth of other faiths than do other Christians. The burdens of possible relativism fall most heavily on these believers, and the state and schools have a special moral obligation to be responsive to them. Even where no widespread evidence of increased relativism among students exists, the urging of relativism through the types of teacher statements we found in Modesto can send an illegitimate and alienating message to conservative Christians that schools do not care about protecting their beliefs.

Moreover, research on textbooks used in public school suggests that conservative Christians have reason to be concerned about the treatment of their views in public schools. In an essential empirical study of this issue published in 1986, Paul Vitz reviewed all social studies texts adopted by the states of California and Texas for grades 1–6. While the texts endorsed liberal perspectives on a variety of moral issues, Vitz concluded that they ignored more "traditional" moral positions valued by conservative Jews and conservative Christians.[33] In assessing Vitz's claims, it is relevant to note that he has a strong sympathy for religious conservative critiques of liberal education in general. However, sources without these sympathies that conducted similar empirical studies shortly after Vitz's research reached similar conclusions. The Association for Supervision and Curriculum Development (1987, 12), which favors greater discussion of a variety of religious and moral views in the curriculum, found that public school curricula typically exclude all reference to Christian fundamentalism, with the dubious exception of fundamentalist participation in the Scopes trial. In a 1989 and 1992 survey of North Carolina history textbooks, Warren Nord (1995, 140) found that the texts "typically provide a relatively liberal view of early Judaism and Christianity, emphasizing monotheism, justice, and love; they downplay or completely ignore sin, salvation, damnation, the millennium, cosmology, and faith." These studies are all more than 15 years old, and no similarly rigorous reviews of the curricular treatment of conservative Christian views have taken place since then. Without such evidence, we cannot be sure that the portrait of these older studies remains accurate. Still, given no substantial new evidence suggesting substantial changes in the treatment of conservative Christian views, it is probably reasonable to assume that such changes have not taken place.[34]

None of this research substantiates the overheated claims of right-wing culture warriors that the public schools have a liberal agenda of promoting secular humanism, denigrating conservative Christianity,[35] or favoring religions other than Judaism and Christianity.[36] Besides the obvious fallacy of attributing a consistent motivation to an incredibly heterogeneous public school system and bureaucracy, there are far more credible and benign explanations for the inadequate treatment of conservative Christian views besides liberal bias (Boyer 1996). The sins here are much more of unconscious omission than of intentional commission. The fear of causing controversy has led administrators, teachers, and textbook companies to neglect not only conservative Christian views but a wide variety of religious views. Still, if the claims of culture warriors are exaggerated, the concerns of more measured conservative Christians about a lack of attention to their views seem to have some basis in fact. Public schools must avoid creating world religions courses that offend conservative Christian beliefs, lest they deepen the lack of adequate respect for these views already present in many required social studies and history textbooks.

One important response is for public schools to make a special effort to ensure that world religions courses themselves do not promote relativism, ecumenism, and syncretism. They should provide students with explicit verbal instructions from teachers that the purpose of exposure to alternative religious views is to promote respect for the subjective and not the objective validity of other religions. Schools should tailor the course's lessons and subject matter to reflect the same goal. Exposure to religion for active tolerance should take a descriptive, rather than evaluative, approach. Schools must avoid, for instance, having students read extensively from sacred texts, because this might excessively encourage exploration of the validity of alternative belief systems; they should instead use objective textbooks written by academic religious scholars and testimonies of religious believers about the strength of their beliefs. Classes should only concentrate on the justifications of religions when these are tied inextricably to understanding central practices of religions that students must know about to cultivate respect. Exams and assignments should test students' knowledge about the beliefs and practices of other religions, rather than ask them to assess comparatively the validity of different traditions.

The civic and democratic approach to teaching world religions stands in contrast to the liberal educational approach to teaching about religion, which receives its finest treatment in the work of Warren Nord. Nord's *Religion and American Education* helped blaze a trail for the greater treatment of religion in public schools, by comprehensively detailing the indispensable value of studying religion in a liberal education. In their coauthored work *Taking Religion Seriously across the Curriculum,* Nord and Charles Haynes (1998, 43) explain that a "liberal education requires students to learn something about the major ways humankind has developed for understanding their lives and the world." The neglect of religion denies students basic knowledge of themselves and the world around them on the most crucial of questions. "There are secular *and* religious ways of asking, reflecting on, and answering . . . unavoidable 'existential' questions," Nord and Haynes conclude, arguing, "An *educated* person should have some understanding of the major ways of thinking about them, and the resultant answers" (39).

The liberal educational approach and the civic approach advanced in this chapter agree and reinforce each other on the *need* for a required world religions course. But the same cannot be said about *how the two approaches envision the teaching of a world religions course.* The democratic approach recommends a largely descriptive approach aimed at helping students understand the strength of other believers' faith but not the legitimacy of the religious views themselves.

In its promotion of empathy for other religions, the liberal educational approach to world religions would resemble the recognition approach previously described.

If texts and teachers are to take religion seriously, if they are to be *fair* to members of a tradition, they must let the advocates of that religion speak for themselves, using the cultural and conceptual resources of their own traditions. The point is not to strain their world through our conceptual nets, but to hear what they say and see what they do in the context of their own beliefs, experiences, motives, and worldview—from *the inside,* as it were. (Nord and Haynes 1998, 50)

To provide students with a comprehensive understanding of the world around them, Nord (1995, 191) recommends that students be provided with "as deep an understanding as possible of the alternatives" on contested cultural matters. To ensure the depth of students' understanding of religion from the inside, Nord advises extensive exposure to "literature and poetry and drama," which can help to "imaginatively and vicariously think our way into a religious frame of mind," and to "autobiography, apologetic literature, Scripture, and theology, which may not operate imaginatively but is written from within a religious worldview and uses religious categories and logic" (220).

Unlike recognition theorists, Nord is sensitive to the possibility that his liberal educational approach might conflict with the beliefs of religious conservatives. Having students experience other religions, rather than just grasp their doctrines, is essential to understanding, but Nord (218) firmly rejects the suggestion of other proponents of the educational approach that students participate in a "worship ceremony" of the faiths they are examining. Such participation might require the affirmation of beliefs that violate the student's own faith. A world religions course "must not convey to students that all religious traditions are equally true or false" (Nord and Haynes 1998, 54).

Even if having students identify with other religions is not the intention of a world religions course in liberal education theory, it may still be the effect of the course in practice. If a school were to assign extensive reading from the Qur'an to help students make sense of Islam, for instance, it is relatively easy to imagine some Hindu students misinterpreting this reading as an encouragement to identify with Islam, and it is possible that some Hindu students might conclude after this reading that their religious differences with Muslims are not as significant as they originally thought. Nord (1995, 221) does explain, for instance, that "we take [religion] seriously when we let it question us, when we open ourselves to the possibility that we misunderstand the world and are subject to enlightenment by that religion—when we are willing to be self-critical." The civic course this chapter describes may be critiqued for attempting to thread a needle by encouraging civic respect without recognition. But having students consider religion from the inside without promoting identification seems more the equivalent of passing a camel through a needle's eye.

The likelihood of the course having impermissible effects in practice is particularly significant given the good deal of faith that the educational approach invests in teachers. Under the educational approach, teachers are not just docents describing each faith but, at least occasionally, shepherds into the mysteries of each faith. Even assuming the optimal conditions that teachers are well trained and have the best of intentions, the educational approach allows considerable latitude for bias and misinterpretation of the course's purposes by giving teachers a central role in world religions courses. Modesto teachers, for instance, did receive a fairly rigorous training and had generally good intentions, but several still transmitted to students questionably ecumenicist and syncretistic messages about the course's purposes.[37] Employing a civic approach that primarily focused on description of beliefs helped Modesto to mitigate the effect these messages had. Without this damper pedal, though, the biases of teachers under the educational approach are likely to be more amplified and controversial.

Even assuming an absence of bias in practice, the educational approach to teaching about world religions still has one critical flaw in conception. An essential feature of a *democratic* education in a participatory society like ours is that it should pursue goals that all segments of the society can support. Required courses in particular not only must be free of biases in their classroom execution but must send a message of inclusion to parents and community members. This is not only a practical but also a moral imperative. The civic goal of promoting active tolerance—accompanied with significant checks and balances—found considerable support among conservative Christians in Modesto (as chapter 3 explains) and is likely to find considerable support among conservative Christians elsewhere (as chapter 2 suggests). But it is quite easy to imagine large numbers of religious conservatives and particularly conservative Christians questioning whether helping students to explore religious perspectives "from the inside" is a vital and proper goal of public schools, especially when it involves students questioning themselves and opening themselves "to the possibility that [they] misunderstand the world."[38]

This, of course, does not mean that the educational approach to teaching world religions lacks considerable merit. Nor is it to deny that by taking a more circumscribed approach to teaching about religion, the civic approach to world religions recommended here and adopted in Modesto will fail to promote as well-rounded an intellectual appreciation of religion as the educational approach would. Perhaps in addition to a one-semester required world religions course using the civic approach, schools might consider offering a one-semester *elective* course in world religions based on the educational approach, for students who want a more in-depth understanding of various religions. But the civic drawbacks of a *required* world religions course based on the educational approach outweigh the educational advantages. A course touching on a topic as sensitive as religious conscience must take special care that it does not favor any perspective about religion over any other, and a universally required course on the subject should be based on nearly universal consensus. The democratic and educational approaches are not completely mutually exclusive, but when they conflict, the democratic approach is preferable. The risk of bias in the educational approach is too great, and the reward of a well-rounded intellectual appreciation of various religions is a dubious benefit to many.

## Beyond World Religions: A Special Recognition for Conservative Christians?

A world religions course focused on active tolerance, then, contains more safeguards against biases than the educational approach to world religions and is likely to be preferred by conservative Christians. Still, as welcome as these safeguards might be, they are unlikely to secure widespread satisfaction with required world religions courses among conservative Christians. That conservative Christians prefer the civic approach to the educational approach to teaching world religions does not automatically mean they would prefer a democratically taught course to no course at all. Moreover, the implementation of a required world religions course is a major curricular change. The lack of active resistance to such courses is not sufficient to guarantee their implementation; they need something closer to active support. Active support requires that all sides see world religions courses as mutually beneficial. Non-Christians and secularists committed to tolerance are apt to find these courses in their interests. But even with these safe-guards, many conservative Christians are unlikely to see how the course would prove equally beneficial to them, and they are likely to remain suspicious about the course's syncretistic and ecumenist effects.

They would not be completely wrong to harbor these suspicions. Modesto's administrators, aware of a possible syncretism and ecumenism problem, installed many safeguards and trained teachers carefully to avoid it. At least occasional disregard of these safeguards by teachers is evidence that schools cannot prevent a slight relativistic push, no matter how hard they try. Just because the civic approach to world religions is less likely to encourage the belief that all religions are the same than is the educational approach does not mean it will be acceptably free of this bias. Schools' efforts to prevent syncretism and ecumenism, to be sure, are not futile; they can control the *extent* to which they pervade a world religions course. But given the course's goal of promoting understanding of other religions, some teachers will inevitably, if inadvertently, encourage these beliefs to at least a slight degree, and some students are bound to see their promotion as the course's purpose.

The school curriculum regarding religion merits particularly intense scrutiny. Rights to freedom of conscience are especially precious, and schools must strive to avoid even slight violations of them. To ensure that democratic practice coheres with democratic principles, public schools must go beyond negative steps to prevent recognition, relativism, syncretism, and ecumenism and must take affirmative steps to recognize crucial conservative Christian beliefs in the curriculum. Recognizing conservative Christian beliefs *in* world religions courses is a needed step but is not sufficient. Nomi Stolzenberg (1993) points out that many conservative Christians view the exposure to Christianity as one of many religious options as inconsistent with a robust recognition of Christian truth.

Needless to say, schools must be extremely careful *how* they promote recognition, lest they defeat the purposes of active tolerance and trigger alienation of religious minorities, religious liberals, and secularists. Including a robust recognition of conservative Christian beliefs in courses that all students must take would undoubtedly cause alienation. Such recognition would send a clear message to nonadherents of conservative Christianity that schools value other beliefs more than their own. But elective courses that all students do not need to take often deal with controversial material or material of interest to one segment of the student population and the community. Women's history, African American history, and the Holocaust are all examples of course subjects that might be controversial in the compulsory curriculum but that flourish in many schools as electives. The elective curriculum has become a safe haven for identity politics associated with the left; it is time that identity politics associated with the right receive similar treatment. The treatment of religious beliefs, to be sure, is more controversial and bound by legal and constitutional constraints. But chapters 4 and 5 offer ways schools can teach elective courses in Bible and intelligent design that are consistent with constitutional rules and democratic norms.

Still, if public schools promoting recognition of beliefs is wrong in general, as this chapter has argued strenuously, how could the *special* recognition of conservative Christian beliefs in the curriculum possibly be justified? In a chapter of paradoxes, this is perhaps the most confounding. Not all forms of recognition, however, are the same. The recognition of religion that Charles Taylor recommends is proactive and unalloyed. A stand-alone world religions course encouraging students to accept the objective legitimacy of other faiths would clearly run afoul of religious liberty. This chapter supports a compensatory and heavily conditioned special recognition of Christian beliefs in the elective curriculum. When unaccompanied by a world religions course promoting active tolerance, special recognition of Christian beliefs is clearly unjustified and an even greater violation of religious liberty than a stand-alone world religions course. Such recognition is only defensible when triggered by the implementation of a required world religions course, with its inevitable relativistic push. Conversely, requiring all students to take a world religions course while offering special recognition of Christian beliefs in the elective curriculum would prevent the impression that schools favor one view about religion over another. Requiring world religion courses and providing electives would lead to more active tolerance and less recognition than would having only a required world religions course.[39]

But even if such recognition in electives balances the treatment of conservative Christian views in required world religions courses, it might seem to involve the state in simply taking away with one hand the active tolerance it is giving with the other. If a required world religion course and special recognition of Christian views in electives canceled each other out, why should public schools bother implementing both courses in the first place? An obvious retort is that world religion courses will be required, while recognition of conservative Christian views will be in elective courses. The students who took the former but not the latter would emerge as more committed to active tolerance overall. But a more compelling response is that perhaps it is wrong to see recognition of Christianity in the elective curriculum and the promotion of active tolerance in the compulsory curriculum as necessarily at odds.

Tolerance and recognition, to be sure, *are* often at odds. But when both are framed in the right context, they might interact in a mutually beneficial way. This is far from an uncommon phenomenon. Harvard economist Benjamin Friedman (2006), for instance, has provided compelling evidence that racism and other forms of discrimination have increased during times of economic contraction throughout American history, like the Great Depression, while prosperity produces more tolerance and openness. During tough economic times, according to Friedman, minority ethnic and racial groups are seen as competitors for crucial and scarce resources. More prosperous economic times remove this dread competition and alleviate ill feelings toward alleged competitors. The same dynamic might apply to a public school education that provides special recognition to conservative Christian beliefs. If conservative Christians have their beliefs recognized, they will no longer view secularists and religious minorities as competitors for scarce resources. This might inspire not only increased acceptance of a world religions course but increased active tolerance of religious minorities. If the debate over religion and public schools, however, continues to tell citizens they must choose between no treatment of religion, a liberal treatment of religion, or recognition of conservative Christian beliefs, we should not be surprised if secularists, religious minorities, and conservative Christians continue to view each other as antagonists in the struggle for scarce resources.

Still, even if the education about religion recommended here *could* work in this way, *will* it? Are conservative Christians in particular likely to respond to recognition with tolerance? The next chapter provides evidence from national surveys and interviews that this is not a mere wish. It also identifies the principle of good faith that should determine both what types of conservative Christian beliefs deserve examination in electives and how such examination should be carried out.

# CHAPTER 2

## Teaching Good Faith

The history of universal state-run education is too often a story of power, not principle. Its origins lie less in a humanitarian impulse to spread knowledge and opportunity to all social classes than in the state's desire to harness the energies of its citizens more effectively for its own ends and to favor the privileged and powerful many over the vulnerable few. Public school education in the United States, of course, has not been exempt from these sinister impulses. In one of the most regrettable chapters in American educational history, Oregon voters in 1922 approved a Ku Klux Klan–inspired ballot initiative that required parents to send their children to public schools. The Compulsory School Act was largely an attempt to manipulate reality and rein in diversity through controlling language. Oregon was in the grips of an anti-immigrant and anti-Catholic frenzy. Public schools taught English only, and forbidding their attendance at private schools would ensure that immigrant children received no instruction in their native languages. Fortunately, the Supreme Court recognized this as an unconstitutional assault on parental rights and religious freedom and struck down the act in the landmark 1925 *Pierce v. Society of Sisters* case.

Still, even the most hardened skeptic of public schools would admit that they have *some* necessary role to play in instructing students about a proper language of politics. Democracies trust their citizens to associate freely. Without some shared language, a diverse democracy like the United States would splinter into religious, cultural, racial, and ethnic enclaves. If liberty is not to degenerate into license, citizens must learn how to discuss politics with each other responsibly. Through studying the Declaration of Independence and the Constitution, students acquire a vocabulary of equality and individual rights. Even if such an education borders on the banal and if definition of key concepts remains vague, it gives all students something in common and encourages them to treat their fellow citizens' political views with a modicum of respect.

Public schools today often do not venture beyond this basic instruction in how to talk and think about politics. Heeding the cautionary tales in ours and others' pasts and deterred by the allegedly gaping cultural and political divides in our society, schools provide little or no guidance about how to deal with controversial issues. The opportunities for abuse and bias are many, the safeguards to ensure genuine fairness too few. The controversy includes, of course, the use of religion in politics.

This chapter argues that public schools have an important role to play in encouraging students to think about how to use views about religion in politics. In an effort to avoid indoctrination, schools have gone too far in the opposite direction by refusing to provide even the most minimal and reasonable guidance about the intersection of faith and politics. As passive and even unwitting as their role has been, public schools bear much responsibility for the sad state of America's conflicts over religion and culture. The remedy is to have public schools encourage students to use religion in politics in a way that is consistent with the principle of good faith and to have the public school curriculum about religion model these virtues. This education would address the major concerns of all sides in America's cultural divide. But before this argument can even get off the ground, it must respond to the basic objection that schools have no business guiding students about how to talk about religion and politics.

## IGNORANCE IS NOT BLISS

Religion, many secularists and liberals agree, can be a powerful source of good in people's private lives but does not belong in politics. Americans come from many religious backgrounds, and using religion to explain and justify public policies is bound to be divisive and inaccessible to those who do not share the most widespread of religious beliefs, including those who believe in no divinity at all. The job of public schools regarding how to use religious language in politics is simple, according to this separationist position. Because religion has no place in politics, no guidance about faith and politics is necessary. To provide any guidance is to at least tacitly acknowledge that faith can sustain political views.

The moral conflict of this position with democratic principles will be discussed later. But even if it were morally valid, its impracticality would still be fatal. Religious beliefs have served as a source of political beliefs throughout American history, and polling indicates what Andrew Kohut and John Green describe as a "diminishing divide" between religion and politics. A majority of Americans in Gallup polls from the 1960s opposed church involvement in politics; a majority in a 1996 Pew poll supported churches' "expressing views on political and social issues of the day" (Kohut and Green 2000, 5). Americans between the ages of 18 and 29 are more likely than those over 64 to feel that churches should express political views, by a margin of 58 to 42 percent. Despite popular perceptions that the Christian right is driving this greater injection of religion into politics, increased support for church involvement in politics cuts across political and religious lines. "Remarkably similar majorities" of Republicans (55 percent), Democrats (56 percent), and Independents (57 percent) support church involvement in politics today (ibid., 102). Majorities of Catholics, Jews, and nonevangelical Protestants also believe that churches should play some role in politics (ibid., 40). Religion is correlated with and at least partly explains people's opinions on a spectrum of issues that range beyond sexual and cultural issues and include views on race, the role of government in providing welfare, and the environment.[1]

These numbers indicate that even if the secularist position is neutral in intent, its effects are far from neutral. Every day, religious institutions and families of all faiths are shaping the religious language citizens apply to politics and the choices they make. Churches and families are well within their rights to do this. Problems arise for respect and civility, however, when the information on which they base their advice and choices exaggerates divisiveness. This is the harmful legacy of the culture war industry that has cropped up over the last 30 years in America (J. D. Hunter 1991). Organized by the most extreme partisans on both sides of the cultural divide, their power, support, and funding depend on distorting this divide. By exaggerating the size and nature of the threat posed by their opponents, presenting stark and rigid political positions as their adherents' only options, the culture war industry has, with the help of the media, manufactured dissent. Polls consistently show that the vast majority of Americans on all sides of the cultural divide are open to compromise on controversial cultural and political issues. However, too often convinced by the culture war industry that their opponents do not share their goodwill, they allow extremists to speak for them.

This is not to deny the valid concerns secularists raise about the perils of using religion in politics. Religious rhetoric used to attack other religious groups and the nonreligious can fuel exclusion and alienation of targeted groups. Basing public policies solely on religious grounds can amount to coercion. By stressing what divides us, use of religious beliefs in politics can erode civility, feed cynicism, and encourage apathy. *But all of this is happening right now, partly because public schools implicitly adopt the secularist stance.*[2] When schools fail to provide any guidance about how to use religious beliefs in politics, they become an unwitting coconspirator of the culture war industry. Fools may rush in where angels fear to tread. But fearing to tread near the religion and politics relationship has proven foolish for schools and American society.

A quarter century ago, Richard John Neuhaus (1984) famously complained of the emergence of a "naked public square" stripped of religion. The choice America faces today is not between a naked and a religious public square but between different versions of the religious public square. In the future, are we to have a free-for-all like we currently do, where the loudest and most extreme voices of the culture war industry prevail and civility suffers? Or can we have a more civil and reasonable public square, where religious views are welcome but their more extreme and intolerant manifestations are not? It is only a slight exaggeration to suggest that as public schools go on this issue, so goes our nation. When they ignore religion in politics, they deepen our divisions. When they encourage future citizens to be more thoughtful about what forms of religious language in politics are acceptable and off-limits, they help to heal our wounds.

But perhaps the true offense of schools providing such guidance is not to the principle of separation of church and state but to religious beliefs. Public schools should aim at providing, according to William Galston (2002), maximum feasible accommodation of all religious beliefs. Considering any distinctions between or judgments about religious beliefs at all involves a violation of the spirit of the First Amendment's conscience rights and will inevitably favor religious beliefs held by the majority. Teaching respect for the believer and practical information for respect are proper goals for schools, but providing guidance and encouraging conversation about beliefs and advantaging more "civil" forms of religion is intrusive and can trigger relativism. Maybe public schools are better off simply teaching respect and ignoring how we use religion to talk about politics.

This argument ignores, however, the distinction between solely religious beliefs and those that believers routinely apply to politics (Audi and Wolterstorff 1997, 129). Solely religious beliefs, such as the doctrine of the atonement or views about the sacraments in Christianity or the doctrine of samsara in Hinduism, have, at most, indirect social effects and are not the concern of society and schools. But Christian discussions of prohibitions on same-sex sodomy or of the sanctity of life often influence votes on gay marriage, abortion, and the death penalty. These beliefs affect others' rights and the overall quality of democratic discussion. The greatest threat to vulnerable religious minorities, contra Galston, comes from failing to provide guidance about the use of religion in politics. A free-for-all religious public square leaves them little protection from insults and coercion by public policy.

A strictly descriptive approach to discussing religion is appropriate for solely religious beliefs. But for the sake of religious and other vulnerable minorities, the religiously committed who desire recognition of their religious beliefs, and the overall health of our democracy, a more robust and evaluative approach is necessary for religious beliefs used regularly in politics. None of these arguments are intended to conceal the problems with having public schools provide this guidance. Public schools have too often sanctioned bias to earn a free pass. When they wade into the controversial area of religion, we must watch them all the more closely. But to borrow Winston Churchill's famous quip about democracy, having public schools play this role is the worst option except for all the others. No other social institution has as great a capacity to save us from our cultural conflicts and the industry that perpetuates it.

## THE MODERATE MAJORITY

Few educational goals seem more worthy than using public schools to create an entente in our conflicts over religion and culture. But the cold reality, some prominent secularists argue, is that such an entente is not possible. Conservative Christian demands about religion in the public square are too incompatible with democratic principles. Public school guidance on religion in the public square, on this view, is bound to be unprincipled or unpopular. A compromise conservative Christians could accept would betray democracy. A form of guidance consistent with democracy could never garner the support of conservative Christians and be implemented. "Perhaps in the end," concludes Stephen Macedo (1995, 478), "our politics does come down to a holy war between religious zealots and proponents of science and public reason." If so, there is little schools can do; they can only sit back and watch the shouting continue. To defend a deliberative education about religion from these charges requires investigating what some prominent secularists say about evangelicals and seeing if they are right.[3]

The chief democratic sin of evangelicals and fundamentalists, according to their political opponents, is their aggressive injection of sectarianism into politics (Hauerwas and Willimon 1996; Macedo 2003; Crapanzano 2000; Lynn 2006). According to Martha Nussbaum in her recent book *Liberty of Conscience,*

> An organized, highly funded, and widespread political movement wants the values of a particular brand of conservative evangelical Christianity to define the United States. Its members seek public recognition that the Christian God is our nation's guardian . . . It threatens to undermine the very idea that all citizens, no matter what they believe about the ultimate meaning of life, can live together in full equality. (Nussbaum 2008, 4)

Evangelicals view the political process, their opponents argue, as a vehicle for imposing their religious preferences on those with different beliefs and none at all. Polls consistently show that evangelicals are by far the most active of all American faiths. Asked if "Christians should get involved in politics to protect their values," 79 percent of committed evangelicals agreed that they should (Kohut and Green 2000, 101). More than 9 out of 10 evangelicals believe that Christians should be trying to change American society to better reflect God's will and that "converting people to Jesus Christ" is "very important" (C. Smith 1998, 36).[4]

All interest groups want to see their cause triumph, but religious interest groups have an obligation to be more restrained. An overly aggressive approach is bound to provoke conflict and alienation, and imposing narrow religious preferences on citizens with different views violates the spirit, if not the letter, of the First Amendment. This is especially the case because evangelicals aim to regulate the most fundamental and intimate decisions we make. By legislating about homosexuality, abortion, and euthanasia, evangelicals seek to control how we die, what we do with our bodies, and how we behave in the privacy of our homes.

The true measure of a reasonable democratic citizen has less to do with what they believe than with how they hold their beliefs. If a group is open to argument and willing to compromise, there is hope that even if their private beliefs are less than tolerant, they can be persuaded not to act on these beliefs in public. Acceptance of the "burdens of judgment," in John Rawls's memorable phrase (Rawls 1993, 54), distinguishes ardency from intransigence. God may have made humans in his own image, but realizing the limits of our understanding and how different backgrounds could have reasonably led others to different beliefs and lifestyles helps us to realize that we fallible humans are not supposed to imitate God's example by making others over in our image through politics.

Unfortunately, according to their political critics, evangelicals are beyond such democratic conversion. Despite a theological belief in original sin, evangelicals believe that they are the recipients of God's revelation and that the Bible provides clear religious, moral, and political guidance. Their beliefs, according to their critics, are characterized more by certainty than by humility. Democratic debate is thus largely pointless, and there is not much use in taking into account other peoples' opinions and religious beliefs. Christian Smith (1998, 144) remarks that evangelicals "are aware of alternatives to their own version of faith" but that "this does very little to undermine their own beliefs and commitments." Important social science research shows a positive correlation between religious certainty and intellectual rigidity, on one hand, and intolerance and prejudice, on the other (McFarland 1989, 327; Altmeyer and Hunsberger 1992).[5]

Effective democratic deliberation requires that participants have at least a minimal concern with fairness and reciprocity, which evangelicals, as presented by their critics, appear to lack. Critics maintain that evangelicals want the right to pursue power over mainstream culture but refuse to accept the rules of tolerance and civil dialogue toward those with different views. Why should secularists and liberals worry about extending respect to the political arguments of evangelicals, if evangelicals show no interest in deliberating and playing by the rules of the democratic game? If separatism and unwillingness to listen are accurate and representative of most evangelicals, teaching deliberation would not be practically possible, let alone effective.

Much hinges, then, on determining whether the portrait of intransigent yet overbearing evangelicals is accurate or a useful fiction. Skepticism about making such a determination immediately rears its disapproving head. With such an abundance of divergent accounts about our conflicts over religion and culture, is it realistic to think we can arrive at an accurate account? Are there any sources that we have particular reason to trust? Accounts from activists on both sides of the culture war are most clearly disqualified. While the anecdotes about the extremist behavior of their opponents may be true, their desire to draw publicity to their cause and raise funds leads them to turn the exceptional into the typical. Mainstream media accounts of culture war disputes are little better. The media's desire for simple-to-follow story lines and its usual "If it bleeds, it leads" mentality exaggerate the influence of extremists.

Public opinion research offers a more promising route, but not all such research is of equal worth. Close-ended survey questions, for instance, can be of great value. Strictly limiting the number of possible responses to questions allows pollsters to easily compare results of different surveys and thus track changes in opinions over time. But the apparent clarity of close-ended survey results can often conceal as much as it reveals. Providing the polled with a limited range of options to describe their beliefs and policy preferences often fails to capture the nuance, ambiguity, ambivalence, and intensity of their beliefs.

To choose only one of numerous examples, a 2005 poll conducted by the Pew Forum on Religion and Public Life to examine Americans' views on evolution and other topics found that 67 percent of white evangelicals favor teaching creationism along with evolution and that 46 percent favor teaching creationism *instead* of evolution.[6] The latter result in particular seems to confirm the worst fears of secularists about domineering evangelicals. But a good deal of information is missing from this survey. It is not clear how intensely evangelicals favor the teaching of creationism and how strongly they are committed to changing the status quo. Without this information, it is difficult to determine how evangelicals' beliefs about teaching creationism in schools will translate into action in concrete situations. Evangelicals might be willing to steamroll opposition to achieve their goals, but they also might be willing to listen and compromise when faced with arguments from their opponents. These results also lack context and are difficult to evaluate in isolation. Perhaps evangelicals personally favor the teaching of creationism but are equally or more committed to accepting America's religious and political pluralism. Results of close-ended surveys about evangelicals are less the final word than they are the first. Open-ended and in-depth interviews fill the gaps left by close-ended surveys. They allow for the expression of more detailed, nuanced, and ambivalent responses. They enable researchers to better gauge the intensity of preferences and how belief might translate into action.[7]

The portrait of evangelicals that follows is based primarily on the sociological research of Christian Smith and Alan Wolfe. Combining close-ended survey results with open-ended interview results, they provide the most comprehensive information available about evangelicals. The story their research tells runs strongly counter to what the culture war industry and the mainstream media would have us believe. "Examining the views of ordinary evangelicals (as opposed to a handful of outspoken evangelical elites) in all of their depth and subtlety (instead of compressed and over-simplified in rudimentary answer categories on surveys)," observes Smith (2000, 60), "reveals a diversity and complexity that contradicts conventional wisdom about evangelicals."

Just as many myths have a grain of truth, the secularist portrait of evangelicals is not all wrong, according to Smith's and Wolfe's accounts. Neither researcher disputes, for instance, the strength, bordering on certainty, with which evangelicals hold their beliefs; their serious objections to aspects of mainstream culture; and their often fervent wish for a culture and a politics that conforms more to their Christian values. But alloyed with a commitment to basic democratic principles and a reconciliation to America's religious pluralism, these beliefs are far less of a threat to civility and an obstacle to finding common ground than they might at first appear.

A significant majority of evangelicals in Smith's interviews expressed a solid commitment to the basic political freedoms of speech, thought, and religion.[8] A commitment to these basic freedoms can still ring hollow in the ears of secularists and religious minorities when the group expressing them is aggressively committed to creating a Christian nation. But according to Smith (2000, 37),

Perhaps the most surprising yet most consistent theme that emerged on the topic of "Christian America" in our interviews had to do with the proper Christian response to the loss of American's [*sic*] Christian heritage. The almost unanimous attitude toward those who the evangelicals see as undermining this heritage was one of civility, tolerance, and voluntary persuasion.[9]

This acceptance for religious pluralism made most evangelicals willing to put their commitment to basic freedom and respect into practice.[10] Evangelicals accepted the gradual and occasionally frustrating nature of democratic politics. "Almost all of the ordinary evangelicals we interviewed," reports Smith (1998, 195), "were studiously committed to and confident about expressing their views through voting and polite lobbying." Civility in a democracy depends not only on accepting the legitimacy of voting outcomes but on the way groups express their views during democratic debates. Most evangelicals demonstrate a clear desire to respect the boundaries of propriety and decency in democratic debate. Exactly two-thirds of the evangelicals in Smith's survey (1998, 133) said they try "hard not to offend people with their Christian views." Many evangelicals believe that extremism in the pursuit of justice can be a vice.

Evangelical tolerance not only extends to many of the political and religious rights of their opponents, according to Wolfe, but also covers large swaths of mainstream culture and moral behavior. For their secularist critics, evangelical aloofness from mainstream culture is a democratic problem because it involves a refusal to engage with and possibly learn from those with different beliefs. Reciprocity demands that groups in a democracy aiming to rule and be listened to must tolerate being ruled and listen to others. But Wolfe questions the intensity and extent of evangelicals' opposition to and wish to separate from mainstream culture. Tolerance of moral freedom is the dominant American cultural paradigm, and it is one that evangelicals are becoming increasingly reconciled to. While their language condemning homosexuality or euthanasia can often be harsh, use of this language is far from prevalent among evangelicals, and most are notably reluctant to act on their criticisms. Absorption into mainstream culture has tempered evangelical zeal. "If anything," concludes Wolfe (2003, 254), "the problem American believers have is lack of confidence rather than excessive arrogance."

Smith, too, rejects the secularist portrayal of evangelicals as resident aliens. Evangelicals "speak of 'the world,' . . . almost always as something to be present in and engaged with" (Smith 1998, 126). They are open to being influenced by mainstream norms and institutions—as long as mainstream norms and institutions are open to their influence. A large majority of the evangelicals Smith interviewed, for instance, supported the ideal of public school fairness to different faiths and ways of life. Their main complaint is that public schools are currently not faithful enough to this ideal. "Regarding issues of morality and religion in public schools," Smith (2000, 132) found that "most of the changes that evangelicals would like to see are framed in a way that at most calls for 'equal time' for the Christian viewpoint, rather than the 'Christianizing' of public schools."

Secularist critics might contend that evangelicals are wolves dressed in sheep's clothing, that their moderation is not a commitment but a tactic to be discarded once evangelicals have secured political and cultural hegemony. Democratic citizens only have an obligation to those who have taken democratic principles to heart. Evangelical support for democratic principles, it is true, may not be based on the secular principles their critics prefer, but it is not necessarily less sincere or permanent for that. Many evangelicals root their preference for persuasion in deeply held religious and moral values. Evangelicals' predisposition to harsh moral judgments is often held in check by their belief in a God of love and mercy and their appreciation that Jesus used not coercion but persuasion (Wolfe 2003, 261).

Principled justifications for persuasion are, of course, mixed with self-interest. God commands evangelicals to bear witness to their faith, notes Smith (1998, 135), and evangelical resistance to giving offense often stems from a feeling of being constantly "on stage." Religions in American society must compete in the marketplace, Wolfe reminds us, and Americans, including evangelicals, often switch faiths. Evangelicals are well aware that harping on sin, restrictive morality, and coercion will make it difficult to retain the committed and attract the uncommitted (Wolfe 2003, 256). Besides, as Wolfe explains, many evangelicals believe that offensive proselytizing is just bad manners, and evangelicals are as sensitive to charges of impoliteness as most other Americans (187). Although less than altruistic on the surface, these self-interested considerations are distinct from the mere egoism related to domineering behavior. The constant sense of auditioning their faith—concern with attracting converts and about not sticking out too much—suggests that most evangelicals are concerned about the impression they make on others and how mainstream culture perceives them. Since the mainstream culture in American society is linked intimately with democratic practices and moral freedom, this concern provides evangelicals with a powerful incentive to abide by these practices and norms.

## IS A DEMOCRATIC EDUCATION EVEN NECESSARY?

Perhaps, for the purposes of this chapter, Smith and Wolfe prove too much. Most Americans, they argue, including a large majority of evangelicals, are not moral, religious, or political extremists and are generally willing to play by the rules of democracy. Smith and Wolfe acknowledge that their conclusions apply to most, but not all, evangelicals. Still, if almost all Americans already accept democratic norms of civility and respect, a public school education for applying religion to politics in a way that encourages these norms would appear superfluous.

What our cultural conflict lacks in breadth, however, is often made up for by intensity among elite minorities. While James Davison Hunter, the most well-known proponent of the culture war thesis, concedes to Wolfe that the culture war model does not fully capture the views of average evangelicals, Wolfe concedes to Hunter that the model is often apt in describing the interaction of elites and intellectuals (Hunter and Wolfe 2006, 20, 49). The extremists on both sides of the cultural divide may be small, but thanks to the culture war industry and a helping hand from the mainstream media, they are often highly visible.

An isolated extremist may not be much of a threat to democratic norms of civility and respect, but an extremist with a *Hardball* or *O'Reilly Factor* invitation or even just an Internet connection is a different story, even if that extremist lacks many hard-core followers. Technology has greatly increased the capacity for mischief and harassment. Many of the statements extremists make about religious minorities and their cultural opponents are profoundly alienating in and of themselves. The alienation is compounded by the fact that extremists' ability to make themselves heard in the public square leads religious minorities and their cultural opponents to get the impression that they command the full allegiance of a large cadre of loyalists.

Religious minorities and other targeted groups would not be *completely* wrong in forming this impression. Most ordinary evangelicals, for instance, may express strong support for democratic freedom and the tactics of persuasion rather than coercion, but this does not mean that they never express hurtful and alienating political beliefs. Wolfe (2003, 46) stresses that abortion and gay marriage were not particularly salient even to evangelical voters. But "out of the mouths of my interviewees," he states, "came some pretty strong language condemning homosexual lifestyles" (47). He acknowledges that offensive proselytizing often goes too far "in regions in the United States where evangelicals constitute the dominant majority, such as small towns in Texas or South Carolina" (214). Similarly, the majority of evangelicals may not be willing or even intentional soldiers in cultural battles, Hunter explains, but elite activists exercise considerable influence on them.

> The majority of Americans were not self-conscious partisans actively committed to one side or the other but rather constituted a soft middle that tended one way or inclined toward the other. But the options they ended up with were framed by elites in the parties and special interest organizations, their respective institutions, and the rank-and-file supporters who formed the grassroots support . . . Thus, when push came to shove, Americans—even in the middle—made a choice. (Hunter and Wolfe 2006, 33)

The culture war, Wolfe concludes, is "not a division between red state and blue state America; it's a division inside every person" (Pew Forum on Religion and Public Life 2006). Despite their commitment to democratic rights and institutions, the faith of many evangelicals leads them to tolerate statements by extremist elites and even to utter deeply alienating opinions themselves at times. Smith (1998, 210) describes this ambivalence as "voluntaristic absolutism": "By this we mean, in short, that many evangelicals think that Christian morality should be the primary authority for American culture and society *and* simultaneously think that everyone should be free to live as they see fit, even if that means rejecting Christianity."[11]

True democratic inclusion for religious minorities requires that Americans holding moderate views not merely abstain from discrimination themselves but openly disdain the discrimination practiced by extremists. Given the prominence of the culture war industry, Americans must not only refrain from using illegitimately sectarian and deeply alienating forms of religious arguments in politics. A truly civil and respectful democratic dialogue requires that Americans distance themselves actively from the illegitimately sectarian and deeply alienating forms of religious arguments made by others and often used in their names. Most evangelicals Smith (2000, 43) interviewed "were keenly aware that many evangelical televangelists and political activists are creating a bad reputation for Christians." The respect our democratic principles demand require that they be more vocal in repudiating this extremism.

Public schools can perform an essential service by providing guidance about the use of religion in politics. Evangelical extremists in the culture war industry misrepresent the views of ordinary evangelicals in a way that often deeply alienates religious minorities and other targeted groups. The silent majority of evangelicals too often fail to set the story straight. Public schools can persuade this silent majority to distance themselves openly from the illegitimate sectarian justifications and harsh language employed by those who claim to speak in their name. Many ordinary evangelicals themselves are torn between a commitment to respectful democratic discussion and sectarian commitments. Public schools should not, of course, encourage evangelicals to temper, let alone abandon, their sectarian commitments. These commitments often enrich our diversity and frequently provide a powerful challenge to morally questionable mainstream commitments. But schools should encourage evangelicals to present their commitments in public argument in democratically acceptable terms.

Smith's and Wolfe's research suggests that many evangelicals are themselves concerned about their reputation and would be open to this influence. But evangelicals will only truly accept such guidance if it is reciprocal. Practicality and, above all, fairness require that schools recognize that responsibility for our frequently poisonous cultural conflicts lie as much on the left as on the right. They must address the deliberative transgressions of secularist extremists as much as those of evangelical extremists.

Chief among these transgressions is the tendency of secularist extremists to exaggerate the antidemocratic sentiments of most evangelicals. Ordinary secularists occasionally indulge in these stereotypes themselves and are more often culpable by doing nothing to combat their use by elites or the media.[12] Not only are these exaggerations wrong, but they are counterproductive. Stereotypes of evangelical extremists become a self-fulfilling prophecy. Portrayed as beyond engagement and ignored by secularist elites,[13] evangelicals become more resistant to speaking or listening in civil dialogue, more prone to extremist statements themselves, and more susceptible to endorsing or at least accepting the extremist statements of elites. In his interviews of evangelicals, Smith (1998, 37) found,

> Particularly striking are evangelicals' perceptions of hostility from the mass media, public schools, and feminism. In all cases, evangelicals are between one-third to almost three times more likely to view them as hostile to their own values and morals than are mainliners, liberals, Roman Catholics, and nonreligious Americans.

An even greater threat to respectful democracy lies in the philosophical framework that fuels the exaggerated claims of secularist extremists. Secularist extremists believe there is no place for religious language and justification in democratic discourse. They exaggerate the intolerance and closemindedness of evangelicals to urge exclusion of evangelicals from political discussion, which in turn allows them to avoid serious engagement with actual evangelical political arguments and critiques of culture.

If public schools should persuade evangelicals to express their arguments in more democratically acceptable language and to distance themselves from disrespectful arguments of extremists, they have an equal obligation to persuade secularist students to avoid indulging in stereotypes of evangelicals and to distance themselves from the exclusion of evangelicals that is preached by secularist elites. Evangelicals want not only tolerance of their rights but inclusion and serious consideration of their arguments. Encouraging such mutual engagement can enable secularists and religious conservatives to have a clearer view of each other and can prevent the vicious cycle that fuels their conflicts over religion and culture.

## THREE MODELS OF DEMOCRATIC DISCUSSION

Perhaps the optimism of the preceding conclusion is premature. The silent majority of evangelicals and secularists may not be as extreme as the media makes them out to be, but this does not mean that there is a specific model of respectful democratic discussion that both sides would agree on. Even if

we discover a model that constitutes common ground for the silent majority on both sides, we still need to show that it is truly fair and consistent
with democratic norms. We cannot automatically dismiss the possibility
that the extremists on either side are right. Allowing any religious views to
be used in politics may violate the separation of church and state. Encouraging restrictions on the type of religious arguments democratic citizens
use may involve the establishment of a favored religious point of view. To
determine what guidance public schools should provide on the use of religion in politics, we need to examine what restrictions on the use of religious language are legitimate and likely to be accepted.

Before we arrive at this destination, however, it would be helpful to first
review the major variants of democratic theory and what general restrictions each places on the language and reasons used in political debate.[14]
These variants offer three basic approaches to the state's role in encouraging civic deliberation among ordinary democratic citizens: provide no or
little guidance, encourage civic unity, and provide substantial advice about
what arguments citizens are obligated to take seriously and what arguments they must avoid using. The proceduralist democratic theory of
Robert Dahl (1982) and William Riker (1982) is most closely associated with
the first position. With roots in James Madison's pluralist conception of
democracy, where the invisible hand of private interest expression serves
the public interest, proceduralists emphasize that bargaining and compromise recognize each group's interest adequately. Civic education about
what language and reasons to use in democratic debates is superfluous.
William Galston, as we have already seen, reaches the same conclusion, although for the exact opposite reason. "Religion," for Galston (2002, 39), "is
a clear example of a matter that in principle should not be subject to collective determination." Providing a civic education about religion will inex-
orably favor the language and reasoning that religious and secular majorities use. To prevent a sense of alienation and exclusion among religious
minorities like the Amish and Christian fundamentalists, schools must
practice maximum feasible accommodation.

Since I have already addressed the problems with public schools ignoring religion, my comments here are brief. Even if proceduralists' dubious
claims that pluralism is an adequate protection for the basic rights of minorities are right, they ignore the effect of a free-for-all discussion of religion and politics on the *quality* of civic deliberation. Even if used by mi-

norities impotent to achieve discriminatory policy results, excessively sectarian language and reasoning can make their religious and secularist targets feel like less-than-full citizens. Secularist caricatures of evangelicals
and attempts to exclude all references to religion in the public square can
feed a sense of exclusion even when they fail to convince the majority of citizens. Uncivil language on both sides can fuel social and cultural conflict.

Even if Galston is right that civic education about religion would feed
alienation and exclusion, having schools ignore religion can heighten the
exclusion and alienation of non-Christian religious minorities and secularists. But Smith's and Wolfe's research gives us reason to question the extent
of the exclusion that public schools would cause by providing guidance
about religion and politics. Sizable majorities of evangelicals and religious
conservatives accept core liberal democratic values and processes and express at least qualified support for public schooling. These majorities seem
open to public school guidance about the civil use of religion in political debates, as long as it is reciprocal and reasonable. They are unlikely to feel the
exclusion Galston fears.

Traditionally, the major alternative to proceduralist democracy has
been civic republicanism, which has its roots in Jean-Jacques Rousseau's
concern with the ills of factionalism and self-interest that plague modern
politics. Encouraging citizens to develop and share a robust conception of
the public good is the solution, and civic education is an essential tool in instilling this conception. Through civic education, government carefully and
often intrusively shapes the language and justifications that citizens use in
political arguments. Association with the evils of twentieth-century totali-
tarianism has alienated contemporary democratic theorists from
Rousseau's enthusiastic embrace of the general will, but Rousseau's legacy
lives on in a much modified and more moderate form. Communitarianism
shares Rousseau's concern with the lack of communal spirit, and John
Dewey has lamented the loss of a unified public discourse. But among the
heirs of civic republicanism, Benjamin Barber's work is of most interest
here, because of its direct consideration of the boundaries of legitimate political language and discussion.

Barber (1984, 148) acknowledges the limits of Rousseau's "unitary"
model of democracy and rejects the suppression of conflict in democracy.
Averse to imposing common interests, he advocates a "strong democracy"
that "aspires to transform conflict through a politics of distinctive inven-

tiveness and discovery" (119). This transformation takes place through considering how to frame arguments in a way that appeals to other moral beliefs and, even more, through open-minded listening to others' opinions. Democratic citizens, for Barber, must be willing to at least renegotiate the margins of their identity and at times rescript large portions of the way they think about themselves. We are not equal participants in a common democratic endeavor unless we all risk equally departing from our narrow perspectives.

The virtues of Barber's approach address the deficiencies of the proceduralist approach. Barber (1984, 159) is correct that effective democracies require collective action and that civic education can be essential in preparing citizens for such collective action. The strong democratic approach is also consistent with tolerance and an active distancing from extremist arguments. External and legal checks on violations of liberty, such as those found in the Constitution and enforced by courts, are not sufficient to ensure the rights of vulnerable minorities. Judges are often appointed by politicians swayed by majority opinions, and many serious violations of liberty and democratic norms of respect take place in the private sphere and are not legally actionable. Even if perfectly enforced, legal protections against rights violations are still too passive and negative. An atmosphere of respect for all citizens requires that a significant number of citizens actively reject or distance themselves from offensive political language. Strong democracy emphasizes that the state has a role in promoting citizens' internal restraint and in making citizens responsible for being respectful even when legal sanctions do not apply (Barber 1984, 160).

But strong democracy is too strong of a model for civic education about religion. Barber does not aim to eliminate disagreement among democratic citizens, but he does seek to reduce the scope of disagreement. The price for admission to the public square is that self-interested points of view must transform themselves into civic-minded ones. Barber defines points of view as self-interested when they are concerned only with the interest of the individual or the group to which the individual belongs (Barber 1984, 119). This definition still leaves considerable room for interpretation, which Barber never clearly resolves. It could, for instance, include religious views about abortion that rely on the notion of sin. Since only Christians or certain types of Christians care about sin or believe that the salvation of their souls depends on living in a society that forbids crucial sins like abortion, we might consider these views to be concerned exclusively with the interests of Christians.

Even if these religious views can be construed as self-interested, there is an essential difference between them and other self-interested views. Consider, for instance, different types of self-interested views concerning whether to protect the environment. A logger might oppose deforestation regulations because this will reduce the logger's profit, and a manufacturer of hybrid cars might support restrictions on miles per gallon because this will help the manufacturer sell more cars. These views are clearly self-interested according to Barber's definition, because they are only concerned with the economic self-interest of the individuals themselves (and their companies and families). The National Association of Evangelicals recently signed on to an "Urgent Call to Action" statement supporting government policy to prevent climate change, pollution, and the extinction of rare species. They justified their policy positions in large part by citing the requirement in Genesis that humans be good stewards of God's creation (Fitzgerald 2006). Using Barber's definition, many nonevangelicals who do not feel called by divine authorities to be good stewards might see these views as self-interested. But the evangelicals who signed on to the call for action would disagree sharply. From their standpoint, the commandment to be good stewards is one that applies not only to evangelicals but to all humans; the salvation of individuals and society as a whole depends on following God's commandments.

Civic-mindedness alone does not make points of view acceptable in a democracy. There have been many victims of what Saul Bellow called the Good Intentions Paving Company, and generosity can no doubt be oppressive. But if our lone concern is with whether a point of view is self-interested or civic-minded, it seems clear that many religious views are more civic-minded than, for instance, narrow economic calculations and are more entitled to a place in democratic discussion.

Even if Barber's strong democracy was to make a place for religious arguments that critics consider to be self-interested, its emphasis on transformation and open-mindedness would still disqualify it as the basis of a religious education for deliberation. Citizens, strong democracy demands, must begin by setting aside certainty about their beliefs. "Politics," contends Barber (1984, 127), "is the search for reasonable choice, which must be made in the face of conflict, and in the absence of independent grounds for judgment." Elsewhere, he argues that strong democracy makes "preferences and opinions earn legitimacy by forcing them to run the gauntlet of public deliberation and public judgment" (136). This suspension and risking of one's core beliefs and identity is noxious to many religious believers. Many believers are certain about their beliefs and hold that their derivation from personal revelation or a religious text is sufficient proof of their truth. Encouraging a sense of distance from religious beliefs, however temporary, is the equivalent for many believers of encouraging relativism.[15] Encouraging citizens to discover common ground they already share (but are not aware of) is more consistent with the rights of conscience than is encouraging an ironic distance from deeply held beliefs. Barber's contention that citizens must risk personal as well as political transformation of their deepest beliefs causes it to run afoul of religious liberty.

The importance of having a well-functioning democracy, Barber might respond, outweighs the violation of religious conscience that transformation involves. But this assumes that some form of moral consensus is strictly necessary for a well-functioning democracy, a claim many democratic theorists find implausible (Deveaux 2003, 786). Smith's and Wolfe's research suggests reasons why evangelicals can be respectful democratic citizens *even if they are certain* about their beliefs. Respect for pluralism and democratic liberty could restrain evangelicals from supporting a coercive imposition of their beliefs on fellow citizens. Concern for the norms of politeness, together with reflection on Christ's example of persuasion and message of love, can prevent evangelicals from an overly harsh criticism of religious minorities and targeted groups, even when they feel certain that the behavior of the latter is wrong. Not only are evangelicals, according to Smith and Wolfe, capable of making this distinction, but many currently do so. This suggests that we can build a respectful democracy without resorting to the conscience violations that transformation and listening involve.

Deliberative democratic theory occupies a middle ground between the proceduralist and civic republican visions. Deliberative theorists, unlike procedural democrats, recognize the need for restraints of civility on political speech; not only are these restraints instrumental ones that lead to the formulation of better policies, but they play an expressive role in promoting mutual respect (Gutmann and Thompson 2004, 21). Improving civic discourse should not, however, include the imposition of shared values or thick constitutional principles. Deliberative theory treats justice and morality not as given prior to democratic debate but as largely outcomes of proper democratic debate. It favors inclusion of a wide range of moral arguments. In their discussion of surrogacy contracts, for instance, deliberative democracy's two most prominent advocates, Amy Gutmann and Dennis Thompson (1996, 237–66), argue that legislatures and citizens should be able to use moralistic and paternalistic arguments, including those drawn from liberty.

Citizens from disparate backgrounds may not, Gutmann and Thompson acknowledge, be able to find shared ground on hotly disputed political issues. Greater and more open-ended discussion of political issues could lead to even greater disagreement, and societies should not attempt to impose common ground where none exists. Deliberative theories leave room for reasonable disagreement after debate has taken place. But democracies should try to "economize" and civilize disagreement. Disagreements, argue Gutmann and Thompson (1996, 82), should be governed by a principle of civic magnanimity that calls on citizens and officials to acknowledge the moral status of the positions they oppose. As Gutmann and Thompson maintain, the principle of economy of moral disagreement requires that "in justifying policies on moral grounds, citizens should seek the rationale that minimizes rejection of the position they oppose" (84).

The inclusive version of civic education implied by Gutmann and Thompson's deliberative democratic model would seem to have considerable appeal for conservative Christians, who suspect that attempts to impose consensus on shared values or constitutional principles come too often at the price of excluding religious beliefs. Using deliberative democracy as the basis for a civic education for talking about religion would not require the transformation for consensus that strong democrats seek. Recognizing that their opponents' beliefs deserve a moral status and place in public debate is an external gesture of respect that is a far cry from the suspension of belief Barber wants. Deliberative democracy's openness to diverse justifications for moral and political positions in politics would seem to address conservative Christians' greatest concern—the exclusion of points of view with a religious basis.

But the door for religious points of view that Gutmann and Thompson's deliberative model seems to open with one hand is shut with the other. The root of their ambivalence and ultimate exclusion of many religious views lies in a legitimate concern. Deliberative democracy allows justice and morality to be defined largely through democratic debate, but this openness has its limits. What if citizens wish to support racially segregationist policies using racist language in a democracy? If these citizens are in the majority, their behavior would threaten the fundamental rights of African Americans. Even if they are a relatively small minority, their speech and arguments would lead to disrespect and alienation. Deliberative models must steer between the Scylla of sanctioning injustice and the Charybdis of exclusion. Too many restrictions on beliefs could lead to an exclusion of legitimate beliefs, but too much inclusion of beliefs could lead to injustice.

To minimize unreasonable and harmful pluralism, Gutmann and Thompson introduce three basic principles to govern deliberation: reciprocity, publicity, and accountability. The latter principles apply mostly to politicians, but the principle of reciprocity applies to ordinary citizens and is most relevant for this chapter. According to Gutmann and Thompson (1996, 56),

> Deliberative reciprocity has two related requirements. When citizens make moral claims, they appeal to reasons or principles that can be shared by fellow citizens who are similarly motivated . . . When moral reasoning invokes empirical claims, reciprocity requires that they be consistent with relatively reliable methods of inquiry.

The application of reciprocity to the use of religion in politics is not completely clear. Gutmann and Thompson (1996, 56) do reject explicitly the right of "religious fundamentalists" to use literal biblical arguments to justify the restriction of liberty. But such arguments constitute a decreasing percentage of the religious arguments that evangelicals use in politics. For moral as well as practical reasons, many evangelicals have muted or simply rejected the use of overtly sectarian religious appeals and literal biblical arguments in politics. Not only are such arguments likely to be unsuccessful in persuading those with different beliefs, but they are inconsistent with the democratic norms and code of mainstream civility that many evangelicals subscribe to. Political arguments that stress the social consequences of policies that they oppose have come to accompany and at times replace the explicitly sectarian arguments in evangelicals' political arsenal. Often, these arguments depend on empirical claims based on some form of scientific research.

Evangelical opposition to partial-birth abortion, for instance, is still driven by an insistence that all fetuses are due protection from the moment of conception. But evangelicals also cite scientific research claiming to show that fetuses are capable of feeling pain from abortion procedures quite early in a woman's pregnancy. Describing women who choose to abort fetuses as murderers in political dialogue has grown less frequent; focusing on postabortion stress syndrome is more prominent. Many evangelicals now cite research showing that many women who abort their children come to regret their choice and develop psychological problems at abnormal rates (Bazelon 2007; Reardon 1987; Cougle, Reardon, and Coleman 2003). The Supreme Court cited research like this in its most recent decision upholding the congressional ban on partial-birth abortions (*Gonzalez* 2007). Condemnation of homosexual relationships and marriage as a sin against God can still be heard in arguments presented for public consumption as well as in evangelical church sermons. But religious conservatives and evangelicals increasingly stress—at least in their public pronouncements— the effect that allowing homosexual marriage has on the family. Many evangelicals tout studies suggesting that gays and children raised by gay parents are more prone to a variety of psychological disorders (Blankenhorn 1995; Popenoe 1996). They emphasize the increase in divorce rates and family breakdown in nations that have legalized homosexual marriage (Blankenhorn 2007; Kurtz 2007). Even some of the more divisive voices in the culture war industry seemingly stress science more than religion. In their treatment of homosexual marriage, the Web sites of Focus on the Family and the Family Research Council stress statistics at least as much as sectarian condemnation (Focus on the Family 2009; Family Research Council 2009).

Determining what religious arguments have a rightful place in respectful and reciprocal democratic discourse is no longer as simple as it was, for instance, in the early 1980s heyday of the Moral Majority. The explicit and exclusive sectarianism of the political arguments that Jerry Falwell and his acolytes put forward clearly ran afoul of reciprocity. Many evangelical arguments today are, at least on their surface, complex tapestries with religious, secular, and scientific threads intertwined.[16] For this reason, I describe them as "hybrid arguments."

Many secularist critics have been quick to reject these hybrid arguments as merely clever manipulations. Evangelicals offer these arguments for public consumption to gain a more sympathetic hearing in public discourse and legal forums, but their motives remain primarily sectarian. As evidence, secularists point out not only that evangelicals often maintain and at times voice their sectarian beliefs alongside their scientific beliefs but the allegedly shoddy nature of the scientific beliefs themselves. The mainstream scientific establishment strongly rejects allegedly scientific claims about the capacity of the fetus to feel pain in the first trimester of pregnancy. Mainstream psychologists and social scientists have likewise rejected evidence alleging postabortion stress syndrome or the high rates of depression among children raised in gay families (Patterson 1995; Wyers 1987; Ghazala 1993; Russo 2005; Stotland 1992). Secularists point to the source of these studies to substantiate their claims. The scientists responsible for these studies come from strongly sectarian or evangelical backgrounds, and their work is published not in leading mainstream, peer-reviewed journals in their respective professions but in journals sympathetic to their cause.[17] Committed more to finding results favorable to their cause than the scientific method, these scientists select methods and evidence that will yield conclusions favorable to their sectarian bias.

Robert Audi, one of secularism's leading philosophical voices, contends that for hybrid arguments to have a legitimate place in democratic discourse, their secular attributes must be independent and autonomous of their sectarian attributes, and they must be "evidentially adequate" (Audi and Wolterstorff 1997, 29; Audi 1993). Most of the political arguments advanced by evangelicals would, according to their secularist critics, fail this test. The empirical and logical basis of these claims is so inadequate that they could only be convincing to someone who has a prior religious inclination to accept them.

Gutmann and Thompson's discussion of hybrid arguments at first seems more nuanced: they stress that their emphasis on reciprocity "does not exclude religious appeals per se" and that "empirical claims need not be completely verifiable" (1996, 56). But this apparent openness is swiftly and strictly qualified. Like Audi, Gutmann and Thompson support an accessibility test, maintaining that citizens cannot require others to "adopt one's sectarian way of life as a condition of gaining access to the moral understanding that is essential to judging the validity of one's moral claims" (57). In other words, arguments are not welcome unless they are convincing independent of their religious underpinnings. Like other deliberative models, Gutmann and Thompson's model emphasizes the use of reason and logic in public debate. At the least, they argue, logical claims and arguments on issues where empirical claims are irrelevant or unavailable must meet a "plausibility test." "Plausibility is no doubt partly subjective," they recognize, "but at the extremes which the requirement comes into play, we can usually find a sufficiently objective test"; similarly, religious claims "should not conflict with claims that have been confirmed by the most reliable of available methods" (56).

The stringency of several of these requirements is notable. Citizens have an obligation to familiarize themselves with the "most reliable of available methods" and to make sure their logical and empirical claims are consistent with them. Religious arguments are not accessible unless they are completely independent of religious underpinnings and completely persuasive to those with different beliefs. *Any* nonrational element of an argument that is not plausible invalidates the entire argument.

Despite Gutmann and Thompson's avowal that some religious arguments have a legitimate place in public debate, their criteria seem to leave little room for any religious arguments, and their two books on deliberative democracy provide no example of a legitimate religious argument. They do cite the participation of religious groups in a 2002 presidential commission for bioethics, which examined cloning (Gutmann and Thompson 2004, 52). But they congratulate the groups on this panel for sticking to reasons that were commonly acceptable. The participation of these groups was only legitimate because they emptied themselves out completely of their sectarian beliefs. The only reasonable inference is that civic education based on Gutmann and Thompson's deliberative model would recommend to students the exclusion of almost all religiously based arguments, including those hybrid arguments that include logical and empirical elements.

The common ground that Gutmann and Thompson claim to identify turns out to be more partisan than it at first seems. Religious conservatives and evangelicals would reject its applications to politics and civic education as unfair because of the heavier burden of proof its criteria impose on arguments with faith elements and controversial logical and empirical claims. More depressingly, our consideration of different democratic approaches does not appear to have made much progress toward a solution to the civic education dilemma that is acceptable to all culture war combatants. The deliberative democratic model appeared to hold out the most promise because of its openness to different forms of reasoning, its relatively open-ended attitude toward definitions of justice and morality, and its willingness to tolerate civil disagreement even after extensive deliberation has taken place. Gutmann and Thompson, however, imply that true deliberative democracy would make little room for religion in public debate. Fortunately, Gutmann and Thompson's model is not the only possible application of deliberative democracy to religion. The next section presents a deliberative model concerning religion that is more faithful to the basic principles of deliberative democracy than Gutmann and Thompson's model.

## THE GOOD-FAITH APPROACH

Gutmann and Thompson's account suffers from two oversights. First, what counts as good reliance on logical reasoning and empirical evidence is less straightforward than they make it out to be. Their use of strict standards when it comes to natural science claims is plausible. Citizens should not cite studies claiming to show that fetuses are capable of feeling pain at as early as eight weeks if establishment science suggests that there are good biological reasons for thinking that this cannot be the case. But such strict standards are less appropriate when dealing with controversial claims about social phenomena that involve complex moral judgments and weighting.

That some empirical social science studies are more reliable than others should not invalidate completely the use of the less reliable studies or the reasoning they are based on. Mainstream social scientists as well as abortion rights groups, for instance, have called into question the methodology and conclusion of studies alleging that postabortion stress syndrome is fairly widespread. Even if mainstream studies were to show reliably that postabortion syndrome is less extensive than its ardent supporters claim, this does not mean that discussion of postabortion syndrome has no place in the abortion debate. Whatever the exact number of women affected, clearly some women do suffer from depression as a result of having an abortion. Furthermore, there is room for reasonable moral disagreement about the significance of this suffering. Even if studies show that postabortion syndrome is clearly less prevalent than its supporters claim, that women's right to choose should trump the suffering that some will come to feel is no moral slam dunk.

The disputes over empirical studies about the effects of homosexual marriage on families and on children raised in gay families similarly do not automatically disqualify the use of these moral arguments in the debate over homosexual marriage. Even if these studies do not provide significant evidence that there is a present effect on the family, this may have less to do with the complete absence of an effect and more to do with the limits of empirical and statistical research. Society and the family are complex and delicate fabrics. That the effects of a more liberal attitude toward homosexual marriage may not be perceptible or tangible in the present does not mean they do not exist or will not in the future (Devlin 1968). Liberal philosophers like to follow John Rawls in preaching that we appreciate the burdens of judgment and restrain ourselves from imposing sectarian beliefs on others. But the burdens weigh both ways. Secularists should not be so quick to assume that the logical and empirical arguments religious conservatives use are illegitimate.

Both critics of using religious arguments and, possibly, Gutmann and Thompson might respond that even if these positions have some plausibility, they still would fail the independence and accessibility test. The great majority of believers in postabortion syndrome or the effects of a liberal attitude toward homosexual marriage on the family hold strong sectarian beliefs. These logical and empirical claims may have some plausibility, but they are far from self-evident, and the religious background of those who accept them surely "tips the scales" in their favor. If faith plays this role, it is unreasonable to expect those who hold different beliefs to accept them.

Religious conservatives could retort that this critique proves too much. The attitude of nonevangelicals toward postabortion syndrome is far from neutral. A belief in abortion rights on other religious and moral grounds makes one more disposed to "tip the scales" against the syndrome's prevalence. But there is an even more serious problem with this critique, which suggests the second oversight in Gutmann and Thompson's attitude toward religious arguments. *The willingness of religious conservatives and evangelicals to put forward hybrid arguments is morally and politically significant even if these arguments are not truly independent or accessible.* Put differently, Gutmann, Thompson, and separationists like Audi focus on whether religious arguments are objectively independent or accessible from the standpoint of an impartial observer. They should focus more on the subjective perceptions of these arguments. It is possible for the independence of logical and empirical arguments to be objectively questionable but subjectively persuasive to those who hold them. Do the religious believers who advance these hybrid arguments believe them to be substantially independent?

The answer for secularists, of course, is a decisive no. Hybrid arguments are merely clever masks intended to conceal sectarian intentions and beliefs. But Smith's and Wolfe's research indicates that this attribution of bad faith is mistaken in the case of many evangelicals. The hybrid arguments many put forth are a reflection of genuine ambivalence. Evangelicals' religious beliefs undoubtedly influence their political arguments. But many who realize that religious beliefs alone are not and should not be sufficient in a pluralistic democracy advance logical and empirical arguments to address this. Still, this might seem to beg the question. Why is the fact that many evangelicals believe their secular arguments are significantly independent morally and politically notable?

The most salient aspect of these hybrid arguments is what they are not. When evangelicals use these arguments, the arguments often replace more sectarian appeals. The evangelical rejection of a liberal attitude about homosexual marriage because of its effect on the family, for instance, often replaces a naked sectarian claim that homosexuality is a damnable sin. On one level, this demonstrates a significant respect for the citizens they are arguing with and for democratic norms in general. Evangelicals using these arguments recognize that other citizens cannot reasonably be expected to accept their sectarian views and that persuasion can only take place on grounds that can be mutually shared. Perhaps more important, presenting hybrid arguments indicates increased respect for targeted groups. It reflects a recognition that expression of pure animus or religious condemnations against homosexuals is not legitimate in civil democratic discourse. This may even have a positive, spillover effect on evangelicals' daily behavior toward these groups. Believers may be more likely to act in intolerant ways toward those they view as enemies of God than those they view as a possible source of social anomie.

When a liberal democratic society takes hybrid arguments seriously, it rightly rewards evangelicals for their principled compromise with democratic norms. When liberals and secularists listen to and engage with these arguments, they strengthen evangelicals' faith in the fairness of our democratic discourse. Inclusion in civil discourse can have a moderating and civilizing effect. The more hybrid arguments are welcome in civil discourse, the more evangelicals are likely to rely on these arguments not only in public disputes with others but in their private discussions and reflections. The more reliance on these arguments, rather than on exclusively sectarian positions, becomes common, the more open evangelicals will become to persuasion. The benefits to evangelicals are reciprocal. The more they use hybrid arguments, the more they will be able to persuade others to adopt or compromise with their views. Promoting a cycle of goodwill and openness ultimately benefits society. Evangelical claims about the effects of gay marriage and abortion may or may not be right, but their general concerns with holding nuclear families together and with the effects of sexual license are too often absent from many Americans' moral compasses.

When evangelicals' good-faith attempts to provide secular arguments meet with liberal and secularist charges of bad faith, the cycle is reversed, and the safety valve is eliminated. Alienated from civil discourse, evangelicals have no incentive to moderate their claims or forgo exclusively sectarian arguments. We should not be surprised if evangelicals, feeling that society has refused to meet them halfway, become even more hardened in their positions, less open to listening and compromise, and more intolerant toward vulnerable groups. With their rhetoric more extremist and shrill and with their attitude more isolationist, evangelical separatists become a self-fulfilling prophecy of the secularist vision, and society is the loser. The more evangelicals view themselves as outside civil discourse, the more others will, too. The valuable contrast that evangelical values provide to mainstream norms will be increasingly ignored.

If our society is to avoid this dismal outcome, talking about religion and politics should be guided not by Audi's principle of independence or Gutmann and Thompson's principle of reciprocity but by the principle of good faith. *Good faith requires that when religious believers make a sincere and substantial effort to balance their sectarian claims with secular logical and empirical claims, other citizens have an obligation to take these arguments at face value and engage with them.* Since the principle imposes separate obligations on those who offer arguments and those who receive them, let's consider these obligations separately, beginning with the former.

The standard of good faith steers a mean between exclusion and inclusion of religious arguments. Believers need not go into denial about their most important religious commitments in order to gain access to political debate. Religious motivations can be the original impetus for the political arguments that religious believers advance in politics. But contrary to Audi's independence standard, religious motivation can continue to exercise a significant influence even after believers have engaged in the formulation of secular logical and empirical claims. If the logical and empirical claims for and against the position appear to believers to be carefully balanced, believers should be able to use their religious beliefs to tip the scales in favor of the more sectarian claim. If one study confirms the existence of postabortion syndrome but another study denies its prevalence, evangelicals can use their religious beliefs to break the tie. Religious beliefs can also be used to give greater weight to one of a competing set of moral demands. If empirical research shows that nations that grant gay marriage have higher divorce rates than those that do not, evangelicals can use their religious beliefs to privilege the threat to traditional marriage over the denial of rights to homosexuals.

If evangelicals need not depart as far from their religious motivations as Audi wants, they also need not seek as far as Gutmann and Thompson want them to. The reciprocity principle's requirement that citizens only use arguments consistent with the most reliable empirical methods available is too strict and too objective. Evangelicals are not free, of course, to invent arguments, and other citizens do not have an obligation to take seriously any argument that evangelicals put forth. Believers can use their religious beliefs to tip the scales or break ties in favor of their preferred arguments only after they have first sought out logical and empirical justifications for their arguments. They must make a genuine effort to go beyond their beliefs. But the principle of good faith gives more credit to evangelicals' subjective commitment to democratic norms than is allowed by the independence or reciprocity principles.

Subjective intentions are impossible to ascertain. If good-faith commitment to democratic norms is the price of admission to the public square, the counterfeiting of motives will be irresistible for some. But even if distinguishing genuine from counterfeit democratic intentions is not an exact science, it is not the equivalent of astrology either. There are signs that strongly indicate the presence of good faith even if they do not count as absolute guarantees. Citizens have a responsibility to engage seriously with arguments that contain these signs. One particularly important sign of a good-faith argument is its significant departure from the sectarian beliefs of its advocate.

This departure can come in the form of shifting focus on a topic away from the concern of a related sectarian belief. The major focus of evangelical sectarian beliefs about abortion is on the violation of the fetus's God-given rights. Arguments concerned with postabortion syndrome focus on the welfare of women who have abortions. Tacitly acknowledging that other citizens might not accept the belief that life begins at conception, arguments concerned with postabortion syndrome mark a significant departure from sectarian pro-life arguments. We can, as a society, agree that protecting women's welfare is important, even if there is radical disagreement about whether preventing abortion does safeguard women's welfare. Biblical arguments against recognition of homosexual relationships focus on the sin homosexuals commit. Concern with homosexual marriage's effect on the family marks a meaningful change in focus and a quest for more common ground. Significant departure from sectarian beliefs need not involve the offering of more secular arguments. A shift to the use of a more general religious argument that does not closely track one's religious beliefs can also be significant. To give yet another example, the case for discussing the theory of intelligent design in public schools is much stronger than the case for literal biblical creationism because the former departs from the sectarian beliefs of its adherents while the latter does not.

If the major obligation of presenters is significant departure from sectarian arguments, the major obligation of listeners is engagement. The obligation to engage with good-faith arguments of religious believers does not, of course, mean that other citizens have to accept the truth of these arguments. When religious conservatives advance good-faith claims, they earn the right to compete in a liberal democracy but not necessarily to triumph. When reasonable disagreement exists, excessive civility is insincerity, and too much acknowledgment of an argument in an attempt to placate an opponent can even be a form of condescension. Taking arguments seriously means opposing them when one disagrees sharply with them.

The obligation of engagement requires more than mere tolerance. Allowing believers to express good-faith arguments and then proceeding to ignore them or merely pay them lip service violates the spirit of true civility. Engagement means taking good-faith arguments seriously, which involves, at a minimum, an obligation to present the arguments honestly and refrain from caricaturing the beliefs of one's opponents. A major cause of our religious and cultural conflicts is the tendency of citizens on both sides of the cultural divide to focus on the most extreme and sectarian arguments of their opponents. The impulse is natural, since depicting the opponents of your positions as extremists means you can write them off. Good faith requires that we confront opposing arguments not at their weakest points but at their strongest. If many evangelicals use hybrid arguments to support their position on gay marriage, supporters of gay marriage should not concentrate exclusively on attacking those evangelicals who put forth extremist and exclusively sectarian arguments.[18] Religious conservatives, of course, have a reciprocal obligation not to dwell on extreme secularist voices. When public schools encourage honest presentation, they check the *O'Reilly Factor* and *Hardball* mentality that shapes our cultural predicament.

Caricaturing is not the only deliberative abuse that increases the religious and cultural divide. When extreme secularists can no longer ignore hybrid arguments but still do not want to take them seriously, they accuse them of bad faith. Some secularists see sectarian intentions lurking in every argument believers put forth. For these secularists, intelligent design is merely the latest Potemkin village biblical literalists have constructed to conceal the ruins of discarded and discredited earlier versions of creation science, and postabortion syndrome is a Trojan horse presented to the Supreme Court and the majority of American citizens who are skeptical that life begins at conception, to finally convince them to become pro-life. Good faith means taking at face value hybrid arguments that significantly depart from sectarian grounds, instead of attempting to unmask their sectarian intentions or redescribing them in sectarian terms. Arguments that depart from sectarian beliefs should not be reduced to sectarian beliefs. If religious conservatives say they are concerned with the effect of homosexual marriage on the family, their opponents should focus on why homosexual marriage does not harm the family, rather than accusing the conservatives of imposing Christian morality on the rest of us. Under the principles of independence and reciprocity, the burden of proof that arguments deserve a serious hearing in the public sphere is placed on believers who advance them. The principle of good faith shifts the burden of proof to the opponents of these arguments. They must show the substantial current resemblance between hybrid and sectarian arguments—as opposed to merely claiming their sectarian origins—or desist from their accusations of bad faith.

Secularists might still object that the principle of good faith expects them to take too much on faith. Objective standards like the independence and reciprocity principles may risk filtering out legitimate religious arguments, but they also provide a legitimate line of defense against arguments that deserve no place in the public square. Good faith would strip secularists of this defense. Smith's and Wolfe's research suggests that secularists of little faith may be rewarded by compromising with evangelicals, but the possibilities for abuse of good faith seem rife. Evangelicals may aspire to St. Augustine's heavenly city, but they still live in the earthly city, where practical checks, not wishes, must ensure good behavior. Our spotlight must thus shine once again squarely on public education. Providing guidance to students about how to talk about religion in public schools is the only way to ensure that believers talk and act in good faith and that they are worthy of other citizens' trust.

## TEACHING GOOD FAITH

John Tomasi, in his provocative and elegantly reasoned work *Liberalism beyond Justice* (2001), argues for a public school education about religion that "gently affirms" faith. Concerned with the "spillover" effect that teaching such liberal values as tolerance and neutrality can have on robust religious beliefs, he recommends that schools teach students how their commitments as liberal democratic citizens could flow from their religious tradition. Stephen Macedo, in his *Diversity and Distrust* (2003), argues that the public school curriculum should embody a "liberalism with teeth." A liberal society needs distinctive liberal virtues, such as tolerance and respect, for pluralism to sustain it. Students from families and religious communities that do not stress these virtues can only get them from public schools. Public schools play a central role in sustaining liberal democracy by challenging the intolerant and illiberal beliefs of these students.

Tomasi's and Macedo's positions represent two familiar poles of the debate about religion and public education. But there is one position that has been omitted from this debate: that public schools can gently challenge and gently affirm religious beliefs *simultaneously*. This chapter suggests that this is what public schools should do in dispensing guidance on how to talk about religion and politics. Although this mandate appears contradictory, its plausibility will be clearer if we better understand what type of challenge and affirmation public schools should engage in.

Challenging of religious identity does not, of course, mean that schools should encourage students to rethink their religious commitments. Principles of religious tolerance, let alone the Constitution, forbid this. Schools must explicitly stress that the guidance they offer only applies to religious belief students intend to use for politics. The divide between public and private must be honored. Schools should stress that while students may talk about politics in as sectarian a way as they want at home or church, they should be cognizant of the rules of civil discourse when talking with those of different faiths and none at all. Believing in biblical condemnations of homosexuality and abortion and discussing these condemnations with family and fellow believers are not inconsistent with democratic norms. These rules do not banish religion from the public square. But schools should encourage believers to only present arguments to others in ways that are consistent with good faith. Schools should urge students to look beyond their sectarian beliefs for empirical and logical evidence and to seek to cast arguments in hybrid terms. Sectarian religious beliefs can break ties or tip the scales in favor of one's preferred argument, but only after a good-faith effort to find logical and empirical support for one's position. Students should feel free to present any empirical or logical arguments that they find plausible but should be open to changing their political—but not their religious—beliefs when empirical or logical evidence contradicts their arguments.

Affirming religion does not mean schools should teach the truth or justifications of any belief, some beliefs, or all beliefs. It certainly does not involve converting atheists into believers. Schools should stress, though, that not only is religious commitment compatible with democratic citizenship, but American democracy thrives on the good-faith contributions religious groups make in the public square. If the religious must learn to forgo the exclusively sectarian, secularists must learn not only to tolerate but to engage with religious arguments that significantly depart from the sectarian beliefs of those who advance them. Genuine hybrid arguments, schools must emphasize, must not be ignored, redescribed as sectarian, or accused of bad faith.

With this philosophical framework in place, we can now be more specific about how schools can provide this advice to students. Jay Wexler, whose contributions to the religion and civic education debate are pioneering and essential, provides one possible avenue for transmission. Wexler (2002) calls for providing students with an extensive introduction to the religious justifications of political views held across the religious and political spectrum. Students would learn the religious basis of evangelical views on abortion and gay marriage and Catholic views on antipoverty programs and the death penalty, among other points of view. Wexler's proposal acknowledges that, like it or not, religion is part of American political discourse. Introducing students to religious arguments is necessary to prepare them for citizenship and is the only way they will be able to understand and respond to these arguments.

Unlike the approach advanced here, Wexler would not accompany this introduction with substantial guidance about how democratic citizens should treat these arguments or what types of arguments are compatible with democratic norms. This means that his approach includes too little and too much. Wexler (2003, 1218) does argue that having students examine religious justifications for public policy would implicitly suggest that religious arguments have a legitimate place in the public sphere. But this message might be too subtle for students. Exposing students to religious justifications might lead to serious and respectful engagement but could also lead to increased ridicule and aversion, and it is likely to do the latter among hardened secularists and separationists. This outcome would hardly be consistent with the tempering that Wexler himself (2003, 1201) desires for the culture wars.

The greater danger is that Wexler's laissez-faire approach would reconcile students who are not hardened secularists and separationists to accepting too many religious arguments in political debate. It provides no guidance about which arguments are faithful and unfaithful to democratic norms or which arguments deserve to be taken seriously and which do not. The most likely result of Wexler's proposal is that it would reconcile students to the status quo treatment of religion in politics. But the status quo is the problem, and understanding the status quo better will do little to change it.

The good-faith approach to teaching about religion and politics also stands in sharp contrast to the liberal educational approach.[19] Warren

Nord's discussion of how to handle the intersection of religion and politics in the classroom is not as explicit and detailed as Wexler's. But this is largely because it does not have to be; the proper way to handle religion and politics flows quite naturally from the overall liberal educational perspective. The perspective emphasizes providing students a well-rounded intellectual appreciation of the distinct religious worldviews a variety of believers inhabit, which makes its goals distinct from Wexler's civic approach.

In practice, however, Wexler's civic approach and the liberal educational approach converge. Teaching religion from the inside, the educational approach emphasizes, requires taking "seriously religious claims to truth *as truth is understood within various religious traditions*," as opposed to "reconceptualizing positions in terms of competing, privileged positions" (Nord 1995, 50, 163). Broadening students' understanding of the world and the possible worldviews open to them requires particular focus on what makes each religion *distinctive.* Several times, Nord invokes the image of an education that catches for students the essence of religious worldviews, an essence that eludes the inadequate "conceptual nets" of secular worldviews.[20] The liberal educational approach, then, should strive to capture and concentrate on the sectarian inspirations and justifications that believers use in their private lives and their communication with each other. "If students do not understand something of souls," asks Nord (207), "how are they to understand the abortion debate?" The implication is that focusing primarily on more empirical and logical claims that believers draw on in politics, as the good-faith approach does, would provide students with a truncated understanding of the worldviews these believers inhabit and would be unfair to both believers and their worldviews. But would it?

The sectarian justifications that the educational approach would focus on are undoubtedly a real and sincere part of the worldviews of most conservative and evangelical Christians. Then again, so is the willingness to adapt and align these political arguments with democratic norms. In determining whether the focus of the good-faith approach on empirical and logical arguments is selling conservative religious beliefs short, it is surely significant that an increasing number of conservative Christians themselves do not seem to consider the reliance on these arguments to be unfair to their religious views. If schools are committed to presenting students with a comprehensive understanding of how most conservative and evangelical

Christians live their religion overall as opposed to what their theological doctrine and scriptures say—Nord emphasizes providing students with the "experience" of inhabiting other religions—empirical and logical arguments are entitled to a place at least equal to sectarian justifications in the curriculum about religion and politics. Thus, the good-faith approach can be justified on liberal educational as well as civic grounds.

Still, advocates of the liberal educational approach might well respond that all this argument proves is that schools should expose students to *both* the sectarian and the empirical and logical political claims of religious conservatives. The good-faith approach goes further, of course, and supports *only* teaching the empirical and logical claims and largely ignoring the sectarian, while emphasizing that sectarian beliefs can be used as tiebreakers.

One reason to prefer the good-faith approach to the more inclusive educational approach is the alienating civic effects that discussing sectarian views in the required curriculum would have on religious minorities, secularists, and vulnerable groups targeted by these views.[21] But the educational reason for preferring the good-faith approach is even stronger. Sectarian points of view at the intersection of religion and politics tend to be far more eye-catching than empirical and logical claims. Students in the classroom are likely to attend to and discuss extreme sectarian views more than moderate empirical and logical claims. Indeed, this likelihood is the case in our current political discourse. Both extreme sectarian and more moderate claims are available for public discussion, but the media and many secularists choose to focus on extreme sectarian views, largely because it is financially profitable for the former group and politically profitable for the latter. There is little reason to believe that things would be different in the classroom. Discussing sectarian views in required classes would most likely not address the shortcomings and distortions of current political debates but simply reproduce and aggravate them. Just as important, such discussion would be unfair to conservative Christian worldviews and believers, because it would reduce often complex and nuanced worldviews to extremist sectarian caricatures. If we want students to get a more accurate and comprehensive sense of the views of most conservative Christians about politics and religion, schools should focus on the empirical and logical claims ignored by the media and many secularists, while ignoring the extremist sectarian claims these groups dwell on.

If, in its struggle for respectful discourse, American society is not merely to hold its ground against the culture war industry but to reclaim more civil space, it must provide the type of explicit and robust guidance about the intersection of religion and politics that Wexler's proposal and the educational approach forgoes. The required world religions course in Modesto introduced students to America's tradition of religious liberty and encouraged a respect for all faiths' rights to free religious expression. Even this brief discussion had a significant impact on students' respect for religious liberty. This discussion could have been and should be broadened to include an extended discussion of the good-faith obligations of the presenters and recipients of religious arguments.[22] In Modesto, discussing concrete cases like the controversy over the Pledge of Allegiance or the right of Sikh students to wear ceremonial daggers was indispensable in helping students to interpret the general principles their teachers conveyed, and such discussions must play a similar role in presenting good-faith principles. Abortion, gay marriage, the death penalty, and the environment are only several of the controversial issues that schools could mention.

If schools are to avoid fanning the flames of these controversies, application of good-faith principles to them must be careful. In particular, schools should remember that *what* schools teach cannot be considered in isolation from *how* schools teach. With its emphasis on participatory learning and serious engagement with other citizens' beliefs, Joe Coleman's pedagogical method of "democratic learning" seems to share a special kinship with the principle of good faith and would seem to be the preferred method for discussing the application of good-faith principles to controversial subjects. Coleman (1998, 756) observes that "we are probably more tolerant and respectful of differences embodied in real people that we have to interact with," and he emphasizes an approach that links

> education to empowering experiences especially vis-à-vis the ends which education is to serve or students' abilities to shape and determine their school environment. This form of pedagogy reflects the introduction of democratic modes of decision making into the school and classroom. Students are empowered to help determine rules, standards of behavior, the nature of their academic evaluations, and the topics which they will study. (751)

Coleman's democratic learning theory has the potential to be too robust in the case of religion. Allowing students to establish the principles governing discussion of religion without the benefit of historical insight and teacher guidance would be too messy and might create more cynicism than consensus. In communities with dominant religious majorities, classes may arrive at illiberal conclusions. Having teachers "guide" students to good-faith principles would likely be transparent to students and encourage them to treat the discussion as an empty exercise in manipulation. Good-faith principles themselves should not be subject to compromise. But democratic learning can and should play an essential role in the applications of good-faith principles. Students should have wide latitude to discuss which arguments on controversial topics like abortion or the death penalty are consistent with good-faith principles. Teachers should tap the brakes by gently challenging arguments that are exclusively sectarian and secularists who are too quick to disregard beliefs with any religious coloring, but students should be the engine driving these discussions. Good faith is, at its heart, about trust, and students cannot be expected to trust each other as citizens if schools do not trust them.

Nor can trust flourish if public schools fail to practice the good faith they preach in the structure of the overall curriculum. The inclusion of not only topics but classes addressing topics dear to religions can send a powerful signal—not only to students, but to their parents and the general community—that religious views are welcome in the public sphere. Requiring world religions courses and offering Bible elective courses can convey to evangelicals and secularists alike that schools appreciate the role that religion plays in not only the personal but the public lives of its many adherents in American society. Accommodating reasonable requests by religious students to opt out of controversial courses signals to believers that they need not choose between sacrificing their religious commitments and being good democratic citizens. Public schools, like public dialogue, should strive to include those with a serious, if not unqualified, commitment to democratic norms. When parents are willing to allow their children to receive instruction in the principles of respect for religious liberty and pluralism, public schools should show a reciprocal respect for their sectarian concerns. Most important, good faith means taking seriously religious arguments made in good faith in the curriculum. Since intelligent design theory departs significantly from the sectarian beliefs of its proponents, critics have been wrong to portray it as only a moral and religious position. Schools should encourage serious engagement with intelligent design, preferably in an elective, but not required, course. Good faith must begin with a fair account of our beginnings.

But beginning with good faith means more than treating our origins with good faith. If the goal of schools is dedicated to promoting civil discussion about religion and politics, school policy about religion should be conceived in civil discussion. The role of religion in politics is a vital public concern for believers and secularists. Public schools are only public in name if they do not include the views of parents and the community on this vital issue. We should not forget that angels do not govern schools and that communities must check them.

Public schools should strive to include local religious and secularist associations in the implementation of good-faith principles, courses concerning religion, and accommodation and exemption policies. Giving these associations a place at the table in the initial stage of constructing courses and policies can be too chaotic, but having them review school policies before their implementation can prevent egregious bias and ensure goodwill. The Modesto school district, for instance, only implemented its required world religions course after an advisory council of leaders from various religious communities reviewed the course. Administrators attributed the impressive community consensus about the course in large part to this inclusion of the stakeholders.

Local religious groups should play a similar role in demonstrating to students what good-faith democratic deliberation looks like in practice. While first specifying that religious groups should avoid providing obviously sectarian and explicitly scriptural defenses, school districts should canvas an inclusive group of local religious leaders about the hybrid arguments they use on political issues—such as abortion, gay marriage, the death penalty, income distribution, and the environment—and present these arguments to students. Having the examples provided by local religious leaders, rather than teachers and administrators, will head off claims of bias.

## IS COMMON GROUND SOLID GROUND?

Democracy would reap obvious and large benefits from good-faith discussions of religious and political issues and from a civic education modeled on such discussions. But, to borrow Marx's and Engels's famous distinction, is good-faith agreement about religion and politics utopian or scientific? The past few years have witnessed elegant attempts by major thinkers like Stephen Prothero (2007) and Noah Feldman (2005) to resolve the conflicts over religion and culture in our schools and society at large. But these thinkers' solutions qualify as more utopian than scientific, because they do not rely on a detailed empirical analysis of what the major sides in the culture war believe. Many citizens and scholars deplore the culture wars. A growing number of scholars and educational activists and administrators understand that public schools can play a critical role in bringing about a cease-fire. But without showing that a laying down of arms would further the self-interest of most culture war combatants, road maps for peace can lead nowhere. Persuasion, not force, is the best weapon in a democracy's arsenal. Having public schools impose a cultural cease-fire at odds with the basic concerns of religious conservatives, secularists, and religious minorities would be not only undemocratic but counterproductive.

The good-faith approach has a greater claim to science, because it uses empirical analysis to suggest that majorities of each side in the culture war would at least tolerate a good-faith education about religion and politics. But passive toleration of a good-faith education might not be enough. Extremists on both sides may sabotage teaching of good faith, if the majority of its supporters remain silent. Even if implemented, a good-faith education can only have limited impact if its lessons are contradicted or not reinforced by parents at home and religious leaders. Transforming common ground into solid ground requires that significant numbers on all sides of the culture war have motivation not only to tolerate and accept but to support a good-faith education.

If we follow the mainstream media, evangelicals would seem the least likely group to support a good-faith education. But paradoxically, this depiction in the mainstream media may give substantial numbers of evangelicals the strongest incentive to support such an education. Evangelicals have an image problem. Recent poll numbers from the Barna Research Group, which is sympathetic to evangelical Christian concerns, found that 40 percent of Americans aged between 16 and 29 are outside Christianity. Among this group, 87 percent find Christianity "judgmental," 85 percent find it "hypocritical," and 70 percent find it "insensitive" (McKibben 2008, 44). More crucially, evangelicals know they have an image problem, and they care about repairing it. Christian Smith (2000, 87) explains that the evangelicals he interviewed "know that many of their own people have acted offensively, and that this has brought deserved criticisms of evangelicalism as a whole. They are well aware that outsiders often view evangelicals as radically intolerant. And they are both prepared to take a certain amount of responsibility for that reputation, and concerned to remedy the situation."

Yet, if the will for good political relations with other citizens is present, the skills are often lacking. A good-faith education can bridge this gap. By learning to submit to restrictions on political arguments that do not require a complete withdrawal from their faith, evangelicals can improve their image in the world without losing their soul. The principles of good faith allow evangelicals to argue forcefully for their preferred political positions by relying partly on their faith while discouraging the use of the type of purely sectarian arguments that have alienated their opponents and possible allies. A substantial number of evangelicals would likely support an education that enabled them to hone their reputations as respectful democratic citizens while enhancing their ability for political persuasion.

Too often, we ignore that our cultural conflicts have not one but two fault lines. The pitting of secularists against religious conservatives is most apparent to us, but the views of non-Christian religious minorities are commonly overlooked. In part, this is because large numbers of these religious minorities resist assignment to either camp. Many members of these groups share religious conservative concerns about the ignoring and decline of traditional family values and sexual mores and the emergence of a religion-free public square. But many also share secularist concerns about the intolerance and sectarianism of those extremist Christian culture warriors who attempt to dominate the public square (Eck 2002). A good-faith education is capable of generating support among substantial numbers of these groups, because it addresses both of their main concerns. By discouraging the use of strongly sectarian language, good faith would prevent the dominance of public argument by larger religious groups that make non-Christian minorities feel excluded, but it would preserve the meaningful place that these groups cherish for faith in the public square.

The beneficiaries of the status quo are always the most resistant to change. The current treatment, or rather lack of treatment, of religion in the public schools most favors secularists, because it implicitly suggests that religion has no place in the public square. From this vantage point, any introduction of a discussion about religion and politics in public schools may appear risky. Many secularists may indeed not be persuaded that accepting the teaching of good faith is in their interests, but a more farsighted approach may be more beneficial and less risky than conserving the status quo. Encouraging religious conservatives to rely a bit more on logical and empirical arguments and a bit less on purely sectarian arguments may make their arguments more open to persuasive challenges. Citizens usually hold much faster to their beliefs about God and scripture than they do to their views about statistical evidence. Even assuming that most religious conservatives will not change their minds, they may be more likely to accept the legitimacy of controversial political outcomes on issues dear to them. Religious conservatives would prefer, as we all do, that their own policies triumph, but they are often driven to a strident and hostile expression of their views by the sense that their views are ignored or excluded. Secularist triumphs, particularly in the judicial system, are often shallow because their opponents view them as impositions by unsympathetic elites. At times, many religious conservatives react by retreating from political participation because of the perceived bias of the process. On issues like the teaching of evolution (Dean 2005b), perception of illegitimacy often leads to simple defiance. By learning about the principles of good faith, secularists may come to realize that ceding ground on admission of religious views into the public square can cement some of the cultural victories they cherish.[23]

Indeed, Modesto secularists' willingness—after some initial reluctance—to engage with conservative Christians produced a world religions course that achieved the major secularist goal of promoting religious tolerance for all. Turning to the results of this research in chapter 3 will help to show how the principles recommended in the first two chapters can be implemented. It will also provide further evidence that good faith on both sides of our cultural divide is likely to be rewarded.

# CHAPTER 3

## *A Cultural Mystery in Modesto*

A little over a decade ago, gay high school students in Modesto, California, began complaining of discrimination and wanted to form a student club for support. Modesto lies only 90 miles west of San Francisco, but the cultural distance is far greater. Modesto has a large evangelical Christian population, and many residents have taken to calling the city and its surrounding county the California Bible Belt. So it was not surprising that some parents opposed to homosexuality insisted that students receive parental permission before joining such a club, nor was it surprising that school officials initially agreed with them. Some students transferred schools, while others suffered in silence. One of the victims of antigay taunts, Tina Ransom, went to her school counselor for help. The counselor told Ransom that she might not always be gay and that she should accept Jesus into her life (Rowland 2001).

When he discovered that the child of one of his top administrators was the victim of harassment, Superintendent James Enochs took the discrimination personally and decided to act. He told a group of parents, teachers, students, and religious leaders to craft a policy to protect all students from being harassed on the basis of race, religion, class, gender, or sexual orientation. His directive predictably met with strong resistance from conservative Christians. They worried that schools would contradict their beliefs by teaching their children that there is nothing wrong or sinful about homosexuality. All the roles for a protracted and painful religious and cultural conflict were cast.

But Modesto's conflict did not follow this familiar script. In 2000, Modesto decided to engage in a bold and seemingly perilous attempt to use religion as a source of communal harmony. Other school districts include discussions of world religions in subject matters such as history or

English classes or provide independent elective courses on world religions. Modesto is the only school district in the nation to require that all students take an extended, independent course on world religions. No legal controversies or community outrage have erupted. The public schools are no longer the site of cultural battles but a source of cultural peace. The required world religions course does not deserve all the credit for this transformation, but its large contribution is undeniable. This chapter seeks to solve the mystery of how this transformation occurred.


## MODESTO'S VALUE AS A CASE STUDY

Two major sets of questions surround the teaching of a required world religions course in public schools. The first set asks: *Should* public schools teach about world religions? Would world religions courses lead to increased tolerance or highlight differences between students? Do they produce greater knowledge about religion? Might such courses violate the rights of students from atheist and agnostic backgrounds? Will teaching students about many religions encourage the abandonment of robust religious beliefs and traditions?

Even if world religions courses are a good idea in theory, they might be too controversial in practice. This leads to a second set of questions about such courses: *Can* required world religions courses work in communities around the nation? Given disagreements about school curriculum and cultural issues in general, can groups on the right and left find common ground by recognizing the importance of teaching about world religions, or will such teaching inevitably be viewed as too controversial and lead to increased disputes?

Opinions and predictions on these questions abound, but they tend to generate more heat than light. They are often based on anecdotes and personal experiences that mainly reveal the sensibilities and biases of their sources. They do not provide an accurate portrait of the general effects of teaching about world religions. When everyone uses different facts, genuine dialogue is not possible. Establishing common ground on religion in schools requires a shared set of facts to discuss, derived from objective investigation.

Social science is not flawless, and Mark Twain's ranking of "damned lies" above statistics has more than rhetorical value. But the ability of social science to incorporate large amounts of evidence systematically provides more complete and accurate information than anecdotes, and its aspiration to objectivity corrects the biases of mere opinions. If we want to know how world religions courses *will* work, we should look systematically at how one *has* worked. Our best hope for answering the "can" and "should" questions about world religions courses lies in this approach. This chapter presents the results of the first large-scale, systematic social science research conducted on the effects of teaching about religion in public schools.[1]

This research not only addresses important practical questions about teaching religion in schools but examines general theoretical claims and questions surrounding tolerance. For instance, does greater education lead to an increase in tolerance, and if so, why? Tolerance researchers are divided on these questions. Some research suggests that Americans become more tolerant as they gain knowledge about a group. People seem to be more willing to give rights to homosexuals as they learn more about how AIDS is and is not transmitted (Sniderman, Brody, and Tetlock 1991, 31). As people gain knowledge about a group, they feel less threatened by it. But students who learn more about other groups could come to believe that these groups pose a threat to their interests and well-being (Feldman and Stenner 1997). "People sometimes kill their enemies," Stephen Prothero (2007, 18) reminds us, "not because they don't understand them but precisely because they do." Measuring the reaction of Modesto's students to learning about many religions sheds light on these questions.

Besides settling existing disputes, the research addresses an essential question that social scientists have ignored about *religious* respect. The central challenge of respect for religious liberty in a liberal democracy involves making people more active on behalf of other religious groups' freedoms without converting them into relativists. Fashioning this compromise is theoretically possible, but it is not clear that the occasionally crude instruments of educational policy can produce this delicate result. No previous empirical research addresses this issue. Our research investigates whether Modesto's students were able to retain their distinctive religious identities while learning to embrace more vigorously the civil rights of other religious groups. The research allows us to test whether Rousseau (1987, 220) was right to claim, in his *Social Contract*, that "it is impossible to live in peace with those one believes to be damned."

Before examining the research's methods and, more important, the results, it is first necessary to make good on the claim that this research can have a national impact and resonance. We must turn to a discussion of Modesto's religious and cultural history and demographics.

## MODESTO: A COMMUNITY AT A RELIGIOUS CROSSROADS

Modesto, California, which is located in Stanislaus County, has always struggled with the challenges posed by diversity. A century ago, it was in a sparsely populated region dedicated to dry farming. With the development of irrigation, railroads, and highways, the size and productivity of agriculture in the central valley grew exponentially, as did the number of immigrants from other parts of the United States and beyond. Particularly in the last 40 years, the area's religious diversity has expanded alongside its ethnic, racial, cultural, and linguistic diversity.

According to Ida Bowers (2005), a former professor at California State University at Stanislaus, the number of observant Sikhs living in Modesto and the surrounding cities of Hughson and Ceres is approximately 5,000. Two thousand Muslims live in Modesto, 400 attend services regularly, and the center's Saturday school has 180 enrollees, according to the imam of Modesto's Islamic center. Approximately 4,000 Southeast Asians live in Stanislaus County, including significant Cambodian and Laotian populations (Bowers 2005). Much of this population identifies itself as Buddhist, but it also includes Hmong immigrants from Cambodia who practice a form of religious animism. Parmanand Tiwari (2005), a leading member of Modesto's Hindu community, estimates that 6,000 Hindus reside in Stanislaus County and that approximately 1,500 Hindus attend major religious holiday ceremonies at Modesto's Hindu temple.

Mainline Protestant, Catholic, and Jewish communities have retained their popularity amid this diversity.[2] Conservative evangelical Protestant denominations have probably even experienced a rise in membership because of the diversity. Religions stressing more traditional values tend to flourish in times and places of great change. A city of approximately 190,000, Modesto is home to five evangelical Christian "megachurches," which claim over 2,500 members. Evangelicals are "a very visible group and frequently participate in government and public service," according to *Modesto Bee* reporter Amy White (2004). Three of the seven school board members at the time of our research ran on platforms sympathetic to conservative Christian concerns about public schools.

Modesto's evangelicals are not Pat Robertson clones. Resident after resident, evangelical and nonevangelical, stressed the moderate and diverse nature of evangelical Christianity in Modesto. If the conservative evangelical presence "conjures up images as the Bible Belt of the South," associate pastor Paul Zeek (2004) of Modesto's First Baptist Church told us, "it would be very inaccurate." Father Jon Magoulias (2004) of Modesto's Greek Orthodox Church added that Modesto's evangelicals were not "fundamentalists." Amy White (2004) noted "the surprising racial and ethnic diversity" of Modesto's evangelicals and contended that they are less interested in "telling other people what to do" than in defending their children from objectionable influences. Superintendent Enochs dismissed concerns about the evangelical presence on the school board as overblown and described the members as reasonable and willing to compromise. Besides the controversy over homosexuality, complaints from the school board's conservative Christian members have been confined to objections over treatments of sex in the reading for high school English classes. Like the evangelicals in Christian Smith's nationwide study, Modesto's evangelicals hold distinctive concerns, but they are neither as monolithic nor as inflexible as the culture war narrative depicts them.

Modesto is not only religiously but politically diverse. As of 2009, registered Democrats in Stanislaus County outnumbered Republicans by a slight margin of 42 to 38 percent, and the county voted by a slight plurality—49.4 to 48.7 percent—for Barack Obama. But support for Obama was significantly less there than in the rest of California, and the county's voters favored George W. Bush in 2004 by a margin of 58 to 40 percent. In 2008, 68 percent of voters in Stanislaus County supported California's Proposition 8, which amended the California Constitution to ban gay marriage (Stanislaus County Elections 2009).[3]

Modesto's record of respect for religious minorities has been commendable, if not spotless, with regard to overt discrimination. As recounted in the introduction, I did arrive for a visit to Modesto's Hindu temple to find a dead baby calf in front of the temple's gate, a derogatory message placed between its hooves. But the leaders of Modesto's non-Christian religions I spoke with reassured me that this was more an ugly coincidence than a typical occurrence.

Beneath this apparent calm, however, lies a more complex and troubling story that confirms chapter 1's claims about the inadequacy of passive tolerance. Modesto's religious minorities may not have feared overt persecution, but they also did not feel comfortable expressing and celebrating their religious identities in public. Amy White (2004) observed that "since September 11 [religious minorities] are very cautious about being singled out" and "may not want to advertise if they're having a big event." According to Methodist pastor Wendy Warner (2004), Muslims and Hindus who turned down invitations from an interfaith coalition to join in a public memorial to 9/11 victims "expressed fear about participating." Local college professor Sam Oppenheim (2005) surmised that this diffidence stems from the fact that there is "not a lot of understanding in the community between the different groups and not a lot of situations where they can interact with each other easily." Father Joseph Illo (2005) of St. Joseph's Catholic Church speculated that Modesto's tolerance might be at a tipping point. Asked if Modesto is a religiously tolerant community, he responded, "Well, yes, but that's because there aren't too many Muslims here yet."

Christian students in schools often took their dominance for granted, which left the feelings of Modesto's religious minorities unacknowledged. Several of Modesto's high schools, for instance, have Christian clubs that throw pizza parties for their members during lunch hours or after school. Invitations to Jewish students who hid their identity forced them to choose between betraying their faith or revealing their religious differences and facing isolation.

Modesto's religious diversity and short supply of active tolerance made it the type of community that could benefit much from a required world religions course. At the same time, these factors ensured the difficulty of implementing such a course. When she first heard of the course, school board member Cindy Marks (2004) "was apprehensive about how the course was going to work, because there are 50 languages spoken in Modesto and Modesto is in a pocket which is labeled as the Bible Belt." To understand how these doubts were allayed, we must return to a history of the course's adoption.

## A HISTORY OF THE COURSE'S ADOPTION — CONTINUED

When we left Modesto schools in the introduction, they were embroiled in controversy. The 115-member group of parents, students, teachers, and religious leaders that Enochs convoked to craft a policy of promoting respect for all students was mired in a debate on the morality of homosexuality. Enochs brought in Charles Haynes to mediate the meetings (Herendeen 2002).

Haynes told the group to start over. The key, Haynes argued, was to learn how to respect everyone's right to be heard and to believe. Should gay students be harassed in school, he asked? No, everyone agreed. The group set to work on a "safe schools" policy that would reduce taunting and other forms of harassment and that would teach students—and maybe the community—that people should respect each other even though they may disagree (Bird 1998).

Haynes had given community mediation workshops before, but never one in which a community wanted to implement so much of what they talked about in the seminar. The district "took what I said and made the leap," he said, adding, "I didn't think they were going to do it" (Haynes 2006). The committee crafted a package deal. The district adopted a policy in favor of safe schools and instituted a "human relations" seminar to encourage students to get along with one another, as well as a "day of respect" that featured outside speakers talking about various forms of discrimination.

The centerpiece of the policy, however, was the creation of a required course on world religions and religious liberty, to take place over nine weeks in the ninth grade. The district allowed students to opt out of the course but also rejected an elective approach. Elective courses on religion serve a purpose, but their effects are limited because they do not provide students and community members with a collective experience. The students who may need an education in world religions and religious liberty may be the ones least likely to elect to take such a course.

At first glance, a course on religion seems like an odd outgrowth of a controversy over homosexuality in the public schools. In fact, this was only the latest controversy that stemmed from cultural misunderstanding. Instituting a course on world religions helped to increase respect for Modesto's minority religious believers and also helped satisfy conservative Christians, many of whom felt that the school district was not appropriately respectful of their beliefs.

Reconciling the religious majority to the rights of religious minorities was not the course's only purpose.[4] Assimilation is a two-way street, and world religions courses can help conduct the traffic in both directions. Thirty percent of the students we surveyed spoke a language other than English in the home, and recent immigrants as well as others could benefit from a tutorial in the ideas behind our basic rights and liberties. High school civics classes used to provide such an education, but they were largely replaced by amorphous "social studies" courses. Now more than ever, facing the pressures of diversity, school districts find that students (and their parents) need instruction in the basics of civics.

To ensure that students understood the course's relationship to the district's policy for safe schools, the administrators determined that the course should begin with a two-week discussion of the tradition of religious liberty in the United States. Freedom of conscience, the course teaches, is a reciprocal right that must be applied universally to be meaningful. The remaining seven weeks of the course would focus primarily on seven major world religions, in the following order, based on each religion's appearance in history: Hinduism, Buddhism, Confucianism, Sikhism, Judaism, Christianity, and Islam.

Due to time constraints, the course would not discuss in detail the differences between denominations within religious traditions. The approach to religion taken in the course would be descriptive rather than comparative, to ensure neutrality and avoid controversy. Discussion would focus on the historical development and major contemporary beliefs and practices of each religion, but the course would not encourage students to interpret religious texts based on their historical context.

After the basics of the course had been designed and a textbook selected, the district asked religious leaders to serve on an advisory council to review the course. The council drew on members of the Protestant, Catholic, Islamic, Sikh, Jewish, and Greek Orthodox communities; a few other religious communities were asked but chose not to participate. Father Magoulias (2004), who participated on the council, said that there were spirited discussions about how much time should be allotted to each reli-

gion and about the characterization of pivotal events, such as the split between Orthodox and Catholic churches in 1054. But he described the meetings as "generally amicable."

Only approval by the school board remained. Since, according to Gary
Lopez (2005), "there's a strong conservative faction in Modesto, and we
have a few board members who pretty much are aligned with that faction
in town," there was initially "some concern" about the course, expressed
by these members. Once everyone understood that the course was attempting to promote respect and not indoctrinate students in one belief, the
school board's seven members voted unanimously in its favor.

METHODOLOGY

We surveyed approximately 300 to 400 students three times, once in October 2004, before students took the course, and twice after they had taken
the course, in January and May 2005.[5] This was approximately 70 percent
of the freshman students taking the required world religions course at the
five major Modesto high schools.[6] We have no reason to believe that students who were not surveyed differ from those who were. Table 1 reports
the demographics of students from the January 2005 survey.

The survey consisted of 77 to 81[7] questions measuring the course's effects on (a) respect for rights in general, (b) passive and active respect for
religious diversity, and (c) students' level of relativism, syncretism, and ec-

TABLE 1. Demographic Information on Participants in January 2005 Survey (*N* = 355)

| Gender | Ethnicity | Presidential Election Preference | Language |
|---|---|---|---|
| Female: 197 (55%) | White: 145 (41%) | Kerry: 154 (43%) | English spoken in home: 253 (71%) |
| Male: 158 (45%) | Hispanic/Latino: 135 (38%) | Bush: 125 (35%) | |
| | Other: 31 (9%) | Don't Know: 62 (17%) | Non-English spoken in home: 101 (29%) |
| | Asian: 23 (6%) Black: 21 (6%) | Other: 13 (4%) | |

umenism.[8] Modesto students provided fertile empirical ground to test out ideas about religious respect and civic education, because the public school district they live in is religiously diverse and the only one we know of to require a course on world religions and religious liberty.

Extended personal interviews with 23 Modesto students accompanied the surveys and focused on the major issues examined in the surveys.[9] The more detailed answers in the interviews enable us to provide further confirmation of the survey results, get an insight into nuances of students' opinions that the surveys were unable to identify, and better understand the reasons behind students' views and the shifts that took place in their views. Extensive interviews were also conducted with 11 teachers; Modesto school administrators, including the superintendent; school board members; and religious and community leaders in Modesto.[10] While the surveys addressed the "should" question about teaching world religions, the interviews with educators and community leaders addressed the mystery of how a community divided by religion found common ground on a required world religions course.

The presentation of research results in this chapter strives to balance generality with nuance. Missing the forest for the trees is a common shortcoming of human observation, but missing the trees for the forest is often as problematic. Reporting general statistical trends provides an essential summary of the effects of the Modesto course. No course has a uniform effect on every student, and educational policy makers cannot tailor courses for every student. Educational policy must rely on average effects. Inertia is the only alternative.

But reality is messy, and general drifts can obscure disturbing undercurrents that educational policy makers must work to mitigate. Although statistics show that the course encouraged respect for religious liberty, our interviews revealed feelings among several Jewish students that expressing their identity caused greater distance from friends and peers. Not all nuance raises cause for concern, however. At times, close investigation produced pleasant surprises that confirmed the value of the course. Statistics, for instance, showed that students became neither less nor more committed to their religious beliefs as a result of taking the course, but the interviews provided additional evidence to respond to the charge that such courses weaken faith. Several students told us that the course invigorated their flagging faith in their own religion.

## RESEARCH RESULTS

### *Passive Tolerance*

Modesto's policy for safe schools aimed, at its most basic level, to increase students' appreciation for First Amendment rights and especially the rights of religious minorities. This refusal to support discriminatory public policies is the type of tolerance previously described as passive.[11] Upon initial inspection, the surveys students took before the course suggest a passive tolerance deficit, but not a huge one. We asked students if they agreed or disagreed with statements such as "People of all religions should be able to put religious displays outside of their homes as long as the displays are on their private property" and "Students of all religions should be able to wear religious symbols outside of their clothing in public schools." Ideally, every American should agree with these statements. Figure 1 shows that between 75 and 81 percent of Modesto students agreed with them.

But tolerance researchers have long noted that tolerance is easier in the abstract than in difficult cases where it counts the most. To test students' willingness to apply abstract principles when push comes to shove as well as to test their respect for First Amendment rights in general, we asked students if they would extend basic First Amendment rights—such as the right to run for public office, teach in public schools, make a public speech, or hold public rallies—to their "least-liked group."[12] As we suspected, applying rights concretely made most students waver. Figure 2 shows that while half were willing to allow a member of their least-liked group to make "a public speech," 25 percent or less were willing to allow their least-liked group the other three basic rights. Only 15 percent were willing to allow a member of their least-liked group to run for public office.

Though definitely disturbing, these results are perhaps not surprising. When asked about particular groups, Americans have always voiced less tolerant opinions than they should. In a pioneering study of political tolerance in 1954, only one-quarter of the population was prepared to allow a Communist to take a job as a store clerk. By 1973, 57 percent would do so, but intolerance may have shifted by then to new groups, including those on the political right that academics were less likely to measure (Nunn, Crockett, and Williams 1978, 43). Perhaps if Americans knew more about the First Amendment, they would be more committed to it. In a McCormick Tribune Freedom Museum poll, only one of a thousand respondents could name all

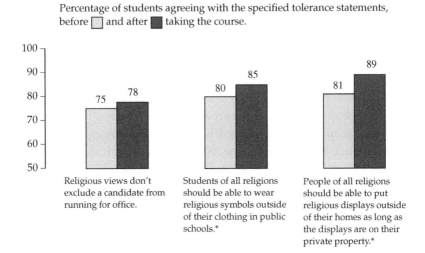

Fig. 1. Passive tolerance. (*Note:* On *t*-tests comparing target group with previous test, * $p < 0.01$; $N$ = between 345 and 365.)

five freedoms in the First Amendment, and only 28 percent could name more than one freedom (McCormick Tribune Freedom Museum 2006). In a recent survey, 75 percent of students thought that flag burning is illegal, and 50 percent believed that the government could censor the Internet (John S. and James L. Knight Foundation's High School Initiative 2004).

We did not expect the course to convert every intolerant student into a civil libertarian. Civic education research tends to show that education has, at most, moderate effects on civic virtue in the short term, and Modesto's course was, after all, only nine weeks long. But we did think that the course would produce statistically significant effects, and our results almost universally confirmed our expectations. Figure 1 shows that agreement with the statements that "Students of all religions should be able to wear religious symbols outside of their clothing in public schools" and that "People of all religions should be able to put religious displays outside of their homes as long as the displays are on their private property" rose by 5 and 8 percent, respectively, after the course.[13] Willingness to grant all four basic rights to least-liked groups increased by statistically significant amounts of between 4.4 and 10.3 percent after the course, as figure 2 shows. Even the

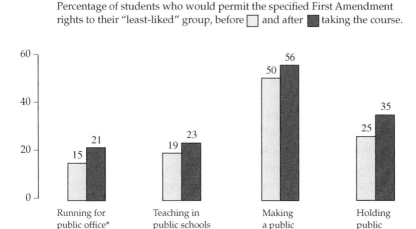

Fig. 2. Tolerance of "least-liked" groups. (*Note:* On *t*-tests comparing target group with previous test, * $p < 0.05$, ** $p < 0.01$, *** $p < 0.001$; $N =$ between 345 and 365.)

posttest results on these questions remain disappointing, but the course did make a significant difference.

As informative as they are, statistics can seem lifeless. Our interviews give a more vivid portrayal of the course's impact on students by adding color and detail. All the students we interviewed agreed that the course made them more respectful of religious liberty. The change in some students' opinions was dramatic. "I had a Hindu person living across the street, and they'd be praying to a statue," a Russian Orthodox student began. "I'd be all confused. I couldn't understand why they were doing it. I thought it was just plain dumb. But I notice now that they had a pretty good reason to."

The interviews also raise warning flags about the course that the surveys did not recognize. Several students reported that their classmates made insulting comments about other religions. When one teacher mentioned that Sikhs treat their holy book, the Guru Granth Sahib, with a great deal of respect by giving the book its own bedroom and bed in Sikh temples, a would-be comedian asked if it also had its own bathroom. Another student told us that students in her class made "little wisecracks" when they watched videos on Islam and Judaism. The course may also have occasionally created distance between students by stressing religious differences. Rabbi Paul Gordon (2004) of Modesto's Congregation Beth Shalom complained that the course raised expectations it could not meet. The course encouraged several students in his congregation to reveal their Judaism to friends and acquaintances, but he felt that their revelations led to more strained relationships.

Schools certainly should not discount the pain that these insults caused, but their occurrence did advance the course's agenda in intriguing ways. Prejudices that might otherwise have remained hidden saw the light of day where classmates and teachers could challenge them. While discussing the origins of Christianity, several students asked Connie Hernandez if the 2004 film *The Passion of the Christ* was right to depict that Jews were responsible for Jesus's execution. The Romans and Pontius Pilate bore more responsibility for the execution than the movie depicted, Hernandez told her students, and even if Jews did play some role in Jesus's execution, Jews today could not be held responsible for what occurred 2,000 years ago. Expressions of prejudice also remind religious majority and minority students alike of the threat intolerance poses, and they provide greater motivation to fight it. Schools should not treat students as means to an end. But unless taunts about religion are a frequent occurrence or regularly lead to fights, neither of which was the case in Modesto, the long-term value of confronting prejudice probably outweighs the short-term discomfort it creates.

More crucially, the students from minority religions we interviewed—including Hindu, Sikh, Jewish, Wiccan, and atheist students—all counted the course overall as a positive experience. Connie Hernandez asked one Hindu student to bring in objects related to her religion and discuss her religion with the class if she felt comfortable. The student proudly recounted to us how she taught her fellow classmates about her religion and corrected their pronunciation of religious terms.[14]

## Active Respect

The course clearly made students themselves less likely to discriminate based on religion, but did it make them more likely to protest discrimination? Active respect involves taking action to defend vulnerable religious groups against insult and discrimination. It can range from small tokens, such as words spoken to a friend, to engaging in political behavior to protect a victimized group. Our democracy not only needs citizens who refrain from preventing religious activities such as student-organized after-school prayer groups or Muslim rallies in public parks. It needs citizens who actively protest the restriction of rights of conscience. The course's designers never intended to promote active respect: improving understanding and respect for basic rights and liberties, they thought, was a worthy enough goal. But after nine weeks of investigation into the practices of major religions and the rights and responsibilities of American citizenship, students might be prone to actively defend rights of conscience and speech more vigorously.

Our research results were mixed. The survey asked students five questions about their willingness to take increasingly strenuous courses to protest religious discrimination in their community. Most dealt with political action, such as opposing a member of Congress, writing a letter to a newspaper, or signing a petition. On all of these questions, the course appeared to have no effects. Such a course appears to be up against strong currents of apathy. Students today—not unlike their parents—show little inclination to take any political action, according to numerous studies on civic education (Conover and Searing 2000, 103). Students with little or no experience of civic participation may have difficulty envisioning themselves writing a letter to a newspaper or participating in the organization of a civic association on any topic.

The one question dealing with a situation students could identify with yielded different results, however. The number of students willing to "defend a student whose religious beliefs were insulted by another student" increased from 55.6 percent before the course to 65.1 percent after—a statistically significant improvement. A change in behavior occasionally accompanied this change of attitude. World religions course teacher Yvonne Taylor told us of a lunchroom incident she witnessed where several students were teasing a Jewish student for wearing a yarmulke. Another group of students confronted the tormentors for their intolerance. Although several interviewed students were concerned about standing out too much or being bullied themselves by larger classmates, almost all said that the course strengthened their willingness to take action by either standing up to the insulter or comforting the victim. "If a person took [an insult] the wrong way," one student told us, "I would go say something. It's not polite to talk about a person's religion because that's what they believe in." "I do try to step up for" classmates whose religion has been insulted, another related, "because I believe in my own religion a lot, and I know what that feels like."

The logic these students used is as notable as their willingness to act. Chapter 1 argued that promoting respect by encouraging students to embrace the truths of the religions they study violates religious freedom. Encouraging students to empathize with the strength of religious minorities' allegiance to their religion rather than with their religious beliefs themselves is more consistent with democracy. Several of Modesto's teachers enlisted this distinction in support of tolerance. "A right for one is a right for all," Yvonne Taylor repeatedly intoned to her students, rather than "A belief for one is a belief for all." The quotes in the last paragraph and our other interviews indicated that students took this distinction to heart.

The previous questions discussed measure active tolerance by gauging how students treat others. But the survey also measures active tolerance by examining how students feel others have treated them. The number of students who reported that they "were made to feel uncomfortable" because of their religious beliefs declined after the course. The survey is not able to tell us if incidents of disrespect actually declined, but the fact that students *felt* less discomfort concerning their religious identity is significant.

Even so, the gains in active respect were underwhelming. Part of this was due to omission. Modesto simply did not aim at active respect. But the course may also be at fault for a sin of commission. The course tended to bathe each religion in what Rabbi Gordon called a "warm and fuzzy light" by avoiding darker aspects of religion, such as incidents of persecution. The district's honorable intention was to avoid controversy, but the effect may have been to undercut a strong motive to protest religious discrimination. We should not expect students to feel outraged about religious discrimination if they are left unaware of the extent of such discrimination at home and abroad. Why should students worry about the civil rights of Muslims in America if they do not know that these rights are in peril? Knowing about the First Amendment and being motivated to act on its guarantees are two different things.

If world religions courses want to motivate students to take action, they should at least tell students about the Holocaust, the European religious wars of the seventeenth century, and New England Puritan persecution of Quakers and other alleged heretics. Discussing religious discrimination in the United States today and especially incidents that have taken place in the local community is essential to helping students realize that religious persecution is not just an abstract threat but a real danger. This is common practice in British religious education. Schools in Sheffield, England, for instance, point out in a unit on Islamic dress that Muslims have been bullied in Sheffield for their appearance (O'Grady 2005, 27).

Highlighting increased incidents of assaults on Muslims is fairly straightforward, but discussion of other types of discrimination can be trickier. Many conservative Christians object to the banning of Christmas symbols on public property and of Ten Commandments statues from courtrooms. Are these instances of religious discrimination or steps necessary to prevent religious dominance? Teaching the controversy is preferable to picking sides or silence, but schools might be better off choosing to spend more time on less ambiguous instances of persecution of Christians today, such as the closing of churches in China. Schools must also avoid spotlighting one religion's role in persecution. Persecutions of Christians in the former Communist regimes of Eastern Europe should balance examples of Christian nations or groups responsible for historical persecution.

Motivation is blind, however, without specific knowledge about what practices religious minorities most want accommodated. World religions courses should describe concrete scenarios for accommodating the reasonable religious demands of each faith studied. Russ Matteson, pastor of Modesto's Church of the Brethren, related that in his previous work as a store manager, he was highly conscious of tailoring work schedules to ensure that Muslim employees could participate in Friday prayer services. Knowing dietary restrictions can help students make more appropriate choices when dining out with friends of different faiths or inviting them over for dinner. Taking time to discuss the correct pronunciation of religious terms can prevent teasing and unintentional gaffes. Being sensitive to the need for modest dress among some believers and to the low energy levels of Muslims in gym classes during Ramadan, for instance, can set the tone for students' respectful behavior (Nesbitt 2005).

Modeling respect for these differences in schools can play an indispensable role in transforming students from believers in religious liberty to practitioners, at a time when respect for religious accommodations is particularly necessary. The number of complaints registered by the Equal Employment Opportunity Commission over workplace religious discrimination has risen almost 60 percent since 1997. Not only are businesses increasingly denying Jews the right to wear yarmulkes and Sikhs the right to wear turbans, but Christians are increasingly being denied opportunities to observe holy days (Diament 2008). Making students aware of these religious requirements in schools can secure their recognition in workplaces and society at large.

## Knowledge about Religion and Religious Liberty

That students emerged from a course about world religions with more knowledge about world religions should come as no shock, especially considering how little students knew about religion to begin with. We were surprised, however, about the size of students' increase in knowledge immediately after completing the course. Students took a five-question test measuring their knowledge of world religions and the American tradition of religious liberty. The questions remained the same each of the three times the students took the test (though fewer took it the third time). On average, student scores improved from 37.4 percent correct in the October test to 66.4 percent correct in January.[15]

Even if it is quite obvious that studying more about religion will make students more knowledgeable about religion, the empirical confirmation of this effect has important implications for our democracy. At a time, as Stephen Prothero (2007) stresses, when Americans need to know more about religion, surveys show that they know increasingly less. As the attacks of 9/11 have turned our focus outward, a greater knowledge of world religions becomes essential for the informed making of foreign policy. "It's as imprudent to ignore the role of religion in foreign policy," writes Sue Rardin (2006, 13), "as it is to pretend that the elephant is in some other room, rather than right here." At home, knowledge about world religions is essential because the willingness to tolerate and respect others is not always sufficient. Accommodating religious minorities at work, school, and in one's neighborhood requires practical knowledge about the requirements of their faiths.

Still, while knowing more facts is helpful, facts must also be placed into proper context. Teaching students only about the Wahhabi form of Islam, for instance, may lead to an increase in knowledge about Islam if they knew nothing previously, but it would not lead to an accurate and complete portrait of Islam. If students do not get this full picture of minority religions from schools, it is unlikely they will get it elsewhere. Extreme and strange practices entice the eye and ear and dominate media coverage of minority and mainstream religions alike.[16] The sensationalistic focus on extremism distorts, rather than informs and exaggerates, the divide between faiths.

Providing a more accurate knowledge about religion need not ignore extreme practices, and schools should certainly not ignore each faith's core beliefs and practices just because they may seem weird. Smoothing out the apparent rough edges of other beliefs to make them more palatable for mainstream consumption should not be the course's goal. Learning to appreciate what appears weird to some students—such as why Hindus pray to a statue of Ganesh or why Sikhs carry a ceremonial dagger—is often the better part of tolerance. But schools can play an essential role in students' understanding by refusing to exaggerate the extreme and apparently weird.

Such accuracy was a major concern of the course's designers. The course, according to Gary Lopez (2005), should help students understand "why some Muslims believe in holy wars, what's their mentality, and why some Muslims are militant and some aren't." All the teachers we spoke with emphasized that the terrorists who carried out the 9/11 attacks were extremists who did not represent the opinions or behaviors of Muslims in general. Jonathan Couchman (2004) asked his students if the terrorists represented the majority of Muslims to a greater extent than David Koresh and the Branch Davidians represented the majority of Christians.

Students we interviewed testified to applying their newfound knowledge about religions to their daily lives. Recognition of and appreciation for the presence of religious diversity in their community and schools dramatically increased. Formerly anonymous buildings they drove by everyday were now properly identified as synagogues and mandirs. Ceremonial daggers were acknowledged as Sikh kirpans. Bracelets were recognized as Sikh karhas. "I didn't know we had so many different religions in just this area," one student commented. "I'm smart," another student boasted about her new awareness, "because I know all these things I didn't know before."

These quotes are inspiring, but would these gains in knowledge last? Living as we do in an age of endless entertainment distractions, Sam Oppenheim (2005) doubted that students would retain many of the facts they learned. Determining knowledge retention is crucial for the debate over the main goals and outcomes of a civic education about religion. Stephen Prothero (2007) has stressed that courses about religion should emphasize conveying knowledge more than modeling citizenship skills. Citizens who know more about religion are better equipped to understand, debate, and at times contest political positions founded in religion on issues ranging from abortion and homosexuality to poverty. But if students are to better evaluate these positions, they need to remember essential facts about the religions they study.

The results of the knowledge test on the May survey calls this capacity for recall into question. Students knew significantly more than they did before the course but significantly less—52 versus 66 percent—than they did immediately after the course. Still, the clear interest students took in the material partly contradicts this pessimism. The more students express an interest in learning about religion, the more likely they are to retain knowledge about the course material and lessons for respect. Students' interest in the course may even inspire a desire for new knowledge about religions in the future, which will in turn contribute to greater respect for other religious traditions.

Nearly 75 percent of students surveyed said they found the course interesting or very interesting.[17] Students' discussion about religion with their parents did not increase on the survey, but they did report engaging in a slightly greater number of discussions about religion with their friends after taking the course. Given the distorted picture of Islam in the media, we also wanted to know if the course would encourage students to learn more about Islam. The percentage of students who agreed with the statement "It is very important that Americans today try to learn more about the Muslim religion" was 42 percent before the course and 50 percent after.[18]

The interviews, however, raised doubts about the likelihood that students would follow through on their intentions. Of the students we interviewed who expressed an intention to learn more, none specified reading they had done or would do. Jonathan Couchman used a grant he received from California to purchase books related to the religions studied in the course, but none of his students asked to borrow the books after the course ended.

Putting the pieces of this puzzle together communicates an important message. The large decline in knowledge on the posttest makes it hard to

believe that students will retain beyond their school years the bulk of factual knowledge they learn in world religions courses. It is especially unlikely that they will remember the highly specific passages from religious
texts that believers of different faiths use to justify political stances. By comparison, schools drill students from an early age in American history and
constitutional law, but many surveys show embarrassing gaps in even the
best students' knowledge.[19]

But even if, amid the competing demands of family, work, and fun, students may gradually grow to ignore their intentions to know more about
religions, the interviews gave no reason to doubt the sincerity of their intentions. Indeed, our survey shows that increase in respect for religious
knowledge remained steady after the course, even as knowledge about religion declined. The interviews also suggest that the knowledge students
are most likely to retain is practical information that receives confirmation
from their daily surroundings. They may forget Hindu, Sikh, and Islamic
theology, but they will not forget how to recognize a mandir or why Sikhs
carry kirpans and some Muslim women wear hijabs.

Prothero might be unsatisfied with this outcome, and it is less than
ideal. But the good news is that it should suffice for the purposes of durable
tolerance. Students will not retain every last detail they learn about each religion, but learning a more balanced account of each faith should sustain
their respect. They will remember that they should not judge Islam by the
*Time* magazine cover depicting extremism, even if they are a bit fuzzy on all
of Islam's core beliefs. Respect will likely be the residue of knowledge.

## Similarity of Religions: A Careful Balance

Distinguishing mainstream from extremist believers is one potent way to
promote tolerance. Stressing the similarities across traditions is another.
Greater appreciation of the common ground between religions increases
students' identification with other religions' adherents and commitment to
their political and civil rights. Teaching that Islam, Judaism, and Christianity share central moral beliefs can balance students' awareness of behaviors, such as terrorism, that do not represent the beliefs and practices of
most Muslims.

Modesto's teachers stressed the major religions' commonalities. They
gave students handouts suggesting that each religion they studied believed
in a version of the Golden Rule. Sherry Sheppard (2004) said that at the end

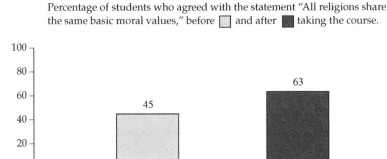

Fig. 3. Moral similarities of religions. (*Note:* On *t*-tests comparing target group with previous test, $p < 0.001$; $N = 339$.)

of each semester, several students told her that the more they studied world religions, the more they realized how they were like each other. "That's exactly the point," Sheppard would respond, explaining, "That's what you were supposed to get from the course." This emphasis produced one of the more dramatic changes in students' views. Figure 3 shows that the percentage of students who agreed that "all religions share the same basic moral values" was 63 percent after the course, compared to 45 percent before the course. "All my life I've been a Christian and that's really the only religion I know about," began one student, who went on to say, "When I take this class I see there are other religions out there and they kind of believe in the same thing I do."

But belief in similarity, as this quote suggests, can lead to the adoption of ecumenism and syncretism and to the weakening of faith.[20] A world religions course must couple emphasis on respect for religious freedom with acknowledgment that religious disagreement can be legitimate if expressed in a reasonable way and if it does not lead to violence or persecution. The syncretist belief that different religions merely provide different roads to God is, of course, a legitimate religious option. But students' arrival at this position should come from serious personal reflection and the teaching of one's parents and religious or spiritual tradition. World religions courses are not intended to advance a position on this question, and many parents and religious communities would be concerned if a large number of students shifted from one position to another as a result of such a course.

Did a weakening of faith commitments go hand in hand with an increase in respect for religious liberty in Modesto? The stakes for religious tolerance could not be higher. The outcome tells us if it is possible in practice to resolve the apparent paradox of religious tolerance chapter 1 describes. Schools have a strong obligation to promote a particularly vigorous form of active respect, but they have an equally strong obligation to avoid the dilution of robust faith. Given the seeming conflict between these two obligations, the triumph of tolerance may be a Pyrrhic victory. But if Modesto's course avoids promoting the dilution of faith in practice, perhaps we can conclude that promoting respect for religion is not so complicated after all.

A sigh of relief seems warranted, at least according to the survey. Asked if they agreed with the statement "I believe that one religion is definitely right, and all others are wrong," students' views *did not change significantly* after they had taken the course, according to either the January or the May posttest.[21] Several interviews suggested that students were conscious about the similarity-relativism connection and consciously avoided it. "As I've been in this class, I've noticed how all these religions tie in in some way," one student said, "but I try not to convert to anything, because I strongly believe in my religion." Students we interviewed seemed able to recognize that even if Christianity and Islam may share some common ground about morality, this does not render the choice between the two faiths futile. The district's choice of a descriptive and historical approach to religion, rather than a comparative approach, deserves some credit, but this result may also be an unintentional by-product of the course's brevity.[22]

More surprising, however, was that 5 of the 23 students we interviewed said the course strengthened their faith. One student told us she learned more "especially about my religion—Christianity. If I had a question about something, . . . I learned my parents may be able to expand on it and give me a little more detail about it. I got some clarification on my own religion and learned a little bit more about it." The course's avoidance of relativism did not go unnoticed by Modesto's conservative Christians. Associate pastor Paul Zeek (2004) expressed satisfaction that students in his evangelical Baptist congregation who had taken the course "have a clearer understanding of the distinctives" about religion and Christianity. A Hindu student testified that the course connected her with her faith by deepening her knowledge. "Some of the stuff I didn't know about my religion, and my parents didn't know either because they weren't from India, they're from Fiji," she told us, "so it's completely different from our religion and they didn't know everything from the past."

Faith-affirming discussions occurred with teachers as well as parents. A Jewish student fasting for Yom Kippur told Connie Hernandez she was "feeling down about her religion" and could not understand why her parents and religion made her fast. Days of fasting in Judaism and other religions are intended for purification, Hernandez urged gently, and the Yom Kippur fast is particularly central to Judaism. Thanking her for the conversation, the student walked away with a more positive attitude about her faith.

None of the students interviewed said they could anticipate converting to a new faith in the near future. But three students did testify they were more likely to change their beliefs sometime in the future because of the course. "I might as well learn about [other religions]," a Wiccan student told us, explaining, "See if I like one of them better than mine, and I can convert and follow that one." "It's kind of interesting because I really don't have religion," another student related, "so I like learning about the other ones and seeing what kinds are appealing to me, and maybe when I grow older I might try one of them."

The casual way these students describe changing their religion as they might describe shopping for new clothes would be reason for alarm if the course was responsible. But as the last student's quote attests, it is clear that the students disposed to experiment with religion were prone to experiment before taking the course. Such a course may encourage religious wanderers to roam more freely, but this involves no violation of democratic neutrality or infringement of parents' rights.

More troubling, however, is that several students had difficulty articulating in interviews what differences between religions caused them to maintain their faith. Out of context, this inability might appear merely a function of students' age and their limited knowledge of their beliefs and might provide little cause for worry. But Stephen Prothero (2007, 34–37) has suggested that moral beliefs, more than theology and rituals, define the religious identity of most Americas today. Christian Smith and Melissa Denton's 2005 study of religion among American teens found that most teens hold a diluted set of religious beliefs, which Smith and Denton described as "moralistic, therapeutic deism." Teens may technically remain in traditional faiths, but shorn of sharp theological distinctions and awareness, their beliefs yield an impoverished sense of religious obligation. Teens are more likely to ask what their religion can do for them than what they can do for their religion. Smith and Denton express concern about a slide toward a "soft relativism" where beliefs are so mild and self-centered that serious religious debate and exploration become irrelevant.

Students' inability to articulate differences could mean that Modesto's course and, even more, a one- or two-semester world religions course could encourage soft relativism in the long run. Most students entering Modesto's course simply took the differences between their religion and others for granted and never felt the need to explain them. By stressing the similarities between beliefs, a world religions course challenges students to search for differences for the first time. Without a proper stress from school, home, and church on theological differences, the longer students search for differences, the fewer they will find. Even if it does not lead to changing or quitting of religion, such an influence could lead to the "emptying out" of religious commitments that is identified by Prothero and by Smith and Denton. The more students view the differences between religion as arbitrary, the weaker their commitments to beliefs and practices may be. It may not be the job of public schools to fight the culture, but they should avoid advancing disturbing social trends.

Even if Modesto's course did not promote soft relativism, the excessive emphasis on similarity occasionally manifested by the course and its teachers provides some reason for caution. Religions are defined as much by their differences as by their similarities. Indeed, many believers value their religion exactly because it is different from other faiths and provides a distinctive identity. Students who do not know the fundamental differences and disagreements between Islam and Christianity cannot hope to understand why Muslims find meaning in their beliefs. Conflating all faiths is an unacceptable price for respect.

Stressing similarity appears to pose a dilemma for world religions courses. It can be a valuable weapon in promoting respect but a Trojan horse for lurking soft relativism. Closer inspection yields a possible path out of this dilemma. The key lies in distinguishing different types of differences and similarities. Stressing the *moral* similarity of faiths is sufficient for tolerance and most appropriate according to democratic theory. Every major faith stresses compassion for others, fundamental human equality, and respect for human dignity, as much as they disagree about their definitions and requirements. These beliefs make each faith compatible with the basic tenets of American democracy. Recognizing that each faith is willing to accept the moral burdens of democracy will give students more confidence in extending the rights and freedoms of democracy to these groups.

The treatment of theological similarities is a subject best left to churches, synagogues, mosques, and mandirs. To compensate for the emphasis on moral similarities and to prevent soft relativism, schools should emphasize theological differences. Since theological differences matter most to conservative religions, there should be a robust discussion of these faiths. Above all, the danger of soft relativism reminds us that implementation of courses gently challenging intolerance based on religious faith must be coupled with curriculum options, such as electives in Bible and intelligent design, that gently affirm faith for conservative Christians. To implement the former without the latter would risk erasing the religious disagreements and diversity on which democracy thrives.

THEORETICAL INTERLUDE: WHY DID TOLERANCE AND RESPECT INCREASE?

Knowing that world religions courses increase tolerance and respect is valuable, but our research contains more far-reaching implications. Today, America struggles to accommodate exploding ethnic, racial, and cultural diversity as well as religious diversity. Public schools bear the burden of preparing young people to accommodate this diversity. Battles over multicultural education attest to the conflicts about the best way to promote diversity. Social science research has a crucial role to play in this debate. It can help to shape school policy about diversity by telling us what factors and strategies best promote tolerance.

Civic education literature has begun to grapple with this issue, but results are inconclusive so far. Tolerance scholars agree that education is the strongest predictor of tolerance (Citrin et al. 2001). But competing explanations exist for *exactly why* education increases tolerance. Education provides knowledge of facts and strengthens the ability to think critically. The substance of knowledge affects response to framing and priming (Ottati and Isbell 1996); that is, greater knowledge can dispel false stereotypes and make people more resistant to the media and politicians who foist false stereotypes on them. As students gain education, they learn more about other groups and are able to put themselves in others' places. Survey analysis has shown that the strength of belief in democratic norms positively correlates with tolerant attitudes (McCloskey and Brill 1983).

Modesto's world religions course offers a rare opportunity to study teaching for tolerance and respect in action. Few studies have focused on the effects of specific school courses on tolerance. Furthermore, a possible defect of Modesto's course turns out to be a research asset. The relative brevity of Modesto's course means that its effect on tolerance may be brief. But it also means that relatively few factors intervened between the course's beginning and end that could account for the rise in tolerance. Other major tolerance studies measure shifts in tolerance over long periods of time. An abundance of historical and social changes could explain the tolerance shifts these studies observe. In our research, we can be more confident that the course and its aspects we were able to observe explain tolerance increases. Examining Modesto's course is thus suited especially well to shedding light on the major factors contributing to increased tolerance.

A basic way to establish the best candidates for explaining the rise in tolerance is to see which factors changed significantly on the posttest along with the rise in tolerance levels. Correlation is not causation, however. Distinguishing contenders from pretenders requires that a plausible logical relationship exist between possible explanations and tolerance. For instance, students were older at the end of the course than at the beginning, and age correlates with the rise in tolerance, but there is no good reason why being three or six months older would make students more tolerant. Three legitimate candidates for significant factors emerge through this method.

I have already discussed the large increases in students' knowledge about religion and appreciation of the similarities of religion, as well as the plausible relationship between these increases and tolerance. The survey also tested the course's effect on threat perception, because of its potential relationship to tolerance. Numerous tolerance studies have found that the perception of threat from an outside group is among the strongest predictors of intolerant behavior (Marcus 1995; Duckitt and Fisher 2003; Sniderman, Brody, and Tetlock 1991). Insecurity breeds intolerance. This may particularly be the case concerning *religious* intolerance among Americans today, given the fear attached to religious differences since 9/11. Teachers

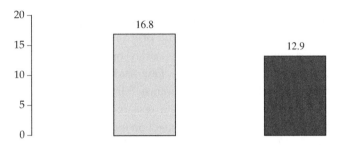

Percentage of students who thought they or their families would likely be a victim of a terrorist attack within the next six months, before ☐ and after ■ taking the course.

Fig. 4. Threat. (*Note:* On *t*-tests comparing target group with previous test, $p < 0.10$; $N = 340$.)

in Modesto, as we have seen, strove to give students a more accurate over-all picture of each religion by emphasizing mainstream, rather than extremist, beliefs. This emphasis, we thought, might ease students' anxiety about threats from religious groups.[23] A significant reduction in threat did occur, as expected. Figure 4 shows that the number of students who thought they or their families would likely be a victim of a terrorist attack within the next six months decreased from 16.8 percent before taking the course to 12.9 percent after.[24]

Regression analysis offers a more sophisticated way to determine the best explanation for tolerance. It enables us to see which of these explanations has the greater relationship to students' tolerance. Table 2 shows how various factors that might predict tolerant behavior compare to each other in explaining one particular behavior, students' willingness to come to the defense of religiously persecuted students.[25] A belief that all religions share the same basic moral values had a positive and statistically significant relationship to active tolerance.[26] The negative connection between threat and tolerance approached but did not reach statistical significance. Religious knowledge explained more of the change in the dependent variables than any other factor. It was statistically significant at the .05 *p*-value level when observed alone, and it remained at an acceptable level of statistical significance when included with other variables. Other analyses for passive tolerance and for a general political tolerance scale found similar results.

A deeper look at the regression analysis suggests that knowledge, similarity, and threat provide a far from complete explanation for tolerance. Our model explains only a small proportion of the variance in tolerance. Much of the difference observed between students' attitudes before and after taking the course remains to be explained. When statistical models and analyses based on surveys fall silent, alternative research methods must be heeded. Our observation of the course and our interviews with students, teachers, administrators, and outside consultants who helped prepare the course help fill in the blanks.

We believe that the missing link evident through these methods, which could not be easily measured in survey research, was Modesto's emphasis on modeling civil discussion about religion. Democratic theorists have long called for greater dialogue among different groups as a way to build community and consensus. Civic education research performed by Pamela Johnston Conover and Donald D. Searing (2000, 119) has found that

TABLE 2. Possible Explanations of Tolerance: Predicting Students' Willingness to Defend Religiously Persecuted Students (regression coefficients)

| Predictors | Religious Knowledge Only | Other Factors | All |
|---|---|---|---|
| Male | | .13 | .11 |
| Non-English spoken in home | | .08 | .14 |
| Religious knowledge | 1.32** | | 1.62** |
| Afraid of terrorist attacks | | −.55 | −.44 |
| Strongly identify as member of a religious community | | .63** | .56* |
| Believe that all religions share the same moral values | | .53* | .39 |
| Grade average | | .21 | .32 |
| Anxiety | | .00 | .07 |
| N | 563 | 222 | 222 |
| Constant | .05 | .13 | −.94 |
| Pseudo-$R^2$ | .02 | .04 | .05 |
| Log-likelihood | −338.57 | −132.66 | −130.25 |

$*p < 0.10$    $**p < 0.05$

social interaction is essential to developing democratic character and learning the basic skills of citizenship. Tolerance is learned by having to interact and get along with people with whom we disagree; confidence in our political preferences is generated when we successfully defend our positions; understanding of issues is enhanced through discussion; and shared citizen identities are nurtured by working together toward common goals.

Modesto acted on this appeal. Teaching students to engage members of other religions respectfully by modeling civil dialogue was a pervasive and persistent concern of administrators and teachers from the alpha of the course's construction to the omega of its classroom implementation. The main purpose of the course, according to Gary Lopez (2005), was to teach that "if you're raised Catholic, not everyone thinks like a Catholic, or if you're raised a conservative Christian, not everyone thinks like a conservative Christian."

Educational consultants prepared teachers for the course by teaching how to mediate controversies and navigate difficult classroom situations. Teachers learned how to discuss religious traditions in a civil and impartial manner. Beginning the course with an extended discussion of the First Amendment and religious liberty shaped students' attitudes toward the religions they subsequently studied. Even the precise placement of the course in the curriculum reflected a careful concern for promoting respectful deliberation. Study of the less controversial topic of world geography preceded study of world religions. Giving the freshmen taking the course time to develop necessary emotional maturity and familiarity with rules of high school classroom discussion helped them to deal with the more controversial topic of world religions.

The students we interviewed understood that the course intended them to use their newfound knowledge about religion as a tool for respectful engagement with members of other religions. "It helps to know about other people's religion when you talk to them," one student told us, "because you don't want to say something bad about their religion that affects them." A Hispanic Catholic student told us she "really want[s] to learn about other religions than my own" because "there are certain things that they may not agree with and in your own religion it's not really that bad." Learning about other religions, she concluded, "helps you treat them with the respect that they want and that they deserve."

Modesto realized that public schools are in a unique position to play a crucial role in modeling civil dialogue about religion. No other authorities—whether journalists, politicians, religious leaders, or parents—regularly stress the importance of respectful deliberation about religion or, more important, teach young people how to engage in such deliberation. Indeed, these authorities often model and encourage civic vices. The media favors extremists who at times discourage religions besides their own. Many politicians exploit religious differences for partisan gain. Perhaps, however, we should not judge these voices of disrespect too harshly. Unlike Modesto's students, their schools never taught them differently.[27] If other school districts hope to copy Modesto's effects, they must pay special attention to replicating the preparation and teaching of the course. An in-depth discussion of these issues is imperative not only to identify how the positive results were achieved but to note the rare mistakes teachers and administrators made that other school administrators must avoid.

## TEACHING THE COURSE: ISSUES AND CHALLENGES

Sports championships, pundits often remark, are not won on paper but on the field. The success of a world religions course is likewise measured by what takes place in the classroom. Having the right game plan for teaching about world religions is critical, but preparing teachers to execute that game plan is as crucial. Modesto administrators understood this. They thought carefully not only about establishing an appropriate teaching program but about providing requirements and incentives to ensure that teachers take the training seriously. Other districts would be wise to follow the example of Modesto, which required teachers to participate in 30 hours of in-service training in preparation for the course.

Teaching world religions for tolerance requires knowing the material and how to model civil discussion for students. Modesto addressed the former requirement by having teachers read texts related to the religions and attend extended classes on each religious tradition with faculty members of the history and religion departments at California State University at Stanislaus. Books and lectures may provide the skeletal structure of each religion's beliefs and practices, Rabbi Gordon (2004) stressed to us, but the flesh and blood of a religion's lived experience must be learned elsewhere.

Modesto's training accounted for this insight by requiring teachers to meet with local religious leaders and visit local religious institutions related to the religions they would teach.

First Amendment Center consultant Marcia Beauchamp supplied the civic context of the course. Beauchamp lectured about the historical origins of religious liberty, the meaning of the First Amendment, and major past and recent court cases interpreting the First Amendment. We all possess inalienable rights that no human authority can revoke, Beauchamp (2007) told teachers, and our responsibilities not only to tolerate but to defend actively others' freedoms flow from the existence of these rights. But respecting students' rights, Beauchamp cautioned, does not mean eliminating differences. Robust deliberation is the lifeblood of American democracy as long as it is respectful. We should teach students the historic struggle for religious freedom in Puritan New England to reinforce this point, Beauchamp urged. Students should take inspiration from Roger Williams, whose heroic insistence on religious freedom and the value of pluralism existed alongside intense religious convictions. The failure of John Winthrop, John Cotton, and other Puritans to accommodate differences should serve as a cautionary tale. Teachers found themselves returning repeatedly to Beauchamp's advice in the midst of trying situations.[28]

Drawing on Beauchamp's advice, but guided also by their experience and knowledge of Modesto's community, Modesto administrators established teaching guidelines to accompany the formal training. They chose to err on the side of caution. The goal of preempting controversy through strict neutrality and limiting teacher discretion permeated all aspects of the course. The first commandment of teaching the course might as well have been "Thou shalt not offend."

The district determined, for instance, that the most neutral way to teach the sequence of religions was to begin with religions appearing earliest in history and end with religions that appeared most recently. Teachers were not free to deviate from this sequence. Avoiding the discussion of overly controversial subjects in class was especially vital to prevent students from getting the impression that the course was calling the legitimacy of any beliefs or practices into doubt. Opting for an approach protective of all religions, administrators felt, would prevent critical discussions of religion that would inevitably single out minority religions. The goal of the course, according to a Modesto social studies administrator, is to convey facts about religion and not to have students engage in any critical evaluation of particular religions or religion in general. Administrators realized that this might chill classroom discussion but felt that allowing teachers too much discretion might aggravate rifts in the community. They trusted their teachers, but they wanted to make sure the members of Modesto's diverse communities did as well.

Sympathetic to the district's concern with preventing controversy, many teachers we talked with felt the guidelines went too far. One teacher even described the guidelines as "districtspeak" for public consumption and maintained that district officials knew they were unrealistic for the classroom. Religion is a complex and abstract subject, teachers told us. Successful teaching requires innovative and creative teaching approaches. Neglecting all critical discussion of religious practices or controversial issues would defeat the main purpose of the course. Inclusive discussions of different religious practices sharpen students' skills in critical thinking, and allowing for greater student participation enhances students' interest in the course. These discussions enable students to develop skills of respectful deliberation in practice and allow teachers to model these virtues. Teachers acknowledged they must scrutinize their own statements and views carefully before engaging in these conversations and must take care not to single out the practices of religious minorities to avoid stigmatizing students. Within these guidelines, however, civility need not be reduced to bland neutrality. Teachers favored a robust neutrality approach that combined fairness with challenging discussions.

Almost every teacher stretched the limits of the district's guidelines to find thought-provoking and balanced ways to address religion and religion issues in the news.[29] A majority of teachers had extended, participatory discussions with their students about a recent Pledge of Allegiance case argued before the Supreme Court, and several discussed a recent news story concerning the right of Sikh students to wear ceremonial daggers, or kirpans, in public schools. Yvonne Taylor noted to her students a passage in the course's textbook that encouraged students to consider the relationship between materialism and religion and indicated that wealthier societies tend to have lower rates of religious adherence.

Asked to provide a representative example of his attempts to promote critical thinking, Jonathan Couchman recounted discussing arranged marriage in Indian society with his students. He began by asking his students if they would want to have arranged marriages. Not surprisingly, all objected. Couchman sympathized with their reasoning. But he added that over half of the marriages among Americans today end in divorce. Students understood his point. His aim, Couchman explained, was not to criticize marriage based in romantic love but to encourage students to realize how Indian supporters of arranged marriage might defend the practice.[30]

Drawing on their own experience to offer students concrete examples and stories about the course's religions was even more effective in bringing the course to life. Students "latched on to the stories that [I] told," Connie Hernandez observed. Hernandez told students of a Hindu wedding she attended. Yvonne Taylor described her visit with other teachers to the local mosque. Another teacher discussed his attendance at his friend's bar mitzvah. Having students from minority religions bring in objects that related to their beliefs and that they felt comfortable sharing with classmates served a similar purpose. Teachers intuited what civic education research has confirmed empirically. Concrete examples and narratives play a crucial role in promoting sympathy and, in turn, tolerance.[31]

## DID THE TRAINING AND GUIDELINES WORK?

Modesto's cautious approach worked to preempt controversy. The survey and interviews indicated that the course satisfied most students' sense of fairness and balance.[32] None of the interviewed students, who came from a variety of religious backgrounds, complained of teacher bias for or against any religion. Sixty-one percent of students on the survey agreed or strongly agreed that "each religion has been treated fairly in the world religion course."

Of course, this number is not as high as it could or should be. Twenty-eight percent of students expressed at least some disagreement with this statement.[33] This raw number requires interpretation. The surveys do not tell us if students felt their own or other beliefs were treated fairly. More important, they do not tell us how serious students considered the violations of fairness to be. Holding Modesto's course to too high of a fairness standard is unrealistic on such a controversial topic. A reasonable standard to invoke is whether the perceived violations of fairness generated legal challenges to the course from parents or the community.

The evidence suggests a general satisfaction among parents and the community at large with the course's fairness. Not a single legal or constitutional challenge has been registered. More crucially, while parents have the right to opt their children out of the course, only about 1 out of 1,000 of each year's students exercise this option.[34] Every religious leader we talked with accepted the course's existence, and none complained that it favored any religion. One pastor of a large evangelical megachurch even told us that he was "thrilled" his daughter was taking the course. Several students in Paul Zeek's congregation told him they felt their teacher made "dismissive" gestures in discussing Christianity but did not make critical remarks. In short, student perceptions of unfairness were rarely strong enough to lead them to register complaints with parents and religious leaders, and even those complaints registered were relatively mild.

In fact, the course's major problem may well have been that the training and guidelines worked too well. Concern with avoiding controversy meant that the course presented religion in a "warm and fuzzy" way, contended Rabbi Gordon (2004). Such treatment exaggerates the similarity of religions. Muting religious disagreements makes these disagreements seem irrelevant and obscures both the causes of intolerance and the need for tolerance. If students are not aware of the controversy religion provokes, how could they possibly understand why people would disagree or persecute each other over religion?

Accuracy is another casualty of the warm and fuzzy approach. Discussing religion without controversy imparts the perception that holding a religious belief is a calm affair that does not trigger strong emotions. Believers just as often experience their religion as turbulent calls to challenge unjust social norms and sinful personal behavior. Much good and bad throughout history has resulted from this turbulence. Sturm und Drang intensity is as much a part of the story of religion as is quiet contemplation.

Avoiding controversy also involves smoothing out the conflicts that exist within each religious tradition. The cost of this oversight is highest to minority religions. World religions courses have a tendency, argues Beauchamp (2007), to treat minority religions as monolithic. We are more aware of differences within faiths familiar to us. Teachers will likely be sensitive to the differences between Catholics and Protestants but are likely to disregard the gulf between Theravada and Mahayana Buddhism. Understanding splits between modernists committed to adapting and assimilating their faith to today's circumstances, on the one hand, and traditionalists committed to holding on more staunchly to long-standing beliefs and practices, on the other, is equally crucial to treating each religion fairly. A historical approach to religion like Modesto's may lead students to pigeonhole minority believers into traditionalist niches that no longer apply to most believers of a faith in America today. Exaggerating the "otherness" of faiths may have consequences for tolerance. The percentage of students who thought "any religious belief or practice is strange or weird" rose after taking the course, according to our survey.

The greatest offense of the overly cautious approach is to agnostics and atheists. Bland neutrality means not only no mention of the advantages of one religion over others but completely ignoring the unsavory aspects of organized religion. The course's textbook devotes only three paragraphs to the use of religion to justify war, persecution, and the oppression of women. But even this exceeds the total neglect of these topics in Modesto's classrooms.[35] At the least, atheist and agnostic students and parents may not feel the course takes their views seriously. At worst, they may feel an implicit pressure to become more religious.

Modesto was right to err on the side of caution, but administrators overcompensated for controversy. Avoiding the perils of the warm and fuzzy approach requires allowing teachers a longer leash to engage in thought-provoking discussions dealing with the benefits and costs of religion in general. Teaching students the conflicts between and within faiths and how different faiths critique each other's moral beliefs and social practices can take place without devolving into crude comparisons about which faith is better than another. Jonathan Couchman's discussion of arranged marriage taught students respect for how Hindus think, but it did not preach the superiority or inferiority of these views.

Fairly representing the views of atheists and agnostics is even more necessary.[36] As we have seen, teachers addressed terrorist acts by Muslim groups by reminding students about violent extremists who had claimed to act in the name of Christianity. This encourages a more accurate portrait of Islam, but many atheists and agnostics would prefer teachers to go farther. Organized religion, many atheists and agnostics believe, inherently favors extremist belief and violent behavior. Zealots and martyrs occupy prominent places in every religion's history. If critiques of religion like these are not politically feasible, world religions courses must at least incorporate a section dealing with humanism, to ensure fairness.[37]

Expanding teacher discretion, however, does not mean relaxing teacher guidelines. The flaws of Modesto's course stemmed not from the existence of strict guidelines but from the content of the guidelines. Instead of banning any discussions that could lead to controversy, Modesto should have spent more energy establishing ground rules for challenging discussions and lesson plans. Teachers, students, and the community suffer when forbidding guidelines create fear. Real controversy lurks, and to say that districts have nothing to fear but fear itself is an exaggeration. But uniting with teachers to create sensible guidelines and training teachers to adhere to these guidelines can prevent controversy as well as provide a more accurate portrait of religion.

## HOW MUCH DO TEACHERS MATTER?

Speaking about the quality of Modesto teachers and drawing on his more than 30 years of experience as a school administrator, Superintendent Enochs (2004) frankly told me that 15 percent of teachers are "great," another 15 percent are "dogs," and the rest lie in the "great gray mass in between." My interactions with Modesto's social studies teachers (admittedly far briefer than the superintendent's interaction with them) left me more optimistic. Most of these teachers were at the least highly motivated, and many described innovative strategies they had used in their world religions courses. Perhaps the awareness of themselves as pioneers in teaching a required world religions course made their job a bit more rewarding and made them more conscientious than most teachers of required world religions courses are likely to be. Still, my experience of the world religions course teachers was consistent with Enochs's central insight that the quality of teachers varies substantially.

This would seem to matter a lot for the legitimacy of implementing a required world religions course. Exaggerating the importance of the average quality of teachers is unfair. After all, schools do and should require biology or history courses even if many teachers in those subjects are less than excellent. Still, holding teachers of required world religions courses to at least a slightly higher standard seems appropriate. Courses about religion are more likely to generate controversy and to be monitored for signs of bias by various religious and community groups. This greater scrutiny is legitimate, because teaching about religion is trickier than teaching other subject matters. To teach religion effectively, teachers must achieve an adequate balance between promoting religious tolerance and not encouraging students to change their beliefs. Exceptional teachers will achieve this balance. But universal world religions courses—like all courses—are taught mostly by average teachers who might not be able to achieve this balance. Perhaps it is simply better to make the course elective and leave the teaching of it to the most motivated and innovative teachers.

The evidence from our research addresses these concerns in several ways. A natural temptation might be to assume that the quality of teaching performance depends on the teacher's own religious background. Teachers with strong commitments to one religion might lack sufficient appreciation for promoting tolerance toward all religions, while agnostic and atheist teachers may not appreciate enough the need to protect the views of students with strong beliefs. Our interviews with teachers found no evidence to support either claim, and our surveys found no statistically significant correlation between a teachers' religious views and gains in tolerance. Increases in tolerance and the lack of change in level of commitment to their faiths were generally the same for students of teachers with many different personal views about religion.

While our sample size is admittedly small and may not be representative, the professional commitment of Modesto teachers to the stated goals of the course consistently trumped personal religious views. Two of the teachers we interviewed described themselves as atheists, but both evinced sympathy for students with strong religious beliefs. Conversely, several teachers we spoke with held firm religious commitments but evinced deep concern about ensuring respect for all religions. Mary Kappas described herself to us as holding firm Greek Orthodox beliefs but ranked among the three most innovative and motivated teachers of the course. For instance, she cowrote a successful proposal to receive a grant from the First Amendment Center's First Amendment Schools project, which funded the purchase of videos on the major world religions to show in her course.

What the best teachers shared in common was not a particular religious background or view about religion but an elevated capacity for self-awareness and an openness to learning from students, inspired by a fitting sense of humility. The best anecdote we encountered that enunciated these appropriate virtues for a successful world religions teacher came from outside Modesto. Jim Antenore originated and taught a high school comparative religions course in Irvine, California, for over 30 years. Antenore was recognized as both a National High School Association Teacher of the Year and a California League of High Schools Teacher of the Year, in large part for his work on this course.

In his early years of teaching the course, a visit to his class from a local rabbi had a profound effect on his teaching philosophy. By phone prior to the visit, Antenore (2009) told the rabbi, "I want my students to understand what it means to be Jewish." Upon his arrival, the rabbi began by telling Antenore's students, "I want you to know that your teacher is a fool." "There is no way you can ever know what it means to be Jewish," the rabbi continued, "unless you are Jewish." Instead, the rabbi proposed to explain to students "what Jews believe and why they believe it." Antenore, who developed a warm and lasting friendship with the rabbi, told us that the experience served as a constant and appropriately humbling reminder about his limits as a teacher. Going forward, Antenore made sure to emphasize strenuously to his students that he could not convey the full experience of the religions he was teaching them. Antenore's advice is consistent with the balance this book prescribes between promoting tolerance and not encouraging changes in belief. He stressed that humility meant focusing on the core beliefs and practices of religion in class, while telling students that if they desired a deeper understanding of the faiths they were studying, they would need to explore them on their own with members of these faith communities.

Our interviews thus undercut one possible myth about teaching, by yielding a list of important virtues exceptional teachers from all religious backgrounds did display and can acquire. Our statistical analysis should undercut an opposing tendency to take the emphasis on exceptional virtues and teachers too far. As noted previously in this section, our surveys indicated that student increases in tolerance and lack of increase in relativism did not vary according to the religious views of teachers. In fact, our results for "teacher effects" were even broader. The increases in religious tolerance and lack of increase in relativism did not vary in a statistically significant way for the students of every teacher. Our surveys did not detect a statistically significant correlation between the quality of teachers and the effect of the course on students.

These statistical results, of course, do not prove that the quality of teaching makes no difference on students' development of tolerant attitudes or their knowledge and understanding of the material. Anecdotal information from interviews with Modesto administrators and students suggests that teaching matters quite a lot, and more sophisticated and nuanced questions than our survey had time to ask might have revealed some significant teacher effects. Still, the basic results of the survey remain highly relevant here. Teaching quality may matter a lot, but our surveys suggest that average teachers were able to produce significant gains in tolerance without producing a shift in level of faith commitments—exactly the balance needed in world religions courses.

This is yet a further testament to the effectiveness and importance of Modesto's guidelines and teacher preparation. Misguided in some details, as the previous section suggests, the guidelines did generally what guidelines should ideally do. They gave teachers a basic skill set that enabled even average teachers to produce adequate and statistically significant results related to the course's goals. *Most crucially, what happened in Modesto is a reminder that rather than being an obstacle to successful implementation, the vigorous monitoring of courses about religion by religious and secularist groups can actually help to ensure that these courses are balanced and fair.* Concern about controversy was one of the factors motivating Modesto administrators' careful crafting of guidelines and teacher training.

Teachers of courses about religion should hold themselves to a high standard. More specifically, they should aspire to the type of self-awareness and reflection that Jim Antenore described and that several Modesto teachers displayed. Public school education about religion would better approach the ideal if all or most teachers did so. But if Enochs's "great gray mass" of teachers does not ascend to these heights, this should not be cause for excessive concern. Modesto shows that effective teacher training and guidelines can ensure that even average teachers produce significant and positive results.[38] Where teacher training and these guidelines can on average produce the very good, we should not allow unrealistic aspirations to the perfect to be an enemy.

## CONCLUSION: THE MODESTO MYSTERY SOLVED

When Modesto administrators made a courageous choice to implement a required world religions course, they appeared to face daunting odds. All the elements of a perfect cultural storm—a large evangelical Christian population, an active group of politically and culturally liberal residents, and adherents of a wide range of religions—were present. A recent dispute over tolerance for homosexuality was an ominous portent.

Today, not only is Modesto's course accepted by all of its diverse communities, but many voices from the left and the right celebrate the course as the best way to treat religion in schools. On consecutive days in Modesto, I interviewed Russ Matteson, pastor of the liberal Church of the Brethren, and Paul Zeek, associate pastor at Modesto's evangelical First Baptist megachurch. During the course of our conversation, Matteson (2004) condemned the Bush administration's "hyperpatriotism." Zeek's office prominently displayed a framed picture of Ronald Reagan. If these men were to sit them down in a room together to discuss religion and politics, there is not much they would agree about. But both heaped praise on the world religions course.

Modesto's bold experiment provides strong evidence that world religions courses *should* be implemented. Students' respect not only for the rights of religious minorities but for the First Amendment rights of all vulnerable groups rose considerably. Knowledge about religion sharply increased, as did appreciation for the common ground shared by faiths. Fears about rampant relativism and teacher bias turned out to be more imagined than real.

Still, the deeper mystery proposed at this chapter's outset remains unresolved. How did the course manage to survive, let alone flourish, in such a divided community? The answer has important implications. The key to solving the cultural mystery in Modesto can be used to implement world religions courses in all or almost all American communities. With its burgeoning religious diversity and thriving evangelical Christian community, Modesto's religious makeup and its accompanying tensions mirror those of the nation at large (Eck 2002). Indeed, Modesto is not less but more religiously and politically divided than most American communities. If common ground on teaching about religion in public schools could be found in a community as strongly divided as Modesto, it is more than reasonable to expect that it could also be found in many similarly divided communities *as well as the majority of American communities less divided than Modesto.*[39]

Explaining the course's success must begin at the beginning, with the course's originators. The district officials responsible for the course realized it might be a hard sell. These officials cared deeply about and diligently cultivated community support. They listened to all sides and worked hard to tailor the course based on what they heard.

Religious leaders, school board members, and teachers all stressed that extensive consultation with community members in the initial stages of the course was essential to the acceptance of Modesto's course. Everyone agreed that Charles Haynes's mediation provided the framework of respectful discussion and disagreement that enabled the course's establishment. Instituting an advisory council of religious leaders was vital in clearing away misconceptions about the course and preempting criticism. "Bring all the stakeholders to the table at first," Gary Lopez (2005) advised other districts considering a world religions course. "You can defuse a lot of the controversy about what it is and what it's not, and what you're trying to accomplish," he explained, adding, "If you give [community members] ownership in it, you have a better chance to mitigate a lot of the controversy." Religious conservatives, who often feel excluded from public school decision making, particularly welcomed this stakeholder approach. "If you have tensions in your community where religious conservatives are distrustful, if that distrust is so high," Haynes (2006) told us, "you have to say 'we're going to listen to you, we're going to take you seriously.'"

Districts should not take consultation too far, though. The consultation process with the community and advisory panel only worked well, cautioned a Modesto social studies administrator, because the district presented them with a well-structured model of the course. An approach allowing the community or an advisory panel of religious leaders to determine the basic framework and content of the course, she warned, would be too contentious.

The best salesmanship would not have worked without a sound product. District officials realized that courses in world religions can be framed broadly enough that all are able to see them as a repository for their hopes while no group is able to claim exclusive ownership. Simply including a robust discussion of religion in the curriculum won the approval of all the advisory committee's members. Father Illo (2005) recalled that when the course was presented to the council, "all [the members] congratulated the schools on actually talking about religion because that's usually a pariah in schools and academia." "But it makes sense," Illo continued, "because you just can't pretend that religion hasn't had an effect on world culture."

Talking more about religion held particular appeal for Modesto's evangelical Christians and religious conservatives. Like their cohorts around the nation, they lamented that ignoring religion trivialized its role in people's lives and society. Aside from the dubious exception of the Scopes trial, public school curriculums have a history of completely ignoring evangelical beliefs (Vitz 1986). Modesto's course punctured this telling educational silence, teaching students that whether they agree with it or not, religion matters.

If conservatives mostly wanted recognition of religion, liberals and religious minorities mostly wanted tolerance. Prior to the course, Russ Matteson (2004) related, several students in his "liberal congregation had uncomfortable or bad interactions with students from evangelical denominations . . . who believe that Jesus is the way, the truth, and the life, and that Jesus' truth is unique." The course's emphasis on religious liberty and its connection with the policy for safe schools appealed to Matteson. Focusing on world religions instead of just the Judeo-Christian tradition would open students to the wisdom of other faiths. Matteson approved of the way students in his congregation "used the course to incorporate different religions into their perspectives." "Enabl[ing] students to realize that God is present in other places around the world" is crucial, he argued, to enhanced tolerance and respect.

But the course was not just a success because it gave each religious group what they most wanted. Policies that satisfy opposing groups can still founder when suspicion and mistrust are high. The deeper secret to Modesto's triumph was that what liberals and evangelicals wanted was not as far apart as the two sides themselves thought initially. Modesto provides a case study of successful deliberative democracy in action. Once the ground rules for civil discussion were in place, dialogue transformed perceptions by unearthing some common ground. Conservatives may have stressed recognition of religion in schools more, but liberals thought it was a good idea, too.[40] Liberals may have wanted tolerance more, but conservatives valued safety.

Even where genuine disagreements existed, they were less severe than imagined. Liberals learned that conservatives understood that schools are for teaching, not preaching. "Would all of the distinctives that we as followers of Christ would want pointed out get pointed out?" asked Paul Zeek (2004). "No," he admitted, "but that's not the main purpose of the course." Zeek stressed that despite theological disagreements with more liberal communities, "we could find common ground [because] we all want kids to be safe." Conservatives learned that liberals understood the difference between tolerance and enforced agreement. Both sides ceased to view each others' political and cultural beliefs in black-and-white terms and instead recognized these beliefs as the many-threaded tapestries they most often are.

The terra firma that most united Modesto's citizens was a belief in the value of religious freedom. Disagreements over the status of homosexuality and parents' authority over their children do not lend themselves to easy policy solutions. Communities, however, do not need to resolve all of these issues once and for all in order to prosper. The success of America's experiment with democracy relies not on shared policy views but on a shared commitment to fundamental democratic rights. Indeed, in a sense, all our freedoms have their roots in the freedom of conscience and the right to make up one's own mind about the most important things. This freedom includes the right not to endorse positions with which one disagrees. The mainstream media too glibly dissolves Americans into competing religious and cultural communities defined by their differences from each other. Modesto's example shows that for all their sincere and often serious disagreements, Americans' creedal commitment to religious freedom makes cultural peace possible.

The consensus around the Modesto course, as impressive as it is, does not mean that all curricular disputes over the discussion of religion are likely to find a similarly successful resolution. World religions courses clearly reflect the principle that "a right for one is a right for all," which Yvonne Taylor emphasizes to her students—a principle that is at the heart of Americans' creedal commitment to religious liberty. But the debate over teaching evolution and creationist theories seems to inevitably pit the religious freedom rights of some against the religious freedom rights of others. The next chapter considers whether this inevitable conflict is real, or whether public schools can address the issue of our origins in a way that respects the religious freedom of all.

CHAPTER 4

# An Intelligent Democratic Design to Teaching about Evolution

Science emphasizes observation and evidence, but you might not know that from reading various evolutionary biologists' appraisals of creationism's future. Writing in the immediate aftermath of the 1925 Scopes Monkey Trial, Harvard biologist Ernest Mayr boasted that "this trial was the end of the fundamentalist attacks on evolution" (Larson 1997, 228). After the Supreme Court struck down the teaching of creationism in Louisiana in 1987, Stephen Jay Gould (1999, 182) contended that "it ended an important chapter in American social history, one that stretched back to the Scopes trial of 1925." Three years later, Ohio State University biologist Tim Berra (1990, 207) predicted,

> I suspect there will be an evolutionary ending. As future generations acquire more knowledge through education, simplistic answers based on belief will become increasingly unsatisfying. Those religions that cannot reconcile their beliefs with advancing scientific knowledge and common sense will lose followers to the more flexible, less dogmatic religions.

The evidence shows that it is evolutionary biologists who have failed to adapt, by allowing their faith in science to obscure their powers of observation. Americans remain as deeply divided over the truth of evolution as ever. A May 2006 Gallup poll found that 36 percent of Americans believed that God guided the process of evolution, 46 percent believed that God created human beings "in their present form in the last 10,000 years or so," and 13 percent believed that God played no part in evolution.[1] Similar polls taken in 1991 and 1999 show that the divide between creationists and evolutionists has not declined over the last 15 years.[2] Close to a majority of

Americans express a belief in either young earth (YE) creationism, which adheres to the literal story of creation in Genesis, or intelligent design (ID) theory, which accepts the world's age as 4.5 billion years old but rejects the theory that one species is capable of evolving from another.

Like many scientists, Berra claims that where improved education and access to knowledge exist, acceptance of scientific claims is inevitable. But the divide over evolution has persisted even though—or perhaps, as I will suggest, precisely because—most public schools teach evolution, while all ignore creationism. In light of this evidence, federal judge William Overton's prediction that "the controversy between biblical fundamentalism and evolution is one which will continue, I believe, forever" seems more accurate (Larson 2003, 184).

If scientists are mistaken that the controversy will disappear, at least in the near future, our best hope for consensus on this issue is to establish a treatment of evolution and creationism in the public schools that most Americans can accept. In recent years, our society has moved further away from that goal. A major theme of this book is that the mainstream media often exaggerates the conflicts over religion by focusing on exceptional controversies. But national headlines in recent years about teaching evolution and creationism in schools in Kansas; Ohio; and Dover, Pennsylvania, are more representative than inflated. In August 2005, the National Center for Science Education reported 78 clashes over the teaching of evolution in 31 states over the previous year—more than twice the typical number of incidents (Wilogren 2005).

The major obstacle to resolving the controversy, this chapter contends, is the exclusive focus by both sides on the scientific legitimacy of creationist theories. Even if science offers conclusive answers, relying on science has proven unable to generate a consensus among the various religious and secularist groups. The democratic or civic approach outlined earlier in this book holds out greater promise of resolving the evolution controversy. Not only are its principles of active respect and good faith those that all sides in our disputes about religion can agree on, but it entails taking into account and attempting to satisfy the main concerns and interests of each major group. The scientific approach endorses an evolution-only approach fueled by fear and caricatures of what conservative Christians want. Accused of bad faith, many conservative Christians have responded by rejecting the evolution-only approach as exclusionary and elitist. The democratic approach, by contrast, attempts to listen to and take seriously the concerns of each group involved in the evolution controversy, and it strives to determine if and how these concerns can be reconciled with major democratic values.

## TWO ROADS NOT TAKEN

Both evolutionists and creationists seem to agree on one aspect of the controversy: that its resolution must be scientific. Most supporters of YE creationism and all ID supporters accept that their claims must be scientifically valid or not true at all. Having judges, school boards, and educational administrators determine the scientific validity of creationist theories would seem to be the most sensible way to decide if and how creationism should be included in the curriculum. An influential court case (*McLean* 1981) has reached this conclusion, along with many prominent law professors and scholars (Ruse 2005; Greenawalt 2005; DeWolf, Meyer, and Deforrest 2003).

If this obvious alternative is available, why should we instead favor the democratic approach to the controversy? A basic problem with the science approach is that it is not clear which scientists should get to decide on the scientific validity of creationism. Evolutionists claim that all forms of creationism, including ID, do not qualify as scientific views. They contend that ID supporters with scientific backgrounds most often hold degrees in fields unrelated to evolution and do not publish in peer-reviewed scientific journals related to evolution. ID supporters claim that the logic of evolutionists is circular. They maintain that the reason ID supporters are not in fields related to evolution and do not publish in peer-reviewed journals is because their views are discounted automatically by these fields and journals. Since they claim to constitute a significant minority of scientists, ID supporters contend that students should be taught about the alternative views on evolution within the scientific community.

To determine which scientists' views should count, many judges and academics have turned to the philosophy of science (Ruse 2005; Greenawalt 2005, 96–115). It attempts to determine which explanations count as science or nonscience by considering such factors as the falsifiability, predictive power, and elegance of the explanation. But mainstream philosophers of science themselves at times disagree about how to distinguish or demarcate scientific from nonscientific views. A minority ask if it is even possible to make such demarcation (Laudan 1996a; Quinn 1996). Even those mainstream scientists who agree on demarcation criteria sometimes disagree about whether these criteria disqualify creation science or ID as forms of science (Laudan 1996b).

Chaucer's Parson in *The Canterbury Tales* memorably asks, "If gold rust, then what shall iron do?" With due respect to the often exceptional intelligence of judges and educational administrators, we should not expect them to reach an irrefutable conclusion about the scientific status of creationism when expertly trained philosophers of science disagree on this issue. The philosophy of science is a highly specialized field whose members receive years of academic training. Lacking such training, judges and educational administrators must rely on experts. But their lack of training is an impediment to choosing the most qualified experts, and disagreement among philosophers of science means that even excellent choices of experts can trigger claims of bias.

More critically, deciding the evolution controversy by relying on scientific experts is unlikely to generate public trust in the outcome. Decisions relying on abstruse expert testimony are difficult to explain and justify to those who are not specialists. Unable to understand the reasoning about why their side has lost, many people are likely to believe that judges have manipulated the use of expert testimony to satisfy their predetermined biases. This approach will create, rather than quiet, controversy and will undermine the possibility of a commonly accepted solution to the controversy.

Similar problems plague another alternative to the democratic way of resolving the evolution controversy. Perhaps if there is no clear consensus to whether creationism is a science, we can at least determine if it is a religion (Beckwith 2003, 153; N. Miller 2001; Wexler 1997; Greenawalt 2005, 90). If it does qualify as a religion, it has no place in the classroom. But the Supreme Court's standards for what counts as a religion are vague. It has vacillated about whether beliefs are religious mainly because they are theistic or because they function similarly to conventional religious beliefs. Legal scholars have criticized the Court's decision to use one set of criteria to determine a religion in free exercise cases and another set to determine a religion in establishment clause cases. The Court ruled in *United States v. Seeger* (1965) that a conscientious objector was entitled to protection under the free exercise clause because his humanist beliefs qualified as a religion, but a federal appeals court in *Smith v. Board of School Commissioners of Mobile County* (1987) concluded that teaching of humanist beliefs in public schools did not qualify as religious according to the establishment clause. In cases such as conscientious objector controversies, courts have no choice but to decide if a belief is religious or not. But in cases where a clearer and less specialized basis for decision is available, as I will argue is the case with creationism, it is better for courts and school administrators to avoid the debate about what counts as a religion.

Let us assume, for a moment, that every single scientist and philosopher of science in highly esteemed universities and professional associations agreed that creationism is not a science. Should this end the debate about the inclusion of creationism in the curriculum? Relying on science to resolve this debate ignores a basic democratic consideration. Who has the ultimate authority to decide contested questions in a democracy?

Put differently, relying on science in this debate is exclusive in its regard for principles rather than people. It is bound to lead to an even deeper sense of alienation among many parents and students, particularly conservative Christians, from public schools. Parents and students with qualms about the validity of evolution are unlikely to embrace it if they feel it is being forced on them in the public school curriculum without their consent. Perhaps the greatest puzzle in public polling about evolution is that belief in various forms of creationism has remained steady even as evolution is being taught more widely in public schools. This apparent paradox makes more sense when we realize that many parents and students resent evolution even more because they feel they have not consented to the way it is promoted in schools (Haynes 2004).

In fact, requiring the teaching of only evolution in science classes in communities with large conservative Christian populations has often been counterproductive. School boards and concerned parents in many of these communities have successfully placed pressure on teachers to ignore evolution (Skoog and Bilica 2002, 445; Dean 2005b). Even in communities without large conservative Christian populations, the perceived unfairness of the evolution-only approach has motivated many evangelical biology teachers to exclude discussion of evolution or include creationism (Beckwith 2003, 69).

Several esteemed scholars and judges have wondered if excluding both evolution and creationism is not the best solution to the controversy after all. Justice Hugo Black's concurring opinion in the 1968 Supreme Court case *Epperson v. Arkansas*, which struck down an Arkansas law preventing the teaching of evolution, is the best-known expression of this position.[3] Black argued that since many parents believed evolution was an antireligious doctrine, the most neutral approach to the controversy would be to exclude both evolution and creationism from the curriculum.

Concerned with appeasing public opinion, Black's position does little to address the primary concerns of both sides in the controversy. Parents supportive of evolution and providing their children with a well-rounded science explanation miss out on learning about an essential biological concept due to the sectarian complaints of part of their community. Many conservative Christians want their creationist beliefs taken seriously by the public school curriculum, not ignored. Double exclusion also constitutes a loss for democracy. Democracy and mutual respect thrive on discussion and deliberation. An open acknowledgment of differences encourages citizens to learn to engage in respectful discussions with opponents. Exclusion may foster peace on the surface but allow disdain for the position of opponents to fester beneath this calm.

Still, Black does have a point. If the teaching of evolution continues to produce acerbic conflicts like those we have witnessed in recent years, perhaps silence is preferable. Before we reach this pessimistic conclusion, we are obliged to explore if robust discussion can coexist with peace. Perhaps the democratic approach can reconcile discussion and peace to a greater extent than other attempts at solving the controversy.

## THE DEMOCRATIC APPROACH TO THE
## EVOLUTION CONTROVERSY

The democratic approach to the evolution controversy involves asking two questions. What resolution is most consistent with the basic democratic principles of good faith and active tolerance? Can the resolution be accepted by all or almost all of the groups the controversy affects? The democratic approach is strong exactly where the science and religion approaches are weak. These approaches require educational policy makers and judges to be experts in highly specialized fields where they lack training. The basic principles of democratic respect can be widely shared. Judges and educational policy makers not only possess expertise on applying these principles in specific cases but have been specially trained to resolve disputes about these principles. Americans, who are far more familiar with democratic norms than with complex scientific and religious arguments, are more likely to accept a democratic resolution as legitimate.

The science and religion approaches are concerned only with finding a satisfactory theoretical resolution to the evolution controversy. By ignoring public opinion, the scientific approach has produced a backlash against evolution and defeated its own purposes. The democratic approach contends that when deciding school curriculum, schools must take into account what parents, students, and Americans in general believe and feel. Peace must be considered alongside truth. Taking public opinion into account ensures that the democratic approach will yield a theoretically satisfactory resolution that has a good chance of actually being accepted by divided communities and implemented.

## Advocates and Opponents

Concern about qualifying or eliminating the teaching of evolution and the teaching of creationism comes from three main groups. Secularists are concerned that these measures would constitute an establishment of religion and violate the separation of church and state. The secularist position is embraced not only by atheists and agnostics but by many religious liberals and even some religious conservatives who believe that school decisions inspired by religious motivations are inconsistent with democratic principles or infringe on the rights of parents and communities to raise their children according to their religious beliefs (Lynn 2006; Nussbaum 2008; Macedo 2003; Harris 2004). Their support for discussing only evolution is based on the belief that the content of science classes should be based strictly on scientific criteria. If evolution is the best explanation of origins according to the vast majority of the scientific community, the required curriculum should teach it. Religious considerations should not be used either to exclude or qualify the teaching of evolution or include the teaching of creationist alternatives. If parents and religious communities object to evolution, they are free to criticize it and teach creationism to their children at home and during religious instruction. They also retain the right to remove their children from public schools.

Religious minorities are often allied with the secularist cause, but their concerns are not always identical. Secularists do not want curriculum decisions based on religious reasons, and many religious minorities agree. The primary concern of many other religious minorities is that curriculum decisions not be based on the preferences of *dominant* religious groups. Many religious minorities are not committed to the establishment of a completely secular public square and believe that religious and moral beliefs have a place in the public square as long as they are not overly sectarian (J. D. Hunter 1991). This is often a distinction without a difference in practice. Most attempts to change the curriculum for religious reasons or to make the curriculum more accommodating to religious groups come from dominant religious groups. But there are rare cases where attempts to include material in the curriculum take account of the views of many religious groups or where attempts to exclude material based on the objections of many religious groups may find support among many members of religious minorities, even while facing stiff opposition from secularists.

Perhaps the most ardent support for the teaching of only evolution comes from the vast majority of the scientific community, including high school science teachers, academic scientists, and professional organizations of scientists such as the National Center for Science Education. While many scientists are committed to secularism, their primary motivation is to create a scientifically literate population able to distinguish truth from falsehood on scientific grounds. Scientific literacy is not only intrinsically valuable but crucial to America's prosperity. Vast recent improvements in technology industries in countries such as China and India are already posing a challenge to the American economy, and the increasing proficiency in science among students in these nations means the competition will only become fiercer. Even if scientifically literate students do not become scientists themselves, the science and technology sectors of the economy still benefit from an enlightened public opinion capable of evaluating and supporting worthy scientific initiatives (Krauss 2006). Many business leaders in the United States share these concerns with scientists.

Critical of claims that teaching science can be effective without mention of evolution, many scientists stress the centrality of evolution to understanding modern science and technological achievements. In a recent *New York Times* op-ed, University of North Carolina Chemistry Department chair Holden Thorp (2006) argued,

Since evolution has been the dominant theory of biology for more than a century, it's a safe statement that all of the wonderful innovations in medicine and agriculture that we derive from biological research stem from the theory of evolution. Recent, exciting examples are humanized antibodies like Remicade for inflammation and Herceptin for breast cancer, both initially made in mice. Without our knowledge of the evolution of mice and humans and their immune systems, we wouldn't have such life-saving and life-improving technologies.

Scientists may constitute an elite group composing a relatively small segment of American society, but their voices should be given a disproportionately strong weight given their expertise in the relevant subject matter.

At the same time, the assumption by many scientists that admitting a discussion of creationist alternatives into public schools damages the cause of science altogether may be too theoretical and glib. There is little evidence that the lack of belief in evolution undermines a commitment to or the practice of practical scientific trades. In fact, Christopher Toumey's (1994) research about creationists around the nation and in North Carolina (described shortly) found that many of the committed YE creationists among his interviewees were scientific practitioners, such as engineers. "You can be taught that God made the world in six days a few thousand years ago—and that Charles Darwin was a harbinger of contemporary moral nihilism," concludes Eammon Callan (1997, 170), "and still grow up to be a model employee in the research division at IBM." Until there is further empirical evidence from evolutionists to the contrary, Toumey suggests that Callan's claim remains plausible.

As already mentioned, there are two major creationist theories. Young earth creationists hold strictly to the literal account of creation given in Genesis: all species were created essentially in their present form within the last 10,000 years. Throughout most of the twentieth century, the goal of YE creationists was to have evolution excluded from the curriculum rather than to include a teaching of creationism. This goal was largely achieved implicitly in communities with large evangelical and fundamentalist populations. The scientific and technological challenge posed by the Soviet Union's launching of Sputnik brought renewed emphasis on required teaching of evolution and profoundly altered the YE movement. Henry Morris's Creation-Science Research Center and his subsequent foundation of the Institute for Creation Research attempted to provide robust scientific evidence for the literal account. Wendell Bird developed legal and constitutional strategies to defend the teaching of creation science alongside evolution in public schools.[4] The Supreme Court and federal courts repeatedly rebuffed YE creationist attempts to alter the curriculum. In the 1987 case *Edwards v. Aguillard,* the Court struck down a Louisiana law requiring that schools devote "equal time" to teaching evolution and creation science.

"Old earth creationism," better known as intelligent design theory, accepts that the universe is billions of years old and that "microevolution," or some changes within species, have taken place. They draw the line, however, at "macroevolution," or the idea that one species is capable of evolving from another, let alone that all species have descended from a common ancestor. According to ID supporters, the laws of statistical probability and the irreducible complexity of organisms and their parts make it all but impossible that species could have evolved by chance over time (Behe 1996; Dembski 1998). The creation of species by a purposive and intelligent designer is a more plausible scientific explanation. ID has a dual nature as a critical tool and as a positive theory. It involves negative arguments critiquing evolution and methodological naturalism as well as positive arguments used to support the specific claim of intelligent design.

The intelligent designer, however, need not be the Judeo-Christian deity of the Hebrew scriptures and the New Testament. ID advocates staunchly resist attempts to portray their scientific efforts as simply an outgrowth of evangelical Christian theology. The Discovery Institute, the most recognizable and influential voice of ID, boasts Greek Orthodox, Roman Catholic, and Jewish board members. Until recently, it had a Jewish executive director. Baylor University professor William Dembski (2002, 334), one of ID's most prominent advocates, claims that ID is compatible with such views as "pantheism, panentheism, Stoicism, Neoplatonism, deism, and theism."

ID's advocates do, however, stress that ID is mutually exclusive with the methodological naturalism that they claim underlies evolutionism. Methodological naturalism is the claim that only material causes can explain natural events. According to ID's advocates, methodological naturalism and evolutionism are based on circular reasoning. Phillip Johnson, the most well-known ID advocate, explains, "We define science as the pursuit of materialist alternatives. Now what kind of answers do we come up with? By gosh, we come up with materialist answers" (Stafford 1997). Just as ID is compatible with various religious beliefs, evolution is incompatible, its opponents claim, with all religion (not just evangelical Christianity), because it presupposes naturalism. Biology classes may not be shouting to students that God is dead, but they eliminate any role for the supernatural in natural history.[5] Excluding the supernatural from morality, these opponents argue, can only lead to social Darwinism or to the belief, most feared by Dostoevsky in *The Brothers Karamazov,* that "everything is permitted."

These claims are surely exaggerated. Although some of evolution's most recognizable supporters, such as Richard Dawkins (1995), embrace naturalism, many Darwinists deny that accepting evolution presupposes or produces naturalism. Warren Nord (1995, 152), for instance, distinguishes a belief in evolution, which can be designed and purposeful, from the neo-Darwinian belief of scientists like Dawkins. While ID supporters recognize that students in required biology courses are never taught the philosophy of naturalism or social Darwinism explicitly, many claim that these doctrines are implicit and detected easily by students. Less curious students focused primarily on getting decent grades in biology are unlikely, however, to be affected deeply by the metaphysical and moral implications of their textbooks' treatment of evolution.[6]

The claim of many ID advocates that teaching evolution without creationism biases the whole required curriculum in favor of methodological naturalism is similarly inflated. While the truth of evolution may not be challenged directly in biology or other classes, civics, social studies, and English classes stress to students the importance of moral values in the past and the present. English classes encourage students to consider the importance of spiritual values, and world religion courses could do so if they were included in the required curriculum. These views may not quite constitute a fair balance of opinions, but alternatives to purely materialistic and naturalistic ways of thinking are present in the required curriculum.

Still, ID supporters' claims about naturalism have some merit. Within the required teaching about evolution, many students from conservative Christian backgrounds, for instance, are likely to perceive naturalistic implications that conflict with their religious and moral beliefs. These implications are likely to be even more apparent to many parents and community members. Given the prestige of science in our society, it is disingenuous to argue, as many supporters of evolution do, that teaching evolution as a claim to truth held by almost all scientists can be countered easily by teaching critiques of evolution and creationist alternatives at home and in church.

Creationists are divided not only by the form of creationism they support but by the intensity of their beliefs. A minority of conservative Christians are strongly committed to removing evolution from the curriculum, qualifying its teaching, or including YE or ID in the required curriculum. But Christopher Toumey's in-depth study of public opinion about evolution and creationism found that a majority of evangelicals occupy an "evangelical center" position that is distinct from hard-line creationism. The evangelical center shares an appreciation of the religious basis of creationism with hard-liners, and their socially conservative views trigger concern about the moral effects of evolutionism. Concerned primarily with conversion, however, evangelical centrists are pragmatic and keen to avoid a divisively partisan position that would interfere with this mission. Toumey's investigation was over 20 years ago, and no other subsequent research has provided a similar in-depth analysis of evangelical views on creationism. But Christian Smith's research, discussed in detail in chapter 2, suggests a similar split among the majority of moderate and the minority of extremist evangelicals on almost all of the culture war's hot-button issues, indicating that while Toumey's research was not recent, his conclusions are far from outdated (Toumey 1994, 62–67; C. Smith 2000, 150).

Moderation among evangelical centrists, however, should not be mistaken for apathy. These centrists may not be willing to engage in divisive disputes to have creationism discussed in the curriculum, but they would prefer that it be included, and they believe that such inclusion is consistent with basic democratic principles of fairness and state neutrality. Excluding creationism from the curriculum may not lead them to remove their children from public schools, but it does heighten their alienation from schools.[7]

Taking account of the distinction between moderate and extremist creationists also provides a deeper understanding of the opinion polls about creationism and their implications. That a plurality of Americans report believing in YE creationism should not be discounted, but these polling results ignore the intensity of beliefs in YE creationism. Although there is a lack of sophisticated polling on this issue, there is reason to suspect that a significant number of people who profess believing in YE creationism are not strongly committed to only the YE form of creationism. For instance, almost all the attempts to teach creationism in the public schools after the *Edwards* decision have focused on ID and not on YE creationism. This suggests that many who profess YE beliefs are willing to accept the teaching of ID as a legitimate substitute for the teaching of YE creationism. The teaching of only ID might not be ideal for these YE believers, but it seems that their preferences would be substantially satisfied if ID were taught.

Even if believers in YE creationism are willing to accept the teaching of ID rather than YE creationism in the public school curriculum, their willingness to compromise would not appear to be consistent with good faith. Acting in good faith requires a modicum of sincerity. Believers are not free to make up or support existing claims that satisfy democratic norms if they do not believe in them. YE and ID creationism contradict each other logically and directly; the former claims that the earth is approximately 10,000 years old, the latter that the earth is 4.5 billion years old. It would appear to follow that YE believers who support the teaching of ID must be arguing insincerely. If support for ID is insincere and inconsistent with good faith, ID does not merit a place in the public school curriculum.

One possible response ID's supporters could make to the preceding argument is that the support of YE creationists for ID is simply irrelevant to its inclusion in the curriculum. The scientists who put forward ID clearly believe that its truth is independent of sectarian or scriptural confirmation, and a sizable number of ID's proponents do not believe in YE creationism. The insincerity of YE fellow travelers should not be used to impugn the sincerity of these scientists and proponents. But it would also be a mistake to assume automatically that YE believers are necessarily insincere or inconsistent when they advocate the teaching of ID. YE creationists could accept parts of ID theory and reject other parts. It is not necessarily logically inconsistent to accept the ID claim about the irreducible complexity of species and reject the ID claim that the earth is 4.5 billion years old. If this is the case, the willingness of YE creationists to compromise and support the teaching of ID might be construed as consistent with the principle of good faith. By turning their backs on efforts to teach YE, these YE believers might be acknowledging that ID has a more rightful place in the public square, because it is less sectarian, has more scientific legitimacy in their minds, and includes a balanced secular and religious rationale. Despite their continued belief in the truth of YE creationism, the reluctance to push for its teaching in the school curriculum might indicate a recognition that YE is unable to persuade those with different religious beliefs and is more fit for discussion in churches than in public schools.

## DEMOCRATIC PRINCIPLES AT STAKE IN THE EVOLUTION CONTROVERSY

### Active Tolerance

Chapters 1 and 2 suggest that two fundamental democratic principles ought to govern if and how schools treat religious points of view: the principle of active respect and the principle of good faith. Since teaching about origins involves discussing views that challenge existing beliefs, the relevance of the principle of active respect is most obvious to the evolution controversy and should be addressed first. That both sides in the evolution controversy can invoke the principle is perhaps less obvious. Teaching any of the versions of creationism might lead to increased disrespect in schools and society toward non-Christians and even the many Christians who accept evolution. But evolutionary theory directly contradicts the religious beliefs of many conservative Christians, and these believers interpret the failure to teach alternatives to evolution as disrespectful and intolerant. This complexity and others require not only a brief restatement of the principle of active tolerance but an elaboration of features of the principle that were not discussed in chapter 1.

A democratic society, chapter 1 argues, must cultivate active tolerance toward religious groups and particularly minority religious groups and nonbelievers. The absence of open dominance by one religion is not enough. Schools must go further and create an environment where students from all religious groups feel comfortable expressing their identities. This requires encouraging dominant religious groups to restrain their behavior and reassuring religious minorities that schools are welcoming of all expression.

Making sure that the curriculum promotes active tolerance must take into account not only the curriculum's impact on students but its impact on parents and community members. A school district's curriculum affects the ability of all citizens living within the district to express their religious identity. This is not just a point about how current students will treat their fellow community members when they graduate or when they are outside of school. What is taught in the public school curriculum sends a powerful message to community members about their status in the community, because public schools are among the most visible of state institutions. This is why the fights over school curriculum concerning religion are sometimes intense. These battles are not only about what students are learning; they symbolize to citizens that the community either treats all religions equally or privileges one religion over another. A curriculum teaching an anti-Buddhist message or omitting Buddhism from a required world religions course, for instance, would still be undemocratic even if no Buddhist students attended the public schools in that community. It would send a message to Buddhists in the community, the state, and even the nation that American society objects to their religion. This message of exclusion would inhibit the willingness of Buddhists to express their religious identities and talk about their faith in public.

Not only are parents aware of the messages that schools broadcast to their children and the community, but they are often more sophisticated consumers than their children. Both sides in the evolution controversy must take this into account. For instance, sectarian disclaimers about the truth of evolution that encourage students to read about creationist alternatives may be framed in such a way that students are not aware of the religious inspiration and implications of the disclaimer. Students who are not conservative Christians may not be influenced by the disclaimer to read the books or tempted to change their minds about their beliefs, but this does not mean the disclaimer is legitimate. Agendas hidden to students may be apparent to their parents. Parents may know that the disclaimer was supported strongly by a conservative Christian group with an interest in promoting its religious views. Even if students do not receive the message that the schools favor some religions, more perceptive parents may detect this and feel the chill of alienation that stifles democratic discussion. Conversely, schools must also keep in mind that many conservative Christian parents are more aware than their children of the antireligious and sectarian implications of some teaching about evolution.

If non-Christians are entitled to active respect, the curriculum should also not encourage conservative Christian students to embrace the legitimacy of beliefs they believe are mutually exclusive with their own religious views. World religion courses should focus on the subjective value of other beliefs for their believers but not on their objective legitimacy. The conflict between teaching active respect and avoiding recognition in world religions courses has, in fact, turned out to be mostly an illusion. Since teaching active respect does not require the teaching of other religions' truth, there is no need to teach a recognition of other views that alienates religious conservatives.

But what about cases where schools have a particularly strong reason for teaching a point of view that strongly conflicts with the mutually exclusive religious views of a large group of believers? What if there is good reason to encourage students to believe that the offending point of view is true? Failing to teach evolution would be a disservice to students and parents who believe in it and its importance and, according to most scientists, would hinder the nation's technological and economic competitiveness, but many evangelical and other conservative Christians deeply hold that a belief in evolution is mutually exclusive with their religious beliefs. Given the prestige of science in our society, teaching students that the entire scientific community supports evolution encourages students to believe that evolution is true. Evolutionists would not dispute this; teaching that evolution is true and that its creationist alternatives are not is their goal. The evolution controversy, then, is harder to resolve than the controversy about teaching world religions. It seems that schools must make a choice between offending and violating the rights of conservative Christians or offending and violating the rights of those who accept evolution.

Perhaps this either-or approach exaggerates the conflict. In cases concerning the truth of religiously controversial material, schools are not restricted to the options of teaching the controversial material or not teaching it in the required curriculum. One alternative is to teach the material in the required curriculum but allow students to opt out of controversial lessons. If evolution conflicts with the religious beliefs of some students, religious conservative students in required biology courses could be allowed to opt out of classes dealing with evolution or to opt out of the courses altogether. The benefits of this approach appear large, while the costs appear minimal. Schools are able to teach about an important and socially valuable claim to scientific truth, and they can avoid charges by religious conservative students and their parents that the students are forced to consider seriously the truth of a claim conflicting with their beliefs. Given the nature of their religious objections, the students opting out would have been unlikely to accept the truth of evolution had they remained in the class.

While providing an opt-out addresses the concerns of creationists to an extent, it is insufficient to address either their deepest concerns or their basic rights. Keeping a controversial claim to truth in the required curriculum sends a message to students and parents that the school officially recognizes or approves of the claim. Students who agree with the claim may feel emboldened by the school's stamp of approval to place pressure to conform on students who disagree, who may feel that they have to hide their beliefs. Students considering opting out face two painful options. If they choose to remain in the class, they risk offending their parents and their religious beliefs, but leaving risks the stigma that often accompanies open dissent from a socially approved claim to truth. Providing an opt-out but keeping evolution in the curriculum also does nothing to address the alienation of parents and community members who believe that schools are endorsing a claim to truth hostile to their religious beliefs.

A more affirmative step to address the problem of teaching religiously controversial claims to truth is to minimize their conflict with religious beliefs. Providing a safe school and social environment for homosexual students, for instance, is an important social goal that schools should promote. Schools could promote these goals by teaching that homosexuality is not a sin and that homosexual relationships are morally equal to heterosexual relationships. Alternatively, schools could stress that even if some students believe homosexuality is morally wrong, they should respect the basic civil rights of homosexual students. Schools should choose the latter, narrower approach because it is less religiously controversial than the former.

Scientific theories are intended to provide lawlike observations about the natural world, but many theories imply far-reaching moral and metaphysical speculations. The moral and metaphysical speculations usually involve a greater conflict with religious beliefs than the empirical observations. The major social purposes of teaching evolution are to enhance students' scientific literacy and understanding of the natural world. Schools should focus only on those aspects of evolution that are essential to achieving these goals and on providing evidence for the claim that evolution is scientific truth. Controversial moral and metaphysical speculations that conflict with religious beliefs and trigger creationist concerns about the promotion of naturalism should be avoided when they are not necessary to achieve the main goals of teaching evolution. When teaching more controversial beliefs is strictly necessary, schools should make students aware of the implications of the beliefs and that some religions reject these implications.

## Good Faith

Narrowly tailored teaching of evolution is, like an opt-out, a negative step schools can take in the evolution controversy. These steps may contain but cannot extinguish the evolution controversy. Whether in the forms of disclaimers or more robust calls for equal time for creationist alternatives to evolution, many conservative Christians want the state to take more affirmative steps to balance the teaching of evolution. The very existence of opposition is a practical consideration schools must take into account, but the nature of the critique is at least equally relevant, because it touches on a core democratic concern. Many conservative Christians believe that teaching only evolution triggers concerns of fairness that can only be remedied by including a discussion of creationism.

For a more thorough evaluation of these claims, we must turn to the principle of good faith discussed in chapter 2. The principle of good faith welcomes the presence of religious beliefs in democratic discourse but is also aware that the use of religion can be divisive. It establishes guidelines to help determine which religious beliefs are entitled to serious discussion in public and which are appropriate for discussion in the private sphere. The major criterion for entry of religious beliefs into the public sphere is the balance requirement. Believers may use public policy arguments inspired by religion and may use religious considerations to tip the scale in favor of one side or another in difficult cases, but believers must also make a good-faith effort to balance their sectarian beliefs with secular logical and empirical claims. A necessary corollary is that the public policy arguments advanced must involve a significant departure from sectarian beliefs. Both the balance and sectarianism requirements are based on the premise that not all religious references in the public square are equally controversial or disrespectful of others' rights. The most divisive invocations of religion are those that involve a naked appeal to one's own belief systems without an attempt to address the concerns or interests of other citizens.

When the balance and sectarianism requirements are satisfied, however, the burdens of good faith shift from believers to listeners, particularly secularists who would deny religion entry into the public square. The principle of good faith believes that true reciprocity in a democracy means that religious believers deserve to be given credit for adapting their beliefs to democratic norms. Arguments meeting the balance and sectarianism requirements not only deserve treatment in the public sphere, according to chapter 2's argument, but warrant a particular type of treatment. Listeners must take these arguments seriously and at face value. Secularists often accuse public policy arguments related to religion of bad faith and seek to redescribe nonsectarian arguments in sectarian terms. Sometimes this redescription comes in a more allegedly sympathetic form. Barack Obama's claim that their economic vulnerability makes it understandable that small-town Americans "cling to guns or religion" is such a redescription. By treating believers as incapable of knowing and expressing their own interests, the condescension of this and similar statements is no better than outright accusations of bad faith. Taking an argument seriously and according to the principle of good faith means engaging with it *in the form that its adherents sincerely hold it.*

Not all arguments consistent with the principle of good faith are deserving of treatment in the public school curriculum. The principle of active respect can strengthen the claim for a good-faith treatment of certain arguments in the curriculum. The argument based on the principle of good faith suggests that views to which religious believers have a strong attachment deserve consideration in the curriculum. The principle of active respect suggests that this claim is particularly strong when the opposing point of view already receives a robust treatment in the curriculum. The failure to provide a balanced and good-faith treatment of alternative views in these instances sends a particularly alienating message.

Active respect also ensures that undemocratic views that may pass the test of good faith are not acceptable in the curriculum. The principle of active respect forbids any group from using the public school curriculum to claim that one religion is superior to another. Views consistent with good faith that have strongly sectarian implications and associations may send a deeply alienating message to secularists and religious minorities and be inappropriate for treatment either in the compulsory or elective curriculum.

There are degrees of inconsistency with the principle of active respect. Stephen Macedo (2003, 225), for instance, has claimed that if schools sanction the teaching of ID, they must also accept teaching "Christian identity" views that Jews are the instruments of Satan, especially if arguments for tolerance of Jews receive emphasis. The principle of good faith itself rejects the assumption that if some views related to religion are allowed into the curriculum, all views can claim a place. Claims that Jews and homosexuals are instruments of Satan are clearly unbalanced and overly sectarian. But even if adherents of these views were conceivably able to provide versions of their arguments that passed the test of good faith, the principle of active tolerance would still disqualify their discussion in the public school curriculum. Whether creationist views might be inappropriate for the curriculum because of their conflict with active respect will be discussed shortly, but ID in particular does not conflict openly with the principle in the way the views Macedo cites do.

## REQUIRING BALANCED TREATMENT

Is the only measure that would genuinely satisfy most religious conservatives—a robust discussion of creationism in the curriculum—consistent with the preceding expanded understanding of the two guiding principles of active respect and good faith? In *Edwards v. Aguillard*, the Supreme Court struck down a Louisiana law requiring that if schools teach evolution, they must provide instruction in YE creationism. Neither the Supreme Court nor federal courts have ruled directly on laws requiring balanced treatment of ID in required courses. But in December 2005, in *Kitzmiller, et al. v. Dover Area School District, et al.,* federal district court judge John E. Jones III ruled unconstitutional a disclaimer describing evolution as a theory and making resources on ID available to students in schools in Dover, Pennsylvania.

Despite these decisions, arguments for balanced treatment of ID in required courses should not be automatically dismissed. If required biology courses[8] support the truth claims made by evolutionists, then fairness to religious believers whose beliefs are at odds with evolution dictates that schools qualify this support by teaching both criticisms of evolution and the ID alternative. Moreover, legal scholar Francis Beckwith (2003, 148–56) contends that there are two crucial differences between the Louisiana law requiring balanced treatment of YE and proposed legislation to require balanced treatment of ID.

The *Edwards* Court used the *Lemon* test (formulated in 1971 in *Lemon v.*

*Kurtzman*) to evaluate Louisiana's law, and Judge Jones relied in part on the *Lemon* test in the *Kitzmiller* ruling. The *Lemon* test's first prong requires that a law have a valid secular purpose. The alleged secular purpose of Louisiana's law was to promote academic freedom and critical thinking on a crucial scientific, moral, and religious issue. But Louisiana's law required only that school districts teach creationism if evolution was also taught. It gave school districts the option of teaching neither. The commitment to academic freedom and critical thought could not be genuine, the Court reasoned, if school districts could suppress discussion and critical thinking about the origin of life altogether. Combined with statements in the legislative record providing religious justification for the law, the Court concluded that an illegitimate religious motivation was the statute's true inspiration.

Despite its finding, the Court's decision implicitly provided guidelines for constructing a constitutional form of balanced treatment. Assuming that it is wise to investigate the intent of laws, there are at least two valid secular justifications for the balanced treatment of creationism. The Court did not find that promoting academic freedom and critical thought were illegitimate secular purposes, but it found that Louisiana's commitment to them was not sincere. Louisiana's mistake can be corrected by requiring schools to teach both evolution and creationism and by not allowing them to teach neither. Teaching ID could provoke students to reflect on several of the most momentous and meaningful questions humans face, such as the role of purpose, fate, and chance in the universe. Reflecting on these questions could, for instance, enable students to better understand the meditations on these questions by great authors from Sophocles and Homer to George Eliot and Samuel Beckett.

An equally or more compelling justification for the teaching of ID is mentioned less often. Few issues are more important to a nation's success than the moral development of its young people. Many creationists go too far by arguing that evolution necessarily entails social Darwinist conclusions about morality and politics.[9] But many evolutionists concede the conclusion—embraced by some, like Richard Dawkins and Daniel Dennett—that evolutionary biology questions conventional Jewish and Christian views on morality that have been widely shared in Western societies for thousands of years.[10] Darwin himself attempted to suppress the doubts raised about Jewish and Christian ethics by his biological findings, to avoid bringing shame on his wife, a devout believer. These moral views arguably have been a crucial ingredient in the success and social stability of American society and continue to be essential for our flourishing. Teaching only evolution not only could encourage students to doubt these traditional moral views but could give students the impression that the state endorses a view of morality contrary to these views.

In fact, concern about moral effects was among the strongest original motives for objections to teaching evolution in public schools.[11] William Jennings Bryan cited "anecdotal and statistical evidence suggesting that belief in human evolution 'leads people away from God' by giving them a materialistic rather than divine origin" (Larson 1997, 46). He held Darwinism responsible for the horrors of World War I and contrary to the goal of international peace he pursued as secretary of state.[12] According to Bryan,

> There is that in each human life that corresponds to the mainspring of a watch—that which is absolutely necessary if the life is to be what it should be, a real life and not a mere existence. That necessary thing is a belief in God. If there is at work in the world today anything that tends to break this mainspring, it is the duty of the moral, as well as the Christian, world to combat this influence in every possible way. I believe there is such a menace to fundamental morality. (Larson 1997, 210)

The emphasis on the connection between evolution and immorality is more muted today, because science is more ascendant in American culture. But opponents of teaching only evolution continue to cite its moral and political harms. Many creationists link evolution to secular humanism and claim that both encourage students to view themselves as independent of God-given moral constraints.[13]

The causes behind moral beliefs are numerous and subtle. No social scientist has measured the short- or long-term effect that teaching evolution has on students' moral beliefs and behavior. But Christian Smith and Melissa Denton's study of U.S. teenagers' views about religion provides some evidence that holding religious beliefs positively affects teenagers' moral views and behavior. The connection between belief in and teaching of evolution and decline in morality does not have strong empirical support, but neither is it patently irrational or implausible. Teaching creationist alternatives to evolution might be necessary to counter these moral harms.

The final possible secular purpose is the most obvious but also the most controversial. ID advocates argue that the scientific validity of ID constitutes a powerful secular purpose for teaching it. The *Edwards* majority and Judge Jones in *Kitzmiller* rejected YE and ID creationism, respectively, because of their lack of *objective* scientific validity. The principle of good faith suggests, however, that what counts most is not what critics of ID believe but what ID advocates believe about their claims. In the test of good faith, subjective belief of advocates counts more than objective legitimacy as proof of a secular purpose.

ID critics might argue that ID fails to pass even a subjective intent test. The *Edwards* majority and Judge Jones emphasized that creationism was perceived by legislators in both cases as primarily a religious, rather than a scientific, doctrine. Judge Jones further claimed (*Kitzmiller* 2005, 24) that the historical roots of ID in Genesis creationism make ID beliefs religious rather than scientific, and he stressed the overlap between ID and evangelical Christian beliefs.[14] But identifying the historical roots of a belief system in religion does not make the system religious automatically. As Supreme Court justice Potter Stewart noted memorably in *Griswold v. Connecticut*, laws against murder and theft are rooted historically in the Ten Commandments, but these laws are not religious, because additional secular justifications have been provided for them. More crucially, its sectarian religious implications do not disqualify ID as a scientific point of view. By categorizing intents as religious and nonreligious, the *Lemon* test and Judge Jones's argument fail to capture the complex nature of public policy arguments related to religion. Many ID believers would perhaps not hold ID beliefs if they had different sectarian beliefs, but this does not mean that their ID beliefs are exclusively religious. By comparison, if a woman who is a relative of mine runs for Congress, my initial inspiration for supporting her may be my blood relation, but this does not disqualify my support for her policies as an independently valid reason for voting for her.

We seem to be at an impasse. On the one hand, there is abundant evidence that ID beliefs have sectarian origins and implications and may not in fact be independent of religious justification. On the other hand, while some advocates of teaching ID are motivated by pure expediency, many of ID's adherents believe it is an independently valid scientific theory. St. Augustine's stricture that governments are unable to judge the souls of their citizens applies here. When many ID advocates may be hard pressed to judge whether their own primary motivations are religious or scientific, the state is in an even worse position. Still, for democratic and constitutional purposes, the state must determine if ID counts as having a subjectively religious or scientific inspiration. This is where we can return to the principle of good faith. Instead of looking for smoking-gun statements of religious intent by legislators, good faith asks whether the belief advocated for inclusion in the public school curriculum reflects a serious commitment to democratic norms. Commitment to democratic norms is measured by whether the belief includes a balance of secular and religious reasons and involves a significant departure from sectarianism. ID's proponents claim its possible consistency with a variety of religious perspectives. Teaching it does not require mention of any scriptural passage, story, or claim. ID does meet the balance and sectarianism qualifications and should be considered as a sufficiently secular doctrine for the purposes of inclusion in the public school curriculum.

To this point, we have considered the benefits of a balanced treatment for religious groups opposed to evolution. But the democratic approach requires paying equal attention to the rights and beliefs of religious minorities, liberal Christians, and secularists. Is balanced treatment of ID consistent with active respect for these groups? Can these groups accept the approach? These are particularly important questions when discussing the inclusion of creationist theories in *required courses* that all students are expected to take. Compulsory courses send a particularly strong message—not only to the student body, but to the community at large—about what positions schools favor.

Promoting active respect and encouraging the free expression of religious identity requires that schools avoid sending students, parents, and community members a message that the schools favor some religions over others. Since teaching ID does not require mention of religious beliefs and is theoretically consistent with a variety of views on religion, it might appear to be consistent with this criterion. However, almost all ID supporters are Christian or Jewish, including all of the members of the Discovery Institute's board. Furthermore, Jewish, Roman Catholic, and Russian Orthodox ID supporters constitute a small minority of ID's overall supporters and a small minority of their respective religious groups.[15] The overwhelming majority of ID supporters are evangelical Protestants.[16] Despite its nonsectarian claims, the Discovery Institute has at times manifested a conservative Christian agenda.[17]

Not only does ID currently lack support from a wide variety of religions, but its content directly contradicts the central beliefs or origins accounts of a variety of views about religion. Its basic premises are mutually exclusive with the origins accounts of polytheistic or nontheistic religions, including Buddhism, Hinduism, Sikhism, Shintoism, and Native American religions. ID's claim that a purposive creator is responsible for the design of the universe is most compatible with monotheistic religions. But ID also consists of additional claims that are more controversial and incompatible with many monotheistic beliefs. Macroevolution and the descent of humans from a common ancestor are rejected by ID theory but accepted by the Roman Catholic church, various Muslim and Jewish authorities, and many mainline and liberal Christian denominations.[18]

In particular, teaching ID in required courses sends an illegitimate message to students, parents, and community members alike by privileging one religious account of origins. This is especially the case because of the prestige of science and scientific claims to truth in our society. Evangelical students will be encouraged to believe that public schools and society deservedly privilege their beliefs. Many will be inspired to ignore that they need to cultivate active tolerance and help foster an inclusive school environment. Some may even feel that the teaching gives them permission to engage in intrusive proselytizing. Concluding that society favors a religion different from their own, many nonevangelical students will feel more reluctant about publicly expressing their religious identity. Those whose religions have time-honored views on creation will be particularly offended by the schools' implicit message that ID is the only or most legitimate alternative to evolution and that the evangelical Christian view is the most valid religious explanation of creation. It could be argued that students are unlikely to understand the sectarian implications of ID if these are not spelled out in class. This claim is doubtful,[19] but even if it is accurate, nonevangelical parents and community members are likely to be savvier than the students and will feel a heightened sense of exclusion and alienation.

Noting the sectarian nature of ID does not undercut its claim to being scientific or my previous claim that its adherents view its scientific legitimacy as independent of its religious credentials. But the infringement on active respect of including ID in the required curriculum means that the scientific purpose of teaching ID requires a higher level of scrutiny. In Supreme Court cases where a policy conflicts with a fundamental right, the Court applies a strict scrutiny test and requires that the policy further a purpose that is not only valid but compelling. This test is useful and relevant for dealing with school policies that violate the important social goal of achieving active respect. The scientific purpose of teaching ID could be considered compelling if the evidence for ID was overwhelming or if teaching ID were necessary for students to grasp well-supported scientific truths. But the objective scientific legitimacy of ID is controversial, to say the least. Its critics contend that far from being necessary to understand well-supported scientific truths, it undermines belief in them. Placing ID in the required curriculum is problematic not because it is definitely not scientific but because even if its adherents genuinely believe in its scientific legitimacy, it has strong sectarian implications and lacks overwhelming scientific confirmation.

The inclusion of ID in the required curriculum thus comes down to whether the promotion of critical thought and morality qualify as compelling. A necessary corollary of the test of compelling purpose is that the policy proposed is narrowly tailored to achieve its end. If there are two or more ways of achieving the same compelling purpose, schools must choose the way that least conflicts with the fundamental right. Thus, the purpose of critical thought can only be compelling if teaching ID is the only way to promote critical thought on the question of the origin and meaning of life and on the role of chance and purpose in the universe. Many English classes encourage students to think critically about these issues by having students read great literature, including Homer's *Odyssey, Hamlet,* and Hardy's *Tess of the D'Urbervilles.* Many history and social studies classes include a discussion of various religions' accounts of creation. Even if the required curriculum does not currently address these issues to a sufficient extent, there are various ways to enhance critical discussion of these issues in current required courses and be more consistent with active respect—either through a required world religions course or through elective courses that do not privilege ID.

An even more disqualifying flaw of the argument based in promoting critical thought is that teaching ID in required courses will suppress critical thought by restricting the range of answers about questions of origins and meaning that students consider. Learning only about ID in required science classes will give many students the impression that evolution and religion are at odds and that if students reject evolution, they must accept ID. Not only does this discourage students from exploring the creation accounts in other religions, but it ignores the various ways that many religions have attempted to reconcile evolution and their beliefs since Darwin.

The necessary connection between teaching ID and the promotion and preservation of morality, the other possible compelling purpose, is equally questionable. The possible importance of adhering to traditional morality can be and is already discussed in other areas of the curriculum in ways more consistent with active respect. Suggesting to students that they can only lead lives consistent with traditional morality and avoid morally anarchical conclusions if they accept ID also conflicts with the promotion of critical thought. Utilitarians, natural law theorists, and nonevangelical religions, among others, strongly dispute these conclusions.

## Disclaimers and Evolution's Limits

Omitting a positive discussion of the possible scientific validity of ID does not entail the omission of arguments about the limits of evolutionary theory. Indeed, including these arguments might go a long way toward addressing conservative Christian concerns about the religious and moral implications of teaching only evolution.

Disclaimer statements are perhaps the most controversial way to note evolution's limitations. The disclaimer that the school board in Dover, Pennsylvania, required all biology teachers to read to their students reads as follows:

> Because Darwin's Theory is a theory, it continues to be tested as new evidence is discovered. The Theory is not a fact. Gaps in the Theory exist for which there is no evidence. A theory is defined as a well-tested explanation that unifies a broad range of observations. Intelligent Design is an explanation of the origin of life that differs from Darwin's view. The reference book *Of Pandas and People* is available for students who might be interested in gaining an understanding of what Intelligent Design actually involves. (*Kitzmiller* 2005, 708)

Judge Jones's decision to prevent reading of the disclaimer was correct. The disclaimer was rife with sectarian implications that sent an alienating message to students who were not conservative Christians. It suggested that ID was the only possible scientific alternative to evolution, and the only alternative reading suggested supported ID. Creationists reasonably demand that when the state teaches the religiously controversial theory of evolution, it avoid presenting the false impression of a universal consensus around the theory by providing a balanced assessment of its claims. Reciprocity requires that schools provide the same treatment to the religiously controversial theory of ID. Through its various omissions, the Dover disclaimer provided students with a false impression about the validity of ID. The possible flaws in evolution were noted, but not the considerable questions surrounding ID's validity. The disclaimer failed to mention that the vast majority of scientists who question evolution and believe in ID are evangelical Christians. Gaps are routine in even the most well-tested and widely accepted scientific theories, and the disclaimer should have noted that the vast majority of scientists do not believe that the gaps in evolutionary theory invalidate the entire theory (Greenawalt 2005, 114).

The flaws in Dover's disclaimers, however, do not mean that all disclaimers about evolution must share a similar fate. Informing students that many religious believers and especially many evangelical Christians disagree with the truth and consequences of evolution is not only consistent with active respect but necessary for fairness to evangelicals. To avoid sectarianism, disclaimers should focus on critiques of evolution and could note that ID is one among a variety of possible alternatives to evolution, but they should not encourage students to embrace any one alternative. Mention of critiques must be balanced by informing students that a vast majority of scientists believe that these critiques can be effectively countered.[20]

Required biology classes should, indeed, go beyond disclaimers, by devoting class time to examining the limits of science and the possible moral implications of evolution. Teachers should emphasize that science is concerned more with the process of *how* events occur than with explanations of *why* events occur and that many evolutionists, including the noted Darwinian paleontologist Stephen Jay Gould (1999), believe that theological explanations of why species evolved could supplement scientific explanations of how they evolved. More crucially for religious conservative interests, teachers should note that the truth and value of a claim might include other considerations besides its scientific validity. Teachers should note the contention of many religious believers that accepting evolution entails a rejection of their core religious beliefs and of any supernatural presence in the universe or supernatural explanation of natural events. Students should learn that accepting evolution might undermine moral, social, and political ideals many Americans cherish and that Darwin himself was alarmed by the moral implications of his discoveries (Nord and Haynes 1998, 154).

Mention of these concerns is more valid than the Dover disclaimer's emphasis on ID, because a variety of religious believers share them. Conservative Christians are not the only religious believers concerned that an exclusive emphasis on scientific and technological solutions to life's greatest problems is crowding out attention to faith in the private and public sphere. All religions share a belief that spiritual and moral concerns are at least as important as material concerns.

While disclaimers and discussion of evolution's limits might contain the controversy surrounding the evolution debate, they will certainly not eliminate it. The disclaimers and limits make students aware of the possible naturalistic and moral implications of accepting evolution, two major concerns of creationists. Many creationists have recently focused greater attention on including critiques of evolution in the curriculum rather than discussion of creationist alternatives. The Discovery Institute, for instance, did not support the Dover disclaimer, because of its excessive sectarianism. But many creationists will not be satisfied with mention of their disagreement with evolution and of evolution's limits. They believe that evolution is not simply limited but wrong and that ID is the most scientifically valid explanation of origins. Even many members of the evangelical center who might accept these measures to avoid controversy would admit that the measures fail to recognize and address their most important concerns about evolution.

More important, this resolution fails to honor the principles of active respect and good faith. Many conservative Christian parents and students hold that evolution fundamentally challenges their deepest religious beliefs. If schools teach the scientific validity of evolution and fail to recognize and take seriously creationist alternatives to evolution, they send a message to these believers that society and public schools do not respect their beliefs. For all their virtues, disclaimers and discussions of the limits of science still involve an asymmetrical approach to evolution and creationism. Evolution is robustly defended, but creationism is at best merely mentioned.

The outcome of this analysis appears depressing. Schools seem to face a choice between alienating secularists and nonreligious conservatives by teaching ID or alienating conservative Christians by only noting the limits of evolution. Fortunately, we have to this point only considered teaching about the evolution controversy in *required biology* courses. Perhaps teaching about the controversy elsewhere in the curriculum will yield a better resolution.

## TEACHING THE EVOLUTION CONTROVERSY IN NONSCIENCE CLASSES

Concerned about the divisiveness of addressing ID in biology classes, Jay Wexler (2003) cogently argues that the most appropriate place to address the evolution controversy in the required curriculum is in social studies, history, and comparative religion classes. Students would learn about the accounts of creation from a wide variety of world religions and the historical background of the creationist controversy in the United States. Wexler persuasively advocates teaching about religion in public schools to promote important civic ends. In addition to concern with promoting respect for minority religions, Wexler emphasizes the importance of using education about religion to inform students about important public policy debates and to prepare students for political and civic participation. Learning about a variety of accounts of creation will increase students' respect for minority religions and provide students on both sides of the evolution controversy greater information about and sympathy for each other's position. This may not produce an end to the controversy, nor should it, but it will ensure a more civil discussion.[21]

Wexler's suggested changes to the required curriculum are admirable, and public schools should not hesitate to make them. The required world religions course discussed in this book should incorporate a discussion of each religion's account of origins. Conservative Christians would probably not object to these changes in and of themselves. The question remains, however, whether these changes would resolve the controversy. Is Wexler's proposal sufficiently fair to the concerns of conservative Christians, and will conservative Christians accept it as sufficient?

Like disclaimers and the discussion of the limits of science, Wexler's changes are unlikely to satisfy evangelical centrists, let alone more uncompromising creationists. Despite the surface neutrality of discussing various creation accounts in similar ways, creationists would not favor an approach that failed to distinguish their creationist accounts from others. Unlike other accounts of creation, creationists believe that ID has scientific validity. This is also the reason why creationists would object to treating ID in nonscience courses.

Wexler's decision to treat creationist accounts in nonscience courses is, to a significant extent, based on doubts about the authenticity of ID believers' claims that their views are scientific. He (2003, 810) calls into question the independence of scientific arguments for ID from religious arguments for creationism.

> Teaching intelligent design, without talking about history, culture, politics, and especially religion, will not help students understand what the controversy over evolution is really about or help them discuss issues that range over the spectrum of human concerns.

Many religious conservatives and particularly believers in ID, however, believe that the controversy *is* "really about" science. Even if their views turn out, on objective grounds, to be scientifically invalid, the principle of good faith suggests that their subjective claim to indeed hold scientific views is entitled to respect. ID's adherents deserve recognition for advocating a version of creation science that significantly departs from and even rejects crucial sectarian, scripturally sanctioned beliefs. For those who maintain YE and ID simultaneously, the decision to refrain from advocating the teaching of YE may reflect an important understanding of and commitment to the democratic division between public and private.

Claiming to unmask the "true" concern at the heart of ID as religious or moral sends its adherents an alienating message that society and the schools do not take their views seriously. Wexler's arguments here are somewhat at odds with his concern with creating a more civil discussion and understanding between warring cultural groups and with his sympathy for religious conservative concerns about the public schools. Nonreligious conservatives are unlikely to be sympathetic listeners to creationist arguments if they do not take the central claim of creationists at face value, and conservative Christians are unlikely to participate in discussions where the sincerity of their beliefs is questioned. Wexler's suggested changes for the curriculum do not model his concerns with promoting civic discussion.[22]

## TEACHING THE EVOLUTION CONTROVERSY IN AN ELECTIVE COURSE

By process of elimination, the lone remaining alternative to dealing with the evolution controversy is to teach the controversy in an elective class. A recent proposed elective seems to suggest that this path is not promising. A high school in Lebec, California, made national headlines in 2005 by proposing to teach an elective course entitled "The Philosophy of Design." Thirteen parents, supported by Americans United for the Separation of Church and State and other separationist groups, immediately filed a lawsuit, and the school promptly canceled the course.

A closer examination of the course, however, gives some cause for optimism. The Lebec elective included obvious biases. The course focused on YE, rather than ID, creationism and did not mention the creation accounts of any other religion. More important, the course emphasized almost exclusively the flaws of evolution but did not mention the possible flaws of creationism and the response that evolutionists would make to creationist critiques. Of the 24 videos to be viewed by students, all but one advocated the creationist point of view (Barbassa 2006).[23] Perhaps a course constructed in a more balanced and neutral way could receive the support of religious conservatives and secularists alike. This section proposes such a balanced approach and explains why it might gain acceptance from both sides in the evolution controversy.

### The Proposal

For addressing the evolution controversy, this book proposes a semester-long elective course divided into two halves. The first half would provide an in-depth examination of evolution and ID. Unlike Wexler's proposal, the course would take ID seriously as a scientific theory and would examine the support for ID and criticisms of evolution made by prominent ID scholars, such as William Dembski and Michael Behe. Unlike the Lebec elective, the course would provide a balanced account of evolution and ID. Students would examine the responses of prominent evolutionists to criticisms of evolution, as well as the critiques of ID that these evolutionists make. On the issue of whether evolution is merely a hypothesis, students would learn that a large majority of scientists reject this position.

The second part of the course would examine alternative views about the relationship between religion, science, and evolution.[24] Students would examine the views of scientists who believe that scientific evidence supports the reconciliation of Darwinian evolution with ideas of design and purpose in the universe and who believe that it is possible to accept evolution without accepting neo-Darwinian views on evolution and methodological naturalism. They would also examine the works of liberal religious scholars and theologians who use biblical interpretation and historical research to reconcile evolution with fundamental Jewish and Christian religious beliefs.[25] While giving serious consideration to conservative Christian concerns about the moral effects of accepting evolution, the course would also explore the views of prominent thinkers who believe that accepting evolutionary biology does not entail believing in social Darwinism. Finally, the course would examine the possibility that religious beliefs can be true and meaningful even if they cannot be scientifically verified, along with the argument of several prominent scholars that the Genesis account of creation was not originally intended as a literal or scientifically verifiable account. Due to its limited focus and to avoid giving the impression that schools privilege ID, schools would offer the course for credit, but taking the course would not fulfill biology or science requirements for graduation.[26]

## Acceptance by Religious Conservatives

There is little reason to doubt that most creationists and especially evangelical centrists would accept the course, and there are several reasons to believe they would find it an acceptable resolution to the controversy. A 2005 Pew Research Center poll did find that a majority of white evangelicals would ideally prefer that creationism be taught instead of evolution in required courses.[27] But a significant minority (32 percent) of creationists did not support this position, and those surveyed were not asked if they would find fair treatments of both theories an acceptable alternative.

The willingness to compromise is indicated by the fact that recent attempts by schools and legislatures to teach creationism have all focused on teaching creationism alongside evolution. The Discovery Institute's official position on evolution reflects this view. Although the institute does not believe that teaching ID in required courses is unconstitutional, it presently supports only teaching criticisms of evolution in required courses and not mandating the teaching of ID. The institute has opposed legislation in Pennsylvania and Utah intended to mandate the teaching of ID. Even the controversial Dover biology course, opposed by the institute, encouraged but did not mandate that all students learn about ID. A Zogby poll commissioned by the institute in 2001 found that teaching criticism of evolution in required courses satisfied many conservative Christians, appealed to Republican moderates, and overall received the support of 71 percent of respondents (Wilogren 2005). The advocacy of these measures indicates that most religious conservatives desire recognition of the possible validity of their views alongside the teaching of scientific views they believe are hostile to their religious beliefs.

The elective would provide ID not only with recognition but with exactly the type of recognition that ID's supporters desire, by focusing on the theory's possible scientific validity. Since creationists have been willing to accept balanced treatment of evolution and ID in required courses as long as the scientific merits of ID are focused on, there is no reason to believe they would object to such balanced treatment and mention of other religions' accounts of creation in an elective. Taking the scientific merits of ID seriously not only would foster a sense of inclusion among evangelical students but would encourage students who believe in evolution to treat their views on creationism and other matters with more respect and sympathy. This makes the elective more consistent with the democratic rights of conservative Christians than Wexler's proposal.

More ardent creationists might object that discussing ID in required and not elective courses relegates ID to a second-class status. If ID can be taught as a possibly valid scientific theory in an elective, failing to teach it in required courses would seem to be the result of bias. In response, schools should begin by stressing that teaching the controversy in electives would be more advantageous to conservative Christian concerns than teaching it in required courses. In required biology courses, evolution is one topic among many, and only limited time can be devoted to the controversy. Given that the elective is solely devoted to examining the controversy, the scientific validity of ID would receive a more in-depth examination. The elective would also have more time than required courses to focus on the possible negative moral and political consequences of evolution, a crucial concern of many conservative Christians.

Schools should also stress to students, parents, and community members that exclusion of ID from required courses should be construed not as a judgment that it is not science but as an acknowledgment that it is too controversial to be present in required courses. Schools have an obligation to consider not only the scientific merits of points of view but the religious rights of their students. Teaching ID in a required course would send a message to students that the school privileges one religion over others. Such controversial claims are more appropriately treated in an elective.

For similar reasons, while the elective should provide some discussion of YE creationism, it should not provide an in-depth discussion of its scientific merits. Given that many Americans describe themselves as YE creationists, this omission would seem to be grave. Many Americans who report believing in YE, however, may do so by default because they are not familiar with different forms of creationism or are confused about different versions of creationism. The Lebec elective notwithstanding, the support for legislation that criticizes evolution in required courses or teaches ID among large numbers of creationists indicates that many who profess a belief in YE would be satisfied with the elective. The teaching of YE creationism is, in short, not a live issue.

Even if some YE creationists object to omitting a scientific discussion of YE creationism, schools should not accommodate their demands. Given the prestige of science in our society, teaching a point of view as possibly scientifically valid privileges that point of view in the eyes of students and the community. YE creation science is an explicitly sectarian doctrine that is only consistent with one narrow version of religious truth. Evolution can be taught without directly stressing its contradiction with religious views, and ID can be taught without making constant reference to its sectarian implications, but YE creationism cannot be taught without constantly mentioning its sectarian religious results, and defending it in schools would violate active respect and cause excessive controversy.[28] The more serious flaw with YE creationism from a democratic perspective is its refusal to criticize or deviate from the literal account of creation provided in Genesis. That YE creationism so closely tracks and reflects the literal biblical account not only calls into question its independent scientific validity but suggests the lack of a good-faith effort to balance sectarian concerns and inspiration with empirical claims that are capable of appealing to citizens of other faiths and no faiths at all.

Indeed, the concentration on ID and the lack of discussion of YE creationism would provide students with a more accurate overall appreciation of the views most conservative Christians hold. Chapter 2 argued that a concentration on exclusively sectarian political views of conservative Christians in the curriculum would be distracting and unfair to conservative Christians.[29] Their presence in the curriculum would lead students to concentrate on them and would further perceptions of conservative Christians as extremist, at a time when the lived religion of many conservatives is becoming more moderate and conciliatory. The treatment of YE creationism would likewise overshadow any treatment of ID and deepen caricatures of conservative Christians. The democratic position, here as elsewhere, represents a sane mean between two extremes. In this case, it requires giving a privileged place in the curriculum to religious beliefs compatible with basic democratic norms instead of ignoring religion or dwelling on the most sectarian views.

## Acceptance by Scientists, Secularists, Religious Minorities, and Religious Liberals

Contrary to popular perception, secularists, religious minorities, and religious liberals do not object to any substantial discussion of religion in the curriculum. During the 1980s, secularist organizations such as People for the American Way and Americans United were part of a movement calling for increased discussion of religion in the curriculum (Nord 1995, 139). They have, however, objected to discussions of religion that endorse one religious point of view. Privileging a sectarian point of view in the required curriculum, even when discussion of the point of view is balanced, can send a message to the community that schools officially favor this point of view. Privileging of one religious point of view in elective courses does not pose the same threat to neutrality, especially when the course provides a balanced discussion of the privileged view and when alternative views are also presented, as is the case with the elective proposed in this chapter. Since not all students are required to take these courses, students offended by a point of view being taught are not required to learn about it.

More important, there is a common recognition by students, parents, and community members that schools use required courses to deal with issues and views that are important to all Americans. Electives deal with views and topics that are important and often central to parts of American society. Emphasizing one point of view in electives does not necessarily send a message of official favor. For instance, the public high school I attended taught an elective course on the Holocaust but not one on slavery or other historical genocides. African Americans and Armenians, for example, did not protest strongly that their historical tragedies were slighted. Complaints would likely accompany teaching required history courses that focused solely or primarily on the Holocaust or African American history. This does not mean that all electives are legitimate. Courses teaching that one point of view is true or superior send a message of endorsement and clearly violate the First Amendment. For example, Irish Americans would and should complain if schools taught that African American culture was superior to their culture.

Teaching about ID in required science courses sends a message that schools officially favor conservative Christian views and are rewarding these groups for their greater media access and political clout. By placing a robust discussion of ID in an elective students opt into, schools acknowledge that this is an issue of concern to parts of our society, but they do not place an official imprimatur on the truth or greater relative importance of ID to all students. Still, the elective course might conflict with active respect if it encouraged religious conservative students who opted in to more stridently express their opinions or insult and proselytize those who disagree with them. Many conservative Christian students who opt in will likely already be strong believers in ID before they take the course. Their beliefs in ID may strengthen, but only moderately, given their already strong commitment. But the critiques of ID and the alternative versions of creationism will not be familiar to many students. Schools should not encourage students to accept these critiques, but studying them will encourage some conservative Christians to develop greater respect for their opponents and other religions. Like all students who take the course, they will likely emerge with the motivation and information to debate the evolution controversy in civil, democratic terms. The elective will also place ID in context by informing students that ID is held by particular Christian denominations rather than all Christians. Including critiques of evolution and alternative creation views makes the elective more neutral and much less likely to provoke complaints than the Lebec elective.

Furthermore, some of the stridency of conservative Christians results from a feeling that schools completely ignore their views. Many feel that the only way they can be heard over this silence is to speak more loudly and take more extreme positions. Including ID in the elective curriculum will eliminate not only a central complaint of religious conservatives but a source of stridency. An important consequence in many communities will be a greater willingness to accept the teaching of evolution in required biology courses. As noted previously, many localities with large evangelical Christian communities tacitly suppress teaching of evolution even when state regulations require such teaching. Assured that the possible scientific validity of their views is being taught, conservative Christians will be less likely to object to teaching evolution in required courses. The Discovery Institute, for instance, supports the teaching of evolution in required courses as long as the courses include criticisms of evolution. Scientists committed to the teaching of evolution should support inclusion of the elective for this reason.

A final, crucial concern of secularists in particular is that the elective would violate the First Amendment's prohibition against the establishment of religion. In *Edwards* (1987, 594), the Supreme Court concluded that its decision to strike down Louisiana's balanced-treatment law "does not imply that the legislature could never require that scientific critiques of prevailing scientific theories be taught." Francis Beckwith (2003, 159) and Nicholas Miller (2001, 6) have concluded that ID's scientific credentials mean that the Court should and would support a balanced treatment of ID, even though it struck down a balanced-treatment law concerning YE creationism. Even assuming that evolution passes muster as a valid scientific hypothesis, however, the Court's statement in *Edwards* does not mean that it would find all possible teachings of ID legitimate. There are other issues, besides scientific legitimacy, that the Court does and must weigh in establishment clause cases. The Court would clearly not approve, for instance, of a course teaching only ID and not evolution. A great deal thus depends on

how schools teach creationism and ID. To determine if the elective is constitutional, we must examine the tests the Court uses in establishment
clause cases.

The Supreme Court has used three tests in recent years to determine
whether a policy violates the establishment clause. The 1971 *Lemon* test requires that a statute have "a secular legislative purpose" and "principal effects which neither advance nor inhibit religion" (612). In its recent cases,
the Court has moved close to the adoption of the endorsement test first espoused by Justice O'Connor in *County of Allegheny v. ACLU* (1989, 627),
which requires that "government must not make a person's religious beliefs relevant to his or her standing in the political community by conveying a message 'that religion or a particular religious belief is favored or preferred.'" The coercion test, first espoused by Justice Kennedy in *Lee v.
Weisman* (1992, 591), invalidates government actions that "may appear to
the nonbeliever or dissenter to be an attempt to employ the machinery of
the State to enforce a religious [or antireligious] orthodoxy."

The previous analysis in this chapter suggests that while including a robust discussion of ID in a required course might run afoul of the establishment clause, the elective is consistent with all three tests. The most easily
dismissed concerns are those raised by the coercion test. In *Lee v. Weisman*,
the Court invalidated the subtle and indirect coercion employed in a prayer
at a graduation ceremony in which all students participated. A robust treatment of ID in mandatory courses might violate the test, but under my proposal, students are not required to take the elective, and schools could not
provide incentives to students who took the course or punish those who
did not. Teaching ID in required courses might also violate the endorsement test, by sending students, parents, and the community a message that
the schools privilege evangelical Christianity. Placing a discussion of ID in
an elective course is a response precisely to this concern. Including evolutionists' responses to ID and alternative creationist accounts would help
avoid sending students a message of favoritism.

The *Lemon* test—especially its second prong, prohibiting the advance-
ment of religion in general—seems to pose greater difficulties for the elective. The Supreme Court has been careful, however, to stress that a government action cannot have a *principal effect* of advancing religion. Regarding
the treatment of religion in the curriculum, the Court has suggested that
encouraging students to believe in religion or a particular religion would

constitute an invalid primary effect. But the Court has repeatedly stressed that teaching students *about* religion does not have the primary effect of advancing religion. The principal effect of the elective is clearly to encourage students to consider various ways they could think about the questions surrounding the origins of life, rather than to encourage a belief in religion or a particular religion. Finally, the elective is consistent with the first prong of the *Lemon* test, because there are several legitimate secular purposes of the course.[30] The balanced nature of the course would encourage students to think critically about some of the most important metaphysical and philosophical questions of meaning that humans face. The elective might promote morality by provoking students to reflect on the moral consequences of holding different beliefs about origins. Most important, the elective would remedy the current imbalanced approach public schools take toward evolution, and increase social peace by reducing the alienation from public schools that is felt by many conservative Christian students, parents, and community members.[31]

## GOING BEYOND THE CURRENT EVOLUTION CONTROVERSY?

The preceding discussion suggests why secularists and religious minorities should not reject the proposed elective. It does not give reasons for secularists and religious minorities to support such an elective. The following account may not be sufficient to ensure that even a majority of secularists *will* support the elective, but it does claim that secularists and religious minorities *should* support the elective, because of its consistency with several of their central interests.

At the least, the discussion of other accounts of creation of religious minorities will promote recognition and active respect of these groups. Even more crucially, the elective will expand students' awareness of the ways in which religious truth can be conceived. The evolution controversy takes place in black-and-white terms. Many evolutionists argue that the scientific truth of their position means that the account of creation in Genesis is wholly false. Many creationists argue that denying the scientific validity of their beliefs entails denying the truth of core Judeo-Christian religious and moral beliefs.

The reason for this dichotomous way of looking at the controversy is that for all their differences, both sides share a heavy reliance on the scientific mode of reasoning and assessing truth. Science places an emphasis on literal, factual truth and only allows for two possible options concerning the truth of a hypothesis. A hypothesis is *either* true if consistent with the best available evidence *or* false if inconsistent with this evidence. There is no middle ground; hypotheses cannot be partly true and partly false at the same time. This scientific approach to truth is so dominant in modern American life that it often defines the way we think about religion.

But the scientific approach to truth was not always as dominant, at least according to Karen Armstrong (2000, xvi). She distinguishes two different ways used in the ancient world to discern truth. One way, which Armstrong defines as the "logos" approach to truth, involved using "rational, pragmatic and scientific thought." The alternative was the mythical approach to truth. "Myth could not be demonstrated by rational proof," argues Armstrong, because "its insights were more intuitive, similar to those of art, music, poetry, or sculpture."

This conception of myth is largely unfamiliar today. For us, a myth is synonymous with a lie or a falsehood. This view reflects our emphasis on empirical proof; myths are false because they are not consistent with empirical facts. But Armstrong (2000, 15) contends that "myth was not reasonable; its narratives were not supposed to be demonstrated empirically." At the same time, adherents to myths did not think of them as arbitrary inventions. Myths were intended to embody fundamental metaphorical truths about the meaning of events and human experience when that meaning could not be communicated in normal human discourse or proven scientifically. They were particularly appropriate responses to the most complex questions of meaning and the human condition. Although they were neither "true," in our scientific sense of the word, nor intended to be so, they were considered true.

Armstrong claims that societies traditionally valued scientific and mythical approaches to the truth and that the mythical approach was dominant in religious thought. With the increasing prestige of science and empiricism during the Enlightenment came a demand that all truth claims be empirically verified. At first, religious skeptics seized on this emphasis on facts to criticize traditional religious authority and institutions. German higher criticism beginning in the late eighteenth century, for instance, initiated historical investigations into the life of Jesus intended to undermine claims about Jesus's divinity and the truth of miracles. Defenders of traditional religious views adapted their religious views in a way that continues to affect profoundly the way religion is conceived in America today. "Our religious experience in the modern world has changed," contends Armstrong (2000, 17), "because an increasing number of people regard scientific rationalism alone as true, and they have often tried to turn the *mythos of their faith into logos.*"

The exclusive reliance on scientific approaches to truth has considerable pitfalls for both sides in the evolution controversy. The perils are perhaps greatest for creationists, because an essential criterion of scientific views is their ability to be falsified through experimentation. Scientific research in the near future could disprove definitively creationist views like ID in obvious, incontrovertible ways, and most scientists believe it already does. If faced with overwhelming scientific evidence, ID supporters dependent on science would and perhaps already do face a Faustian choice. Rejecting ID would critically weaken belief in their religion, but maintaining scientifically implausible beliefs may drive believers away as well and would contradict their emphasis on science.

The irony for creationists who rely on science is that while they accuse evolutionists of affirming methodological naturalism, they themselves often implicitly affirm that only scientifically provable claims have meaning. According to Christopher Toumey (1994, 57), scientific creationists implicitly accept the

> religion of science and technology . . . in which nothing, not even a basic Bible story, is credible until it is surrounded by technicians, technical equipment, technological jargon, and technocratic authority . . . By alleging that science substantiates the Bible, modern creationism inadvertently makes the Bible answer to secular scientific standards.[32]

Creation accounts conceived as myth rather than science do not stand or fall according to scientific evidence.[33] They are well equipped to outlast and transcend scientific evidence disconfirming the accounts' literal details. Discussing creation accounts as mythical approaches to the truth can suggest an important general point to students about the relationship of truth and religion.[34] It can remind students that there is a distinctive religious approach to the truth that is as important as, if not superior to, the scientific approach to truth and that religious accounts can be true independent of their scientific accuracy or validity. For religious conservative students, it stresses that religious truth can be conceived in ways besides the literal. For atheists, agnostics, and the scientifically inclined, it affirms that religion can teach us insights and answer questions that science is incapable of addressing.

Of course, an elective should not privilege or teach uncritically Armstrong's particular and controversial views[35] about the history of the relationship between scientific and religious approaches to truth. It should present students with a variety of views about the relationship between religion and science. The curriculum might, for instance, acquaint students with Stephen Jay Gould's view that science and religion are "nonoverlapping magisteria," which shares something in common not only with Armstrong's views about the independence of science and religion but also with Alvin Plantinga's support for an integrated, "Augustinian" approach to religion and science, which stands in contrast to Armstrong's and Gould's views (Nord 1995, 286; Greenawalt 2005, 98). Students should also learn that Armstrong's and Gould's views are more favorable to liberal religious points of view.[36]

Having students consider Gould's, Armstrong's, and Plantinga's views as several *possible* ways to reconcile science and religion suggests just several examples of how the elective course might open up the dialogue about evolutionism and creationism. Not only is this dialogue stuck in a rut that breeds mistrust and deepens the religious and cultural divide, but the unquestioned hegemony of science holds perils for creationists and evolutionists alike. Meanwhile, many students and also Americans in general may feel trapped by the polarized discussion and an unhappy choice between atheism and fundamentalist literalism, without realizing that other views on evolution and science offer a way out. Many believers may continue to hold literal views because they believe that rejecting these views would lead to atheism. Many skeptics may maintain their skepticism because they believe that embracing religion would require acceptance of literalism.

It would be unrealistic to hope that in addition to producing a détente in the current evolution controversy, the course proposed here would point the way toward a more comprehensive reconciliation of the controversy over evolution in the future. But at the very least, teaching a variety of views about religion, science, and evolution—while emphasizing ID to avoid the alienation of conservative Christians—will offer more options to those who feel trapped in the current polarized debate, and it is more likely to produce good-faith reflection on views more firmly held than is the current status quo attempt to establish consensus around evolution in the curriculum. To be sure, the least controversial approach to teaching evolution may very well be to maintain the status quo. There may be good reasons secularists *should* not reject and even support the proposed elective course. But this does not mean that secularists *will* embrace the proposed course if it is implemented. Disagreement about the mechanics of the course, such as teacher selection, might lead to more obvious short-term controversy than the status quo. But the status quo, of course, is the subject of constant complaints by religious conservatives. Even if the more obstreperous objections to the status quo were to die down, history suggests that widespread resistance to accepting evolution is likely to persist. Secularists and most scientists would do well to remember that attempting to create consensus around evolution by ignoring all alternatives has only helped to entrench belief in creationism among a large segment of the American public.

Short-term controversy among secularists may be the price public schools and American society have to pay to provide views about evolution with a full, free, and more impartial hearing in the long run. As the experience of countless historical and present-day nations that have sought to establish consensus around religion reminds us, the American path of pluralism is more conducive to peace and a vigorous and free public debate. It would be a shame if we continue to realize this truth in general about religion but continue to neglect it in teaching about evolution. The following chapter explores the pitfalls of a similar attempt to establish religious consensus through teaching required Bible courses and suggests that an even more pluralistic version of the approach recommended here for teaching about evolution is appropriate for teaching students about Judaism and Christianity.

## CHAPTER 5

# The Limits of Consensus and the Civil Politics of Teaching about the Bible

"The Swede," the protagonist of Phillip Roth's *American Pastoral,* yearns for his own Eden. Born Seymour Irving Levov in Newark, New Jersey, he embraces his Scandinavian nickname earned by athletic prowess, marries a beauty queen runner-up, and moves her and his young daughter, Merry, to a dream home in a genteel hamlet in 1950s rural New Jersey. But as in the biblical Eden, hope turns to disaster. As a teenager, Merry takes up with leftist radicals and plants a bomb in the village post office, ostensibly to protest the Vietnam War, before running away from home.

The Swede is kindhearted, and Roth often portrays him as a victim of cultural and political turmoil beyond his control—a casualty of the change in generational norms. But the Swede is not blameless in Merry's predictable rebellion, even if his lack of self-awareness is partly tragic. He fails to realize that the tranquil yet superficial beauty and bland prosperity he surrounds Merry with is suffocating. Her signature stutter is emblematic of her frustration in the face of an overwhelming pressure to conform to the ideals of life in 1950s America. Unable to express herself in words, she does so in violence, as the genial 1950s gives way to the turbulent late 1960s and 1970s.

Roth may not have had the emergence of civil religion or the politics of the vital center specifically in mind in writing *American Pastoral,* but they are major components of the 1950s ethos he evokes. The spreading threat of Communism around the world and, as many Americans believed, possibly at home made civic unity and consensual politics appear a particularly precious commodity. While McCarthy and his followers wished to impose an aggressive conformity, most politicians and public intellectuals on the right and left supported a more benign form of harmony. The politics of "the vi-

tal center," as Arthur Schlesinger Jr. described it memorably in his epony-
mous work, rejected the extreme ideologies of the left and right. Against
the class warfare of Communism and the divisive patriotism of McCarthy-
ism, the vital center's proponents sang the praises of consensus, moderation, and reasonable pragmatism.

Religion, these mandarins of moderation argued, had a crucial role to
play in binding Americans together by giving divine sanction to democratic ideals and practices while distinguishing us from the godless Soviet
empire.[1] Professions of public piety flowered. For the first time, Americans
pledged their allegiance "under God," and their postage expressed trust in
God.[2] But out of sincere conviction and just to be extra sure that our attitude toward faith was more democratic than our enemies', the civil religion
inaugurated in the 1950s and lasting until the mid-1960s was flexible.
Eisenhower captured perfectly the civic emphasis and openness of this
civil religion when he remarked, "Our government makes no sense unless
it is founded on a deeply held religious belief—and I don't care what it is."
Civil religion in the 1950s, quipped William Lee Miller (1964, 19), involved
"a belief in believing." The Protestant establishment's tolerance in practice
extended only to Catholics and Jews fully, but Will Herberg (1960) was
right to note that this marked significant progress in American ecumenism.

This alleged openness and emphasis on consensus concealed an unset-
tling exclusion, however. Besides the obviously discomfiting climate civil
religion created for staunch secularists, it gave little voice to evangelical
Christians. Evangelicals might share civil religion's patriotic inclinations,
but their critique of mainstream culture was suspect, and their emotionalism was unseemly.[3] Norman Vincent Peale's accommodating and tepid
prosperity gospel was more consistent with the taste of the times than
born-again fervency. Roger Williams and Alexis de Tocqueville would have
recognized well that tying religion so closely to the state did neither religion nor the state any favors. Placing its hopes in material enrichment and
national success, civil religion left little time or space to contemplate heavenly rewards.[4] The prophetic politics of a Savanarola may be a bit much,
but states and societies benefit most when religions hold them to a higher
moral standard. The distance from the mainstream that prophecy requires
was the very antithesis of the cozy relationship between religion and society that existed in the 1950s and the early 1960s. By attempting to domesti-
cate religion, the state was harming not only religion but itself.

As justifiable as civil religion may have been in the immediacy of the post–World War II period (Silk 1988, 44; W. L. Miller 1964, xiv), it became increasingly less so as the American religious landscape splintered. Staunch secularists and evangelicals became more numerous, their voices more prominent. These groups came to see the attempts to preserve a centrist consensus in religion and politics as exclusionary and oppressive (Neuhaus 1984; Mathewes 2007b; Perlstein 2008, 747).[5] Like the Eden Swede Levov built for his family, the vital center's attempt to construct an amiable, united nation seems to have backfired. Too long denied a voice by a moderate civil religion, secularists and evangelicals became more vociferous to ensure that they were never ignored or quieted again. Learning from hard experience that the appeal to moderation is too often merely a ploy to rule out their interests, these groups instead turned to discourteous dissent. The excessive emphasis on religious consensus, to be sure, was far from the sole cause of religious and cultural conflicts still with us today, but it is probably a central reason these conflicts have been so full of vitriol.

As chapter 2 has suggested, extremist secularists and conservative Christians distort cultural conflict for political gain and endanger the common ground they obscure. That chapter laid out rules that schools should encourage for political engagement by believers. Overreacting to extremists' influence, as the 1950s experiment with civil religion demonstrates, can imperil religious and cultural peace as well. Using the state's power to fit American religion into a Procrustean bed of moderation is contrary to freedom of religion. Standardizing and taming religion harms both religion and the state. While chapter 2 examined how public schools can counter the threat America's religious margins pose to the moderate political center, this chapter critiques an effort to make political discourse more civil by using schools to challenge countercultural religious beliefs.

The main form this effort takes is in a cogent and novel appeal for teaching about the Bible in the required curriculum. Unlike easily dismissed calls for teaching about the Bible that involve thinly veiled and clearly illegitimate attempts to promote conservative forms of Christianity, the arguments and historical narrative in Stephen Prothero's *Religious Literacy* are frequently compelling and often eloquently expressed and have already proven influential.[6] Indeed, it is precisely because Prothero's account is so cogent that it deserves particularly close scrutiny. Books of such importance demand serious appraisal. But although Prothero's contributions to the debate about religion in public schools are vital and although his call to correct Americans' appalling ignorance about the Bible is on the mark, close examination reveals that the particular way Prothero proposes to correct this ignorance relies on a contestable civic narrative and conception of civic purposes. Prothero's approach to addressing our religious divisions is explicitly based on a disdain for the approach of the vital center. But his narrative does seem to share the nostalgic yearning for lost unity that inspired civil religion advocates, and his preferred education about the Bible reflects a fondness for the centripetal orientation that characterized their proposals. Even if his diagnosis of America's religious ills is right, curing them in public schools in a required Bible course is unwise.

Teaching about the Bible does have a place in the public schools, this chapter argues, albeit in the elective, rather than the required, curriculum. But the approach to teaching the Bible should be more centrifugal than centripetal, more ascending and bottom-up than top-down, and dynamic and future-oriented rather than nostalgic. Rather than seeking to guide Americans to more broadly based religious views, as Prothero's approach does, public schools should provide recognition to the various views of the Bible and of Judaism and Christianity that constitute the actual religious consensus in America today. Such recognition is not only more consistent with democracy but a surer way to religious and cultural peace than the more centripetal approach Prothero recommends. The historical bursting apart of the vital center suggests that we approximate peace as best we can or should by not striving for it directly.

Before directly attempting to parse this apparent paradox, however, attention must be paid to another. As already suggested, the main concern in this chapter seems to contradict the concern of chapter 2. Chapter 2 emphasized the need for schools to guide citizens toward more moderate political expressions of their religious beliefs; this chapter is concerned with protecting religious beliefs out of the mainstream. It is fair to wonder if it is even possible for schools to encourage moderation and civility in political expression while honoring robust diversity of occasionally countercultural religious belief and the prophetic function of religion. A full answer to *how* schools can do this is complex and must wait until the chapter's conclusion. An understanding of *why* schools must attempt this requires a consideration of how Bible courses are different from other courses about religion.

## "TO UNLOOSE THE DOVE OF PEACE"

World religions courses cover many different religions and range extensively. They can have a profound effect on how outsiders view each religion studied, but they are likely to have less of an effect on what believers think about their religion. Devout Hindu students, for instance, will realize that the coverage of their religion in such a course is fairly cursory and does not account for the depth and diversity of their own views on Hinduism. The course on intelligent design proposed in the previous chapter does focus on a set of beliefs associated with one religious tradition. But its concern is narrow rather than comprehensive. It does not seek to present the full range of Christian beliefs, and its concern is ostensibly scientific, even if the implications of its treatment of origins are far-ranging for religion.

A course about the Bible, by contrast, focuses intensively on two religious traditions. As a result, proposals to teach about the Bible must receive a greater level of scrutiny than world religions courses, for two reasons. First, teaching about the Bible sends a clear message to students, parents, and the community at large—particularly to those belonging to faiths other than Judaism and Christianity or no faith at all—that schools are privileging Judaism and Christianity. This message is particularly strong when courses about the Bible are included in the required curriculum.[7]

This privileging does not automatically invalidate teaching about the Bible, but it does mean that a compelling justification or set of justifications must exist to outweigh the effect of this privileging. There is also a more practical reason for this burden to weigh heavily on proposals for required Bible courses. The Modesto example suggests that implementing required courses about religion is not impossible but difficult. Space and money for the materials of a required course in the curriculum are scarce, and political and social capital for such efforts are precious as well. Prothero, for instance, advocates separate required courses on world religions and the Bible. But public schools may face a choice between implementing world religions courses and Bible courses,[8] and attempts to implement required Bible courses will, at the least, drain financial and political resources from attempts to implement required world religions courses. The justifications for required Bible courses must be at least proximate in strength to those for required world religions courses. Even if strong justifications exist for a required Bible course, advocates must show that the course avoids privileg-

ing Judaism and Christianity in a way that violates constitutional standards and democratic values.

The rights of non-Christians, non-Jews, and atheists are not the only
rights at stake in Bible courses. Bible courses inevitably have a far larger impact than world religions courses on the way that Jewish and Christian believers view their own faith. Prothero (2007, 133) may be right to protest that
Bible courses in public schools cannot and should not be similar to Sunday
school courses, but the intensive and comprehensive treatment of the Bible
means that such courses will inevitably have a Sunday school aspect.

Bible courses have a profound ability to shape the way Jewish and
Christian students view their faith and to provide students with a normative and standard definition of what these faiths should include and what
they should not. They have a greater ability to capture and standardize the
religions they treat intensively and to subordinate them to civic purposes.
Much more than other courses about religion, courses about the Bible raise
the question of whether it is possible for the state to teach about religion
without normalizing religion. Their possible effects on how students view
their own religion mean that they have a greater capacity to interfere with
free religious choice than world religions courses. They also provide signals to students outside Judaism and Christianity about which Jewish and
Christian views are more mainstream and acceptable, and this can reinforce the shift in Jewish and Christian students' own perceptions. Unlike
the discussions of good faith recommended in chapter 2, which are confined to guidance about the political use of religious beliefs, the in-depth
examination of two faiths' sacred texts touches more directly on religion.
Once again, the potential for problems are greater in required, rather than
elective, courses, and the former require stronger justification.

Overt and intentional attempts to shape standard views of Judaism and
Christianity are clearly off-limits and certainly not what advocates of required Bible courses like Prothero have in mind. But biases can creep into
these courses in more subtle ways. The Bible is a tremendously heterogeneous text, which believers have used in almost innumerable ways and for
countless causes. In the time Bible courses have to dwell on the nuances of
the text, they must inevitably omit more than they cover. The crux of the
problem is that, as opposed to world religions courses, Bible courses are intensive enough to give students the *impression* that the two traditions re-

ceive full coverage, but they are not intensive enough to provide full coverage of each tradition *in reality.*

If the omissions of such courses favored or discouraged no view of Jewish and Christian faith, they would not constitute a serious problem. But even democratic states have their biases. First, states have an interest in generating obedience and allegiance, and public school curricula are likely to favor dominant groups, entrenched interests, and the status quo. Second, for more practical reasons of generating and maintaining community support, states and schools have an inherent interest in avoiding treatment of controversial and countercultural beliefs. Finally, the state has a natural interest in civic unity and in minimizing the differences between citizens, although this tendency has been more muted historically in liberal democratic societies. This bias toward homogeneity is akin to encouragement to accept the truth value of other religions, which, as chapter 1 argued, violates free conscience and must be strenuously avoided by schools. Combined together, these three impulses make it likely that Bible courses will tilt toward more mainstream and acceptable versions of Judaism and Christianity and away from controversial, countercultural, and prophetic versions, with a particular emphasis on what unites, rather than what divides, the two faiths. In the hands of public schools, intensive treatment of Judaism and Christianity is likely to convert them into "civil" religions in several senses of the term.

Indeed, a brief review of the history of education about the Bible in public schools reflects the presence of these biases. From the mid-nineteenth century until the exile of required devotional reading of the Bible that the Supreme Court imposed slightly over a century later, perhaps the most influential vision of how to treat the Bible in schools originated with Horace Mann.[9] The growing number of Catholic sects and the multiplication of Protestant sects in the nineteenth century made unfeasible the type of avowedly sectarian Bible teaching previously dominant. But if narrow proselytizing was not an option in public schools, neither was the exclusion of religion, at least not for long.[10] Doubt about religious truth may not have been absent in nineteenth-century America, as Abraham Lincoln's private conversations demonstrate, but Lincoln's own second inaugural address is evidence that even the more skeptical of Americans were loath to deny publicly the relationship between religion and morality.

Mann seized on this relationship as the adhesive that could bind Americans together while making them better republican citizens (Bellah and Hammond 1980, 74).[11] Christians may not be able to agree about whether God is three-in-one or just one—although Mann, as a Unitarian, favored the latter—but they could not help but embrace the Ten Commandments. The practical morality Mann believed the Bible conveyed and the Protestant establishment of the time favored the very virtues most conducive to republicanism. No one would benefit more from this education, Mann believed, than Catholic immigrants who came from countries lacking a republican tradition and whose American roots were allegedly not deep.[12]

Teaching the Bible was crucial in these unifying and assimilative processes. The specific form of Bible teaching Mann supported reflected his centripetal and hierarchical tendencies. He maintained that schools should concentrate on the practical biblical morality that binds, rather than the theological points that divide. "In no school," Mann wrote, "should the Bible have been opened to reveal the sword of Polemic, but to unloose the dove of peace" (Boles 1965, 26). Fearful that disagreement would overwhelm consensus, Mann stressed that the Bible should be read without notes or comments (Del Fattore 2004, 239), although his belief that students should read the King James translation of the Bible revealed his somewhat myopic notion of consensus. For someone who believed in an active form of government like republicanism, Mann's form of religious education was resolutely passive.

Mann's assimilative views on Catholics may appear coercive, but to be fair, he rejected firmly the Know-Nothing position that would exclude Catholics, and his nonsectarian education was more respectful of Catholic views than the staunchly sectarian teaching about the Bible that many favored prior to his innovations. Still, Mann's views reveal a lack of imagination. If he really could not foresee a time when the nonsectarian Protestantism he favored would no longer be as dominant, he not only misjudged the future but proved oblivious to the developing religious diversity around him.[13] The moderate, optimistic, rational version of Christianity he advocated, for instance, shared little in common with evangelical Christianity. Mann's reforms remind us that nonsectarianism in teaching the Bible is not the same as neutrality. More pluralistic than the sectarian model it followed, Mann intended his nonsectarian approach to educate and tame religion by excluding important points of view about religion, including not only, most obviously, Catholicism but also atheism and evangelical Christianity.

Mann's myopia is no less evident in his conception of the relationship between the state and religion. He may have believed genuinely that Christian and republican views were compatible, but his excision of controversial views in practice led to the subordination of Christianity to democracy. Religion, Mann seemed to believe, could only help the state when its views justified mainstream political and cultural institutions. Alexis de Tocqueville, visiting the United States at the same time Mann was implementing his reforms, arrived at the more profound view that religion often serves American democracy best when it resists dominant political and cultural trends and ideas.

By transforming reading of the Bible into a civic ritual, reducing Christian belief to general moral bromides, and placing an emphasis on homogeneity, Mann robbed the text of much of its substance.[14] Such ritualistic incantations not only cheapen religion but are antithetical to religion itself, because they ignore the calls to personal and social transformation that give religions much of their power. As Mann's most astute contemporary critic, the Catholic thinker Orestes Brownson, observed, "A faith which embraces generalities only, is little better than no faith at all" (Lasch 1995, 157). The hierarchical and passive approach that Mann recommends for learning the Bible poses a more subtle but equally dangerous threat to religion. "The real objection" to Mann's approach, contends Christopher Lasch (ibid.), "is that the resulting mixture is so bland that it puts children to sleep instead of awakening feelings of awe and wonder."

Concluding automatically that Mann's mistakes are endemic to any attempt to teach the Bible in schools would be a mistake, but so would deciding that their seeming remoteness makes them irrelevant to contemporary proposals. Mann's version of teaching the Bible—with its emphasis on civic unity, exclusion of controversial beliefs, and homogenization of religious views—reflects precisely the biases that states and public schools are likely to manifest when they focus intently on one faith. If these biases are evident in the main source that public schools drew upon for teaching about the Bible for over 100 years, we may reasonably wonder if certain pitfalls of the state's teaching of the Bible are endemic to *any* state teaching of the Bible.[15] Not all nonsectarian approaches to teaching the Bible do or must share Mann's agenda, but we should be skeptical of the neutral credentials of any nonsectarian attempt to teach about the Bible. Not all Bible courses that take account of civic goals do or must degenerate into ritualistic exercises in civil religion, but this is a trap into which state-sponsored Bible courses are likely to fall. Stephen Prothero identifies several of Mann's prejudices, but we must examine whether Prothero's own recommendations are completely free of Mann's biases and whether Prothero's account is able to provide the strenuous justification that required Bible courses need. If it is not, we must then see if any other way of teaching about the Bible in either the required or elective curriculum can meet these criteria.

## DIRECT BENEFITS: A BETTER QUALITY OF POLITICAL ARGUMENTS?

Horace Mann was concerned that Americans knew too much about the Bible. Stephen Prothero is concerned that they know too little. Mann's approach would have students concentrate on the parts of biblical morality they have in common, instead of the theological disputes that divide them. Prothero (2007, 95) reasonably apportions Mann a share of the blame for the appalling religious illiteracy that prevails in America today. The nondenominational approach was a factor in the decoupling of knowledge from faith and the long, slow trek to biblical ignorance that Prothero effectively describes. In a telling image he invokes several times, Prothero laments the loss of the "chain of memory" (80, 146) that once bound Americans and their religion to biblical stories, characters, and theology.

Correcting this ignorance is the foremost raison d'être of the required course on the Bible that Prothero endorses in *Religious Literacy*. Prothero also supports a required course in world religions, to provide students literacy about the many religions besides Judaism and Christianity that are now part of our nation. Like Jews and Christians, Prothero maintains (2007, 116), the more recent immigrants to America have succumbed to practicing "a religion without memory." Prothero assures us that "the Fall into religious ignorance is reversible" (121), but he does not recommend reviving the type of sectarian religious education that once dominated the American public school landscape. The "redemption" he offers is of "a different sort" (121). Still, his book evinces a preoccupation with the restoration of biblical knowledge. Over half of the book's text consists of a historical narrative that identifies the culprits responsible for the decline of biblical literacy. To restore the lost chain of memory that most concerns him, Prothero would teach students not only the major stories and characters of the Bible but its theology as well.

As often convincing as the narrative Prothero forges is, his focus on the restoration of lost links to the past suggests an immediate objection to a required Bible course. The course might indeed restore the links of Christians and Jews to their religious past, but what function can it serve for other believers and those atheists and agnostics who do not wish to be chained to any religious tradition? To offer the Bible as a universal course requires a universal justification. One possible answer is that the Bible's historical, literary, and artistic influence, especially in America, makes a required understanding of it a crucial part of a liberal education. While this argument warrants a greater "natural inclusion" of the Bible in existing required history and English courses, it hardly seems to justify a required, stand-alone course on the Bible. Plato's philosophy had a profound and, some have argued, decisive impact on early Christian theology. Harold Bloom, for one, makes a persuasive case that Shakespeare is responsible for the "invention" of the modern human. The Bible's influence is obviously immense and broader than Plato's or Shakespeare's, but if subsequent influence on Western and American culture is the sole criterion, the justification for privileging the Bible in a stand-alone required course does not outweigh the perception of bias it generates.

To Prothero's credit, he realizes that the influence argument alone is not sufficient to justify a universal course, and he uses civic justifications to supplement liberal educational ones. A civic justification for a required Bible course, according to Prothero, should not be confused with a *primarily* civic approach to teaching the Bible. Unlike Mann, Prothero (2007, 141) supports an education about the Bible that goes "beyond character education." He finds fault with both Jay Wexler's civic education for religion that would inculcate "tolerance, empathy, and mutual respect" and Diana Eck's desire to cultivate a "public commitment" to religious pluralism, because of the implicit threat they pose to firmly held religious convictions. But Prothero does believe that aiming to increase knowledge of the Bible can have important civic benefits justifying the course's universal relevance.

The most immediate, if not ultimately the most important, of these benefits is an enhanced ability to understand political arguments. What secularists, non-Jews, and non-Christians do not know about the Bible, contends Prothero (2007, 12), will hurt them. In a political environment awash in biblical references, secularists armed with biblical knowledge will be better able to recognize and respond to the implicit references evangelical politicians in particular send to their followers. If, however, believers, including the evangelical politicians and citizens most likely to use religious arguments, do not know much about the Bible, as Prothero claims, then the coded messages Prothero warns of have limited political value. In February 2008, National Public Radio's *All Things Considered* interviewed voters, several of whom described themselves as Christians, about three biblical references evangelical Republican presidential candidate Mike Huckabee used in his speeches. According to the reporter, finding people in this informal poll who understood the references proved "almost as hard as getting a camel through the eye of a needle." Interviewed for the segment, Prothero himself commented, "You could imagine that . . . this is [Huckabee's] secret code way that he could speak to evangelicals without alienating more secular people. But the faulty part of that strategy is that evangelicals don't even necessarily know these stories" (Hagerty 2008). What secularists do not know about the Bible will not hurt them if religious believers also do not know much. It may seem that the Bible course Prothero supports is proposing a cure for a civic disease the course itself will create. The course will enable believers and especially religious conservatives to transmit and receive biblical references that outsiders will then be obliged to pick up on.

But a deeper reading reveals a greater consistency in Prothero's argument. Prothero's most prominent civic claim is not so much that American politics is awash in religious references but that it is awash in religious references that have a weak or incorrect basis in the Bible. Prothero highlights, for instance, a recent court case in which a Colorado jury defended its decision to apply the death penalty by invoking the command in Deuteronomy 19:21 that "life shall go for life." If the jury had bothered to pay attention to the whole Bible, notes Prothero (2007, 37), they would have realized that Jesus directly repudiates this command at Matthew 5:38 in the Sermon on the Mount: "Ye have heard that it hath been said, 'An eye for an eye, and a tooth for a tooth'; but I say unto you, that ye resist not evil: but whosoever shall smite thee on thy right cheek, turn to him the other also." If using religion to justify political positions is widespread today and bound to persist in American politics for years to come, Americans might as well get their religious references right.

For Prothero (2007, 10), enlightenment about the Bible is also tied crucially to empowerment. Leaving ordinary Americans in the dark about religion is to condemn them to manipulation by religious extremists who can use the media to claim the religious high ground for ill-informed views. The value, then, of a universal course on the Bible for non-Jews and non-Christians is large, though also largely indirect. The rising quality of biblical references will enhance the overall quality of American politics and benefit all.

Prothero's general argument is commendable, and his position would be incontestable if he were simply exhorting Americans to get their biblical references right. But he is doing more than this; he is arguing that *public schools should help* Americans get their biblical references right. The history of allegedly nonsectarian Bible teaching reminds us that skepticism about neutrality is in order when schools address the Bible. Prothero's recommendation appears neutral on its face, but is it sufficiently devoid of the biases that have plagued Bible teaching traditionally?

Here, the attempt at an honest appraisal of Prothero's recommendations faces a serious obstacle. Understandably for an author concerned with holding the interest of a general readership, Prothero does not dwell on the specific details of how the required Bible course he proposes would work in practice. He does stress the importance of an objective teaching about religion. "Teachers should stick to describing and analyzing these religious traditions as objectively as possible," Prothero tells us (2007, 136), "leaving it up to students to make judgments about the virtues and vices of any one religion, or of religion in general."[16] This objectivity is to apply in matters political as well as religious. Prothero reassures readers that the "purpose" of his Colorado jury example "is neither to provide divine sanction for nonviolence nor to forestall a reading of the Bible in favor of capital punishment, but simply to offer yet another case study in the dangers of religious illiteracy" (38).

While Prothero's proposal is certainly less partisan than Mann's innovations, it is not terribly precise what shape the neutrality he supports will take in practice. The neutrality he supports could entail a stringent requirement that schools refrain from providing students any substantive civic direction. But such a policy would seem to negate the positive civic effects

Prothero envisions. For instance, would students under the same misconception as the Colorado jury Prothero gently chides realize on their own the conflict between the Deuteronomy and Matthew passages, out of all the Bible passages they read? Human nature being what it is, students left on their own are more likely to use the Bible to point out the specks in others' eyes rather than the logs in their own.[17]

Although we cannot be absolutely confident about what Prothero envisions, assuming that schools would take at least a slightly more hands-on approach to his position is more charitable. Required Bible courses need particularly strenuous justifications. The civic justifications Prothero advances, both those already discussed and those yet to be mentioned, fit the bill, and justifying a universal course without them is extremely difficult. Instead of leaving their realization to chance, the Bible course with the best chance of meeting the high bar for justification is one where schools play some active role in ensuring the important civic benefits Prothero claims. Assuming a more hands-on role is also most fair to Prothero's overall philosophy and historical narrative. Prothero, as we will see, composes a forceful narrative about the decline in the quality of American belief. If he is truly devoted to reversing this decline, public schools must play an active role in encouraging students to alter their beliefs.

An active role in shaping students' views about the Bible could mean directly influencing students' understanding about relationships between the Bible and particular political issues. Prothero's account appears, at times, to gesture toward this role. Less charitable critics might even be inclined to see a partisan leaning in the way Prothero envisions schools performing this role. The Colorado jury case is the only specific example he provides of how teaching the Bible would place political views on a firmer biblical footing, and the gloss he provides does favor a liberal political position. Prothero (2007, 86) demonstrates an even more pervasive general concern with popular associations between the Bible and sexual morality, complaining that the "term *Christian*" in contemporary American parlance "connotes opposition to abortion and gay marriage rather than faith in the incarnation and the redemption." He expresses hope that better education about these issues might clear up widespread misconceptions.[18]

Attempting to directly address students' misconceptions about the relationships between the Bible and particular political positions is fraught with problems. Conservative Christian fears about the likelihood of

schools and teachers cherry-picking biblical passages that favor liberal political positions would constitute a formidable political obstacle to implementing such courses. The history of Bible teaching suggests that these
fears are not far off the mark. Public schools might not have used Bible
teaching historically to favor progressive causes, but they have shown a
distinct tendency to favor conventional political beliefs. Prothero's required course appears to be ensnarled in a catch-22. If schools urge students actively to change their views, they will fall victim to charges of partisanship. If they fail to take an active role, they will not accomplish the
civic goals Prothero must rely on to justify a universal course. Fortunately
for his account, Prothero offers a more subtle conception of the active role
schools could take to alter students' political beliefs while avoiding this
dilemma.

## INDIRECT BENEFITS: CAN WE IMPROVE POLITICS BY IMPROVING RELIGION?

While Prothero's occasional concern with particular misconceptions about
the Bible seems to open him to charges of tendentiousness, his main concern is more profound and transcends simple partisanship. The identification of religion with a partisan side in a political debate is not his greatest
worry. He is far more anxious that liberals and conservatives alike too often
associate religion exclusively with specific moral and political positions.
"At least in popular parlance, what makes religious folks religious today,"
complains Prothero (2007, 101), "is not so much that they believe in Jesus'
divinity or Buddhism's Four Noble Truths but that they hold certain moral
positions on bedroom issues such as premarital sex, homosexuality, and
abortion." Prothero believes that the exclusive concentration on religious
morality is a major reason that many religious Americans are comfortable
with ignoring biblical knowledge.

Prothero's concern suggests that he envisions a Bible course addressing
students' political views actively in a more indirect way than the previous
section considered. Instead of targeting specific political beliefs with an ill-
informed biblical basis, Bible courses could aim at expanding students' understanding of Judaism and Christianity. By teaching students about the
Bible, schools would convey the message that knowing about the Bible is

an essential part of being a better Jew or Christian. Students with a greater commitment to biblical knowledge would be more careful about using religion in tendentious and partisan ways in political debates and would be better able to avoid misconceptions when they do.

Not only does this justification appear strong enough to justify a required Bible course, but perhaps even more appealingly, the indirect approach would produce these considerable civic benefits without involving the government in cherry-picking biblical quotes and passages. What could be wrong with a course that, without focusing on specific changes, merely urges Jews and Christians to incorporate greater knowledge of the Bible into their religious and political outlooks? That question verges on being rhetorical.

Still, the history of attempts to teach the Bible serves as a reminder that matters are not quite so simple. Neutral appearances can conceal real biases, and neutral intentions do not necessarily translate into neutral practice. To better assess the neutrality of urging Jews and Christians to incorporate more biblical knowledge into their religious outlooks, we need to delve deeper into the historical account Prothero provides. The account, which occupies over a third of *Religious Literacy*, is central to Prothero's argument. It shares with Jean-Jacques Rousseau's narrative on the state of nature the goal of unearthing the past to hold it up as a mirror to the imperfect present. Evoking regret for what we have lost provides incentive to return to a more golden age. Prothero presents his book's substantive argument in three sections entitled "Eden: What We Once Knew," "The Fall: How We Forgot," and "Redemption: What To Do." Postmodernists and those evangelicals who are often surprisingly sympathetic to their concerns[19] overstate the case when they argue that appeals for greater knowledge always conceal an ideological agenda, but the motivations of such appeals are worth taking into account. Studying Prothero's account of our fall can help us determine if the Eden he wishes our society to approximate by reviving biblical knowledge is entirely different from the type of Eden favored by Mann and the vital center of the 1950s.[20]

Prothero (2007, 59) begins his narrative in the colonies and the early republic, where "biblical wisdom was always in the air." Prothero explains that nine of every ten American households had a Bible (62) and that Bible reading was central in churches, public schools, and colleges. In true Tocquevillian fashion, civil society institutions like Sunday schools sprung up to ensure biblical literacy among the poor, and Bible and tract societies proliferated to ensure literacy in newly formed Western communities. Prothero depicts a time when "knowing what [Jesus] actually did" was at least as "important as having a relationship with" Jesus and when "knowing what the Bible has to say" mattered as much as "believing in the Bible" (86).

History has become more complicated since the original Fall, and there is more than just one tempting apple and sweet-talking charmer in Prothero's account. Mann's nondenominational education occupies a prominent place, as the attempt to teach religion in general discouraged knowledge of any particular religion. The "piety along the Potomac," to use the title of William Lee Miller's book on the topic, Eisenhower encouraged comes in for similar criticism. But while Prothero recognizes that history defies precise weighing of blame, his account does assign dubious pride of place in "our collective Fall" to the rise of evangelicalism (2007, 89). In contrast to an early American religion "about knowledge, learning and reading the word," Prothero contends,

> All that changed, however, with the rise to public power in the early nineteenth century of a new form of Protestantism called evangelicalism. By the end of that century a lack of elementary knowledge of Christianity would constitute evidence of authentic faith. What for generations had been shameful—religious illiteracy—would become a badge of honor in a nation besotted with the self-made man and the spirit-filled preacher. (88)

Born-again experience replaced the need for a well-rounded understanding of theology; ethics focusing on bedroom behavior eventually came to supplant a well-informed biblical morality.

Evangelicals and secularists alike are bound to object to the rhetoric Prothero employs in describing them. Prothero's decision to describe the decline of biblical literacy as a fall from Eden, where evangelicals play major roles (2007, 89), may not be the best way to engender faith among evangelicals that the Bible course he is proposing lacks an agenda. Prothero maintains that the critique that schools should not consider religion because "American political life should be utterly secular and religious reasons out of bound in political discourse" is "so silly that it hardly bears mentioning" (139).

Provocative language is often just a stylistic mechanism to catch people's attention, but the frequency of Prothero's critiques of evangelicals and secularists suggests that these views are not merely rhetorical. Prothero (2007, 106–7) argues that evangelicals in the late nineteenth century chose to "practice" a "Scarecrow faith bereft of a brain" and that "as time went on, Americans by the millions would choose piety and check their intellects at the churchhouse door." In an interview with the PBS show *Religion and Ethics Newsweekly,* evangelicals and secularists come in for dismissal in the same sentence. On the possible objections to his proposals, Prothero claims, "We can't be held hostage to either the secular left or the religious right on this question. Most of us are in the middle" (Abernethy 2007).

Prothero realizes, to be sure, that the changes in America's religious landscape since colonial times make a return to a golden age of biblical literacy impossible and even unattractive. Bible courses should not serve as a blunt instrument to proselytize to those who are not Christian or Jewish or to indoctrinate students into the bland and somewhat empty Christianity Mann prefers. But Prothero's preferred religious landscape is not completely unlike that of Mann or the 1950s civil religionists. He certainly desires Americans to be more informed about the biblical basis of their beliefs than either group, but he envisions using this emphasis on enhanced knowledge to revive a strong center of reasonable, moderate believers who can counter the irresponsible beliefs of religious extremists, who too often dominate the American religious landscape today. Americans are free, in Prothero's vision, to hold many kinds of beliefs and none at all. But the majority of Americans, he reasonably expects will continue to be Christians, and schools have an obligation to encourage them to temper their fervent emotionalism and attention to sexual morality with a sober and studious knowledge of the Bible.

Even granting that American religion and society might be better off with the transformation Prothero envisions and that he acknowledges the changes that have taken place in America's religious landscape, he still seems to overlook the *extent* of the change in America's religious and political consensus. Public schools in a democracy must satisfy the major elements of this consensus to be able to implement courses on religion in practice. As opposed to earlier in the twentieth century, a Bible course in today's religious landscape must appeal to influential and vocal evangelical groups. A course devoted to the transformation Prothero envisions, with its implicit critique of evangelicalism, could not pass this test. Secularists are also more prominent and influential than they once were. Even if secularists were to see an improvement in Jewish and Christian religion as favorable to their interests, the privileging of two religious traditions makes it very unlikely that they would support a required Bible course.

The deeper limitation of Prothero's historical account is not, however, its reluctance to grasp the way the religious landscape has changed but its unwillingness to acknowledge the possibility that this change in landscape may have occurred for good reasons. Prothero's account refuses to concede that religious concerns and consensus on which the age of biblical literacy was founded may simply have become outmoded and that the consensus— or, more appropriately, dissensus—that has emerged in its place may better meet the unique religious and cultural yearnings of America in the early twenty-first century. He ignores, in other words, that Americans might have gotten the religion we desired and perhaps even the religion we need.

Recognizing these possibilities certainly does not entail that Prothero's historical account is mostly wrong. His account has given not only historians of American religion and religious scholars but all Americans who seriously care about religion much weighty and plausible matter to ponder. This chapter leaves in-depth assessment of the accuracy of Prothero's claims to experts in the history of American religion and culture.[21] But Prothero is proposing the construction of a required Bible course aimed at returning us in part to a more golden age of biblical literacy. As a matter of fairness and respect, we must acknowledge that other groups may have narratives of their own about the transformation in American religion. The plausibility of these alternative accounts undermines Prothero's case for a universal course.

Secularists are most likely to find much to dispute in Prothero's causal account of "our collective Fall." The staunchly humanist account of John Dewey in *A Common Faith* (1991), arguing that literal understanding of the Bible loses relevance in the face of modern developments and scientific revelations, may be deficient in accounting for the decline of Bible reading. But so might a historical narrative like Prothero's, which fails to mention Darwinism once. Part of our increased ignorance may also be due to realizing, as a result of a more broad-based education, that, as the Clarence Darrow–inspired character in *Inherit The Wind* puts it, "the Bible is a book. And a good book. But it's not the *only* book" (Lawrence and Lee 1955, 123). Prothero's account is tinged with a sentimentality that often colors the Edens that humans claim to discover. The more distant a society is from us, the easier it is to attribute virtue to its members and ignore its limitations. Secularists are likely to remind us that the weakening of the chains of memory is less a cause for lamenting the loss of nurturing roots than reason for celebrating the elimination of limiting shackles.

Evangelicals, unlike secularists, believe that the decline in religion's prominence is a negative development. But this does not mean that most would share Prothero's views about the causes of the decline. Prothero may find the commitment to emotional faith lopsided in contemporary evangelicalism, but the greater emphasis on emotionalism since the Great Awakening of the 1730s has arguably provided many Americans with a direct, unmediated path to God that addresses their deepest spiritual yearnings. The concentration on matters of sexual morality may appear distorted from the perspective of more moderate and more broad-based Christianity, but to many evangelicals, it is a proportional reaction to the radical cultural shifts on these issues since the 1960s.[22] Evangelical comparisons between the pro-life and civil rights movements may indeed be overplayed and may ignore possible differences between the justice of each cause, but few today would accuse the Southern Christian Leadership Conference of the 1960s of lacking religious perspective because of an intense ethical concern with civil rights issues.

Perhaps more problematic than Prothero's specific slights against secularists and evangelicals is the general philosophy these slights reflect about democratic choice over religion. His skepticism of the free-market, democratic process of religious development is often explicit in his historical account. Prothero (2007, 105) endorses Richard Hofstadter's claim in *Anti-Intellectualism in American Life* that the "demands of democracy" were among the root causes of a turn in American culture where "inborn, intuitive folk wisdom" triumphed over the "broad cultivation" and emphasis on "classical learning" found in the Puritan colonists and the "sages" of the early republic. Prothero proceeds to link the democratization of politics and culture in the early nineteenth century with the rise of evangelicalism in producing the "shift from learning to feeling" that made a "virtue of its ignorance." The true cause of "our collective Fall," then, seems less to be the specific choices that particular religious groups made and more that ordinary Americans had too much unregulated choice over their religion in the first place. Prothero sees state institutions and particularly public schools as a healthy check on the free marketplace of religion. He certainly does not desire to replicate the European historical model by establishing one or more religious views, but he does see public schools as essential to managing the excesses of free religious choice.

The founding generation was not, of course, without its suspicions about democracy as a form of government, and the checks and balances in the constitutional system they put in place reflects these suspicions. But in adopting the First Amendment, its most farsighted members chose to tack a different, more democratic course concerning religion. Madison's famous *Memorial and Remonstrance* (Rakove 1999, 29–36) and Jefferson's *Notes on the State of Virginia* (1993, 252–57), both crucial inspirations for the First Amendment, advocate the creation of a free marketplace of religion that implicitly places trust in the religious judgments of the many. Instead of attempting to freeze religion in place or return it to an alleged golden age, Jefferson in particular predicted that religion would best retain its relevance when government allows beliefs to adapt to new social circumstances.

This trust was not blind. Respecting the robust religious diversity that free choice would inevitably produce meant accepting untutored fringe movements with suspect ideas that might occasionally pull parts of the center along with them. Allowing for the challenge of the existing religious consensus could produce healthy adaptations to cultural developments but also vulgar capitulations to the marketplace. Rather than seeing government as an essential check, however, Madison and Jefferson believed that the best remedy for the excesses of democratic choice over religion was democracy itself. In part, their views rested on an appreciation of the self-correcting tendencies of ordinary Americans' religious choices. But perhaps, unlike Mann and the 1950s civil religionists, they intuited that attempting to freeze the existing religious consensus in place would simply lead to a greater backlash against the center and to more extremism. Our reward for the founders' trust in religious free choice is a nation where religion remains far more vital than in any other Western democracy. This situation not only is fortunate for religion but has been essential for maintaining a diverse culture and has often allowed for the correction of unjust state practices through the countercultural criticisms religions often provide.

Even if this laissez-faire approach has served us well, perhaps the stakes are simply higher today, the fringes more lethal. "Faith without knowledge may or may not be dead," writes Prothero (2007, 146), "but our current mix of fervent religious belief and widespread religious ignorance is surely a dangerous combination." A possible response is that Prothero overstates the extent of the extremist threat and ignores the self-corrections to the alleged problems he identifies with evangelical beliefs. Large swaths of evangelicals and specifically younger evangelical leaders and believers, for instance, are increasingly rejecting an exclusive concern with bedroom morality. More liberal evangelicals like Jim Wallis are urging greater attention to poverty, but even influential social conservative leaders like Rick Warren and Joel Hunter and groups like the National Association of Evangelicals now pay considerable attention to the Christian imperatives of fighting global warming and the spread of AIDS in Africa (J. C. Hunter 2008; Fitzgerald 2006; Kirkpatrick 2007). All of this is happening without state or school involvement.

Still, religious extremists on the right and left remain influential, and this book shares with Prothero a deep concern with the political and social consequences of public schools' failure to address this extremism. Intolerance and a profoundly distorted conflict over religion and culture that drowns out the voices of more reasonable moderates are the costs of this failure. There are, however, more and less intrusive ways to address these problems. Even when the government has the right to challenge religious beliefs posing serious public consequences, it must use the most narrowly drawn and least intrusive means available to accomplish its ends. While tolerance and civil deliberation are crucial democratic concerns, the core principles of religious liberty impose a countervailing commitment. Public schools must strive, to the greatest extent possible, to take religious beliefs as they are and to avoid discouraging strongly held beliefs.

The recommendations in the previous chapters of this book involve an attempt to take these countervailing obligations seriously. The required world religions course endorsed in chapters 1 and 3 is intended to promote tolerance, but its meticulously descriptive nature is intended to avoid the effect of discouraging robust sectarian beliefs. Teaching the principles of good faith, as chapter 2 recommends, is concerned with transforming not extremist religious beliefs themselves but their expression in politics, by encouraging students to reformulate legitimate moral concerns based on religion into less sectarian and offensive political language. To the extent that these courses of action inevitably involve some push away from strong beliefs, they should be countered by curricular changes that recognize the robust beliefs challenged. The principle of good faith itself requires recognition of intelligent design theory in the elective curriculum, and, as I argue shortly, schools should also implement an elective course on Judaism and Christianity that gives voice to strong, countercultural religious beliefs.

Prothero does express a genuine concern with protecting robust religious beliefs. He describes tolerance as "an empty virtue in the absence of firmly held and mutually contradictory beliefs" (2007, 143) and rejects a religious education aimed at "foster[ing] a 'public commitment' to the ideals of multiculturalism" (141). But the protection of robust beliefs that Prothero recognizes in theory is at odds with what he recommends in practice. The required Bible course he supports attempts to improve the quality of religious references in politics by focusing on transforming Jewish and Christian religious beliefs themselves rather than just their political manifestations. Not only are schools likely to emphasize biblical knowledge that favors mainstream over countercultural beliefs in practice, but the very goal of encouraging Jewish and Christian students to incorporate a greater emphasis on biblical knowledge and doctrine into their beliefs constitutes an inappropriate intrusion on religious free choice. The burden of Prothero's proposal falls heaviest on those with conservative Jewish and Christian beliefs. One explicit aim of the required Bible course is to expand the religious horizons of those believers who place excessive emphasis on religious experience and bedroom morality. Adding in the required world religions course Prothero supports only increases the pressure conservative Christians would feel to adapt their beliefs under his recommendations.

Even granting the most charitable interpretation of his recommendations, Prothero's required Bible course is not able to survive the stringent scrutiny such proposals involve. A weaker, hands-off version of the course would not produce the significant civic benefits such a course must deliver to outweigh the privileging of Judaism and Christianity they entail. A more strenuous version of the course emphasizing the enhancement of biblical knowledge might deliver substantial civic benefit by improving allegedly ill-conceived political arguments, but it would come at the inadmissible

price of violating neutrality. A narrower addressing of the political manifestations of religious beliefs that is more consistent with core principles of
religious freedom could achieve the same civic benefits.

## NOT REDEMPTION, BUT ASCENSION

That Prothero's civic justification does not support teaching a required
Bible course does not mean the status quo is acceptable. Students' basic
grasp on the meaning of world and American art, literature and culture,
and causality in world and American history is tenuous at best. The woeful
state of biblical literacy Prothero identifies only further loosens their grip
(Wachlin 2005). Enhancing the "natural inclusion" of the Bible in required
literature and social studies courses is a necessary remedy. But such required courses must cover a lot of material, and the necessarily restricted
discussion of the Bible in these courses will always fail to do justice to its diversity of themes and historical influence. The liberal educational value of
knowing more about the Bible may not be sufficient to outweigh the religious privileging that a required Bible course would entail.

Elective Bible courses that are not sectarian exercises are less likely to
privilege one tradition and feed the perception of privileging, and they do not
require as strenuous a justification. The special and continuing historical and
cultural influence of the Bible is adequate to justify the decision of a state like
Georgia (Jonsson 2006) to provide special support to all schools that provide
an elective course on the Bible. Requiring students to take an extended course
about the Bible can be intrusive, but students of all faiths and none should
have the option of learning more about the Bible if they choose.[23] Prothero
(2007, 35) correctly notes that a significant number of religious believers
across the spectrum, including prominent evangelicals like Mark Noll and Os
Guinness, share his concern with biblical illiteracy and hope that public
schools could provide a greater impetus to their children to learn more.[24]

The strongest argument for having every school offer an elective course
on the Bible is a civic one, although it is not among the civic arguments that
Prothero offers. Schools can maintain the current religious consensus in
two ways. They can mostly ignore religion as they currently do, but this
comes at the impermissible cost of intolerance and religious and cultural
conflict. Promoting tolerance and a more civil dialogue through a required

world religions course, however, can have a syncretistic and ecumenist effect and can send religious conservatives an alienating message that public schools are deaf to their interests. The solution is to provide recognition of the sectarian beliefs of conservative Christians. To do so in the compulsory curriculum would be contrary to the promotion of tolerance and would alienate secularists and religious minorities, but it is less problematic in the elective curriculum. A course with a robust discussion of intelligent design is one form of recognition, but views on evolution are only one part, albeit an important part, of conservative Christian worldviews. Bible courses would provide a more wide-ranging and robust form of recognition to these views (as well as Conservative and Orthodox Jewish beliefs), and many conservative Christians support them. Their inclusion is not only consistent with democratic norms but would have the practical benefit of reconciling conservative Christians to a required world religions course.

Even if ample justification exists for Bible electives in all schools, neutrality remains an obstacle to their implementation. Courses that concentrate exclusively on conservative Christian views clearly offend democratic norms of fairness. Though its partiality is more subtle than the conservative Christian or Mann-inspired alternatives, even Prothero's emphasis on greater knowledge of the Bible reflects a partial agenda. If even the facially neutral goal of encouraging greater knowledge is biased, could any conceivable Bible course survive scrutiny? Concluding that these alternatives are exhaustive and that all attempts to teach the Bible in public schools must suffer from some form of fatal bias would be overly hasty. Fortunately, the recognition argument not only justifies the inclusion of a Bible elective but specifies an acceptably fair approach to teaching about the Bible, which schools should implement.

For all their important differences, the forms of teaching that Mann and Prothero recommend share essential features. Both approaches are top-down, centripetal, and nostalgic. The public school has a definite message that it wishes to communicate to students about the religions examined. This message seeks to maintain the religious consensus in place or to recall features of a previous golden age of religious belief. To ensure that students receive the course's message effectively, academic experts and school administrators are primarily responsible for the construction of the curriculum. Neither religious communities during the curricular construction process nor students in the classroom where the course takes place are conceived as playing an especially active role in defining the course's aim or message.

The recognition argument demands a more ascending, open-ended, and dynamic approach to teaching about the Bible. An ascending approach begins from the premise that even if consensus forms of Judaism and Christianity once existed in America, they no longer exist today. American religion today has no center, and it is not the job of public schools to create one. Rather than communicating a message about better and worse ways to approach the religious beliefs examined, Bible courses using an ascending approach would attempt to avoid giving students the impression that one way of being religious is superior to any other.[25] Instead of attempting to improve on existing beliefs, an open-ended teaching about the Bible would strive to present the different beliefs Americans hold and to give religious communities a meaningful role in the course's construction. By doing so, it would strive to give significant voice to religious beliefs critical of dominant cultural trends. A dynamic approach to teaching the Bible would not attempt to lock in religious beliefs or revert them to an earlier form but would recognize the adaptation of religious beliefs to historical and cultural developments and would allow for future developments.[26]

To summarize, an ascending approach recognizes the choices citizens have made to produce the current state of religious beliefs as valid, and it places more faith in the free market of religion than in government mentoring of religious beliefs. Not blind to the possibility that citizens can make poor choices, the basic premise of the ascending approach is that the free-market approach best preserves the relevance and vitality of religious beliefs, enables American religion to serve the countercultural role Tocqueville and Roger Williams celebrated, and is often more effective than the state in correcting the poor choices it occasionally produces.

Satisfying these requirements may not require a radical break from the status quo after all. One of the most widely used resources in current Bible elective courses is *The Bible and Its Influence* (*BI*) published by the Bible Literacy Project (BLP).[27] The BLP claims the implementation of its curriculum in 181 school districts in 38 states (Bible Literacy Project 2008). *BI* and the BLP aim at enhancing Bible literacy and the recognition of the Bible's historical, cultural, and artistic influence, but these aims are not grounded explicitly in a predisposition about the preferred shape of America's religious consensus.[28]

To ensure neutrality, the BLP commissioned a careful review of *BI* by a wide range of Jewish and Christian groups, including major evangelical groups, prior to publication, and it encourages students to use their own preferred version of the Bible in class. Often sensitive to the divergent ways Jews and Christians think about the Bible,[29] the text is, for instance, careful to describe the first part of the Bible as the Hebrew scriptures rather than the Old Testament. This scrupulous attention to neutrality has paid handsome dividends in the form of endorsements by a spectrum of religious groups, including the National Association of Evangelicals, and prominent evangelicals, such as Chuck Colson.

The consensus around the curriculum is impressive but not perfect. Unanimity is a standard that no public school curriculum could meet, but a particularly wide consensus is more morally imperative and practically necessary when schools address the Bible. Many hard-line evangelical and fundamentalist Christians have expressed unhappiness with *BI*. They have instead expressed support for an alternative curriculum sponsored by the National Council on Bible Curriculum in Public Schools (NCBCPS).[30] Many of the critiques that NCBCPS's supporters, such as the late D. James Kennedy, have leveled at the BLP are the typical fare of a culture war, more appropriate for cable television than serious scholarly discussion.[31] The NCBCPS curriculum itself blatantly favors a conservative, literalist form of Christianity favorable to the religious and political agenda of the religious right, making it strongly inappropriate for implementation in public schools.[32] But a close examination of *BI* does reveal that reason for concern is not completely unfounded and that conservative evangelicals are not the only group entitled to such concern.

Ironically, it is the very attempt of *BI* to avoid controversy that is most controversial. As its title indicates, the overall emphasis of the textbook is to communicate to students the literary qualities of the Bible and particularly its influence on later literary texts. Unit features call attention to the way the Bible figures in works such as Handel's *Messiah* and the works of such artists as Shakespeare and Dickens. This approach would appear above controversy. The Bible's literary influence is indisputable to believers and nonbelievers alike. But the Bible is, of course, no ordinary piece of literature. The Bible makes claims to ultimate truth that go well beyond more limited claims to truth in nonsacred literature, and many Jews and Christians interpret the Bible as literally true.

*BI* meticulously avoids casting doubt on the literal truth of the account in Genesis or the parting of the Red Sea. But many students, let alone parents and community members, are not deaf to the implications of treating the Bible as a literary text. When culture warriors like Paul Weyrich and the late D. James Kennedy criticize *BI* for claiming that the Ark of the Covenant "has become famous in Western imagination," this is surely a case of bad-faith nit-picking. But *The Bible Literacy Report* (Wachlin 2005), sponsored by the BLP and published to assess the current state of teaching about the Bible, found that 20 percent of the 41 teachers interviewed reported issues with students who were "practicing" Christians.[33] "The most common problem with such students," the report found, "was that they became upset if the teacher referred to stories in the Bible as 'myths'" (17). The Bible's literary influence is uncontroversial, but its significance beyond this influence is not.

Recognition of the possible higher meaning of the Bible is not the only casualty of *BI*'s controversy-free approach. Prothero (2007, 134) notes that the textbook confines itself to the literary influence of the Bible but does not address the Bible's "afterlife" in politics and economics. This is generally accurate but not precisely correct. The textbook mostly stays on the safer territory of the past but does occasionally mention relatively contemporary social and political movements based in the Bible. The Hebrew scriptures' prophetic tradition, *BI* notes (Schippe and Stetson 2006, 132), inspired Martin Luther King Jr., Cesar Chavez, Elie Wiesel, and the pacifist work of the American Friends Service committee. The biblical account of Nehemiah's wall and Jesus' humble service to the poor inspired, respectively, the anti-poverty efforts of Rev. Johnnie Ray Youngblood in New York City and Mother Teresa in India (ibid., 187, 246). Readers probably will note that all of the social justice movements that *BI* associates with the Bible are usually associated with the left in American politics. Mother Teresa's ministry to the poor receives mention, but her staunch opposition to abortion does not. An entry for abortion, in fact, is missing from *BI*'s index.

Based on this evidence, a culture warrior might leap to the conclusion that *BI* suffers from a secular humanist bias. But the bipartisan composition of the textbook's consultants, advisers, and reviewers renders this claim implausible. The desire to avoid controversy is a far more reasonable explanation of *BI*'s choices. Abortion and gay marriage are subjects of great dispute in American culture today, but who today disagrees with the justice of equal civil rights and feeding the poor? *BI* focuses on the Bible's influence almost exclusively on past movements of social justice because the causes they fought for have largely been settled; the text avoids deep treatment of current movements for moral or social justice because the causes they fight for have not been settled. Had *BI* been published in the 1960s, we may reasonably wonder if civil rights would have been given the cold shoulder. *BI* has no intention of urging Americans to move their beliefs to the religious center. But its aversion to controversy omits a robust discussion of biblical views critical of the religious and political center and presents students with a biblical religion largely shorn of its countercultural content.

The limits of *BI* reflect the limits of teaching about the Bible by using a single textbook written primarily by religious scholars. When schools use such textbooks, they give students the impression that the views expressed have the special, official approval of the school and the state. The lack of specific authors feeds the belief that the content derives from a universal perspective above the partisan fray. By its very nature, this official status makes it extremely difficult, if not impossible, to recognize countercultural views. Had *BI* decided to discuss how the Bible inspires social movements about live controversies like abortion, gay marriage, and global warming, complaints from the left and right would surely have ensued. Academic-style textbooks are often perceived as the official mouthpieces of the state, and Americans are right to demand that the state in a liberal democratic education speak in neutral tones. The state has an obligation to remain aloof from the endorsement of controversial social causes.

Even though it does not explicitly endorse a single-textbook approach, the approach taken by the other major nonsectarian organization devoted to biblical education has similar limitations, despite its considerable virtues. Like the BLP, the Society for Biblical Literature (SBL) is a nonsectarian organization consisting of teachers, academics, and clergy members supportive of increasing teaching about the Bible in public schools. The BLP and SBL share a concern with exposing students to multiple interpretations and translations of the Bible (Society for Biblical Literature 2009, 13). But the SBL guidelines seem more aware of the possible top-down biases of Bible electives and try to counteract them by emphasizing robust local participation in their construction. The guidelines recommend the formation of committees at the school district level, consisting of "students, parents,

222 TEACHING ABOUT RELIGIONS

teachers, and school administrators," to elicit "responses to the electives, review curricular materials, and make a recommendation to the board" (ibid., 11). Rather than a single-textbook approach, the guidelines "suggest using secondary literature, or assigning several different translations of the Bible, and then supplementing with readings from various academic sources" (13). The guidelines also note that the SBL "hopes to produce specific lesson-plans for high school teachers" in the near future (14).

Without the specific lesson plans in hand, evaluating the effect and reception of the SBL approach is difficult. Still, while its bottom-up features and concern with diversity are commendable, the guidelines offer several strong hints that the prospective SBL curriculum would not go far enough in providing recognition or accommodation of the concerns of all religious perspectives examined, especially conservative Christian perspectives. The guidelines, for instance, eschew a single-textbook approach but assume that Bible electives would focus exclusively on academic sources. They recommend that local communities should have a say in reviewing the curricular materials, but they do not mention the role of religious communities in the selection or preparation of materials relating to their religious perspectives. The guidelines place particular emphasis on teaching the Bible as "ancient literature in its historical context" (Society for Bible Literature 2009, 11), but they pay little attention to exposing students to the dynamic developments in viewing the Bible in America today or the varying centrality of the Bible among different American Jewish and Christian groups today. Indeed, the guidelines themselves seem to anticipate the objection of many conservative Christians. In explaining why a required Bible course would be inappropriate, the guidelines offer,

> Most importantly, students may believe that the very act of approaching the Bible from a critical or academic (rather than a religious) perspective violates their religious beliefs and practices. These students should not be required to take such a course. (ibid., 8)

Bible electives, the guidelines thus imply, must choose between the lesser of two biases. The overtly sectarian approach of the NCBCPS is clearly alienating and unconstitutional (Society for Biblical Literature 2009, 14). But the apparently "objective" academic approach that the SBL and

BLP advocate is bound to alienate many conservative Christians. The ascending, civic approach recommended here, by contrast, offers a mean between these two extremes and a way to recognize a variety of religious perspectives while alienating none.

Rather than attempting to deny controversy by conforming to the existing religious consensus, a genuinely ascending approach must embrace dissensus. Instead of being presented with one academic textbook claiming to be largely above the partisan fray, students in a genuinely ascending Bible class would read several different texts or statements prepared by major Jewish and Christian groups.[34] In the course's section on Judaism, for instance, students would spend equal time reading statements prepared by major Reform, Conservative, Orthodox, and neo-Orthodox committees. Study of Christianity would involve examining views presented by major mainline Protestant, evangelical Protestant, fundamentalist Protestant, Catholic, Unitarian, Orthodox, and Mormon groups.[35] Each group would be free to focus on the major concerns that animate them and that they believe make their views relevant to religious and social circumstances in the United States today.

Unlike the textbook approach, this bottom-up approach would allow for the expression of divergent views on crucial issues. By steering clear of controversy and focusing on the Bible's literary influence, *BI* would give the impression to more literal-minded students that Bible stories are myths. In a bottom-up approach, evangelical groups would be able to express their support for a more literal interpretation of the Bible, just as mainline Protestant groups could express their devotion to a more allegorical interpretation. A bottom-up approach would allow for the expression of divergent views not only about how to read the Bible but about the centrality of the Bible itself to Judaism and Christianity. Indeed, rather than "Introduction to the Bible," a more apt title for the elective course a bottom-up approach requires would be "Judaism, Christianity, and the Bible."

Prothero's proposed Bible course conflicts with democratic norms by encouraging Jewish and Christian students to make biblical knowledge a more, if not *the,* central element of their faith. He intends the emphasis on a more broad-based biblical knowledge to widen the concerns of religious conservatives who he believes are overly concerned with bedroom behavior. But encouraging a greater emphasis on biblical knowledge might also conflict with the views of many liberal Jews and Christians. Though valu-ing the Bible, these believers may give equal or greater priority in their faith lives to modern social injustices that the Bible does not directly address or to shared cultural, ethnic, and historical experiences.

The bottom-up approach would, of course, allow religious groups to focus on their views about the Bible if their faith conception makes the Bible central, and many would undoubtedly choose to do so. But it would also give groups the freedom to stress whatever mixture of Scripture, ex-perience, and morality characterizes their beliefs.[36] Groups could stress that other elements of their faith perspective are as important as and per-haps even more important than their view of the Bible. Even where faith traditions share a belief in the centrality of the Bible to their views, they still believe that the parts of the Bible interact in fundamentally different ways. An ascending approach would enable them to communicate this to students. Making material from religious groups themselves the center of a course about Judaism and Christianity would better allow American re-ligion the room to adapt to new circumstances, as opposed to an academic approach that would more likely prune and shear developments allegedly inconsistent with America's religious roots. Instead of insisting that Amer-ica's religious Eden is past, a bottom-up approach would allow for the possibility that it is as yet unseen and perhaps even in the process of being realized.[37]

Equally valuable is the challenge that a truly bottom-up approach would pose to the cultural, social, and political status quo. Even academic textbooks with the best of intentions, like *BI*, have an inherent tendency to ignore countercultural critiques. To be fair, *BI* chose the lesser of two evils. An academic text seemingly written from a universal perspective that even suggested, for instance, a biblical basis for controversial movements—such as those against abortion and gay marriage and to prevent global warm-ing—would stir complaints that the state is providing official recognition and favor of these movements. At least, critics would argue that this is the impression students would receive. A bottom-up approach is better equipped to walk the perilous tightrope of presenting countercultural cri-tiques without stirring excessive controversy.

Giving voice to religious groups would make clear to students that these views represent the beliefs of some and perhaps many Jews and Christians but not all and that they bear no official state approval. Students would be aware that these critiques come from partial points of view open to question and debate rather than from a universal point of view with implied legitimacy. The fault with single academic textbooks like *BI* discussing controversial views lays not with the discussion of these views themselves in the classroom but with parents' valid concern that governmental approval or recognition of these views is a formidable influence to combat in the struggle for students' minds and souls. Attributing these views directly to religious groups themselves is more consistent with neutrality and likely to be less alarming.

Still, while Roger Williams and Alexis de Tocqueville may be right about the value of countercultural religion in general, the expression of particular critical views may contradict basic democratic norms like active tolerance, which previous chapters of this book endorse. The social concerns some religious groups hold on issues like gay marriage are profoundly alienating. The religious beliefs of others are critical of different faiths and deeply divisive. Allowing groups to express these beliefs could undermine tolerance, even if stifling their expression prevents recognition.

Underestimating this conflict would be a mistake, but appropriate guidelines might go far to defuse it.[38] Schools should encourage religious groups to present positive affirmations and should discourage the expression of negative critiques.[39] Many evangelical Christians, for instance, reject ecumenism and believe that accepting their faith is the only path to salvation. Schools should encourage these groups to focus on why they believe that salvation through Christ's atonement is central to their faith, rather than allowing them to dwell on the alleged errors of those who reject this doctrine. Religious groups concerned with the problem of divorce should focus on the advantages of a stable, two-parent family, rather than castigating single parents or out-of-wedlock births.

Even when such restrictions apply, the criticism religious groups are able to express may still be painful, but the expression of these criticisms need not be the final word. Just as a pluralistic, bottom-up approach allows some religious groups to go on the offense, it allows other religious groups to go on the defense. Mainline Christians and liberal Jews concerned about evangelical Christian endorsement of heterosexual marriage could devote space in their statements to defense of a more open definition of marriage.[40] Indeed, this is a chief advantage of an elective and ascending approach to teaching about Judaism and Christianity.[41]

## CIVIL POLITICS AND UNCIVIL RELIGION

Even if tolerance can survive an ascending approach, civility may not. This potentially fatal contradiction has loomed over this chapter since its outset. A major purpose of teaching about religion, chapter 1 argues at great length, is to smooth out the excessively rough edges of our present democratic discourse. Religion and politics is a combustible mix that could explode if left unregulated. The principle of good faith is, to borrow John Courtney Murray's famous term, an article of peace intended to reconcile secularists and religious conservatives. It would allow believers to rely on their religious views in part, but it would encourage them to rely equally on less sectarian justifications especially in public argument.

A course about Judaism and Christianity, this chapter argues, must strive to preserve the jagged edges of countercultural and prophetic beliefs as part of America's religious landscape. A model based on the classical Greek temple—with balanced, reasonable, and harmonious religions—may be attractive, but the nature of religion in America today resembles more a Gothic church, with its heterogeneity, lack of proportionality, and excess. The ascending approach would allow religious groups to present to students the connection between their moral and social concerns and their sectarian interpretations of the Bible. Recognizing these beliefs runs the risk of implicitly encouraging students to use precisely the sectarian justifications for public policy that the principle of good faith would discourage.

Not only the argument of this book or the coherence of the school curriculum it recommends but also the triumph of America's unique experiment with political and religious democracy hangs in the balance. A successful democratic politics requires reasonable and civil discourse, including restraint on the use of religion in politics. But our commitment to religious democracy and liberty requires the state to take a laissez-faire approach to the development of religion. The balance between the two commitments has been always precarious and at times downright untenable. Prominent members of the founding generation, like Jefferson and Madison, had a faith, perhaps naive, that though the fit between civil politics and uncivil religion could never be perfect, the two could coexist. But the civil religionists of the 1950s denied that the contradiction can be eased substantially. Sufficient political unity in a democracy cannot persist in the face of religious dissensus, they believed, and we must sacrifice some religious democracy for the survival of political democracy. The Constitution, after all, is not a suicide pact, and the spirit, if not the letter, of the First Amendment must yield to concerns about civic harmony.

A comprehensive answer to the profoundly intricate questions of if and how religious and political democracy fit together is beyond this book's scope. What I do hope to accomplish is to suggest tentatively an answer to the general question of whether the two can fit together anywhere, by paying attention to the specific instance of whether the two can fit in the school curriculum. If there is reason to believe that public schools can honor the principles of good faith and religious democracy *at the same time,* then perhaps the larger faith of Jefferson and Madison is not misplaced even today.

A possible solution to the problem begins with the recognition that there is less of a contradiction between the two principles than at first appears to be the case. There is nothing directly contradictory about teaching the principles of good faith alongside a study of the biblical or sectarian basis of moral and social concerns. The principles of good faith not only allow citizens to rely on sectarian arguments in private belief and in discussions with like-minded believers but grant a significant political role for these beliefs as well; sectarian beliefs can serve as the inspiration for political positions and as "tiebreakers." Bible courses can allow believers to recognize the sectarian root of their beliefs and can still encourage them to use more secular arguments in political discussions with those who do not share their beliefs. The course on Judaism and Christianity proposed here could encourage students to maintain or develop countercultural critiques based on their religion and Scripture while simultaneously encouraging them to present these critiques in more nonsectarian terms in the public square.

An even more important misconception to correct, however, is the idea that liberal democratic values and the recognition of sectarian religious views must stand in opposition to each other. Civil religionists of the 1950s held this straightforward, dichotomous view, and many secularists hold it today. According to this view, allowing for the recognition of sectarian views in the school curriculum, even when accompanied by the principles of good faith, would simply give encouragement to religious conservatives to use these arguments in public debate. The recognition of religious conservative sectarian arguments would resonate, but the encouragement of good faith would go in one ear and come out the other. Schools must discourage use of these views and promote more allegedly reasonable religious beliefs, as Mann proposed, or must at least ignore sectarian views.

The history of public schools attempting to suppress or replace sectarian views reveals the simplistic psychological assumptions and lack of imagination of this narrative. Correctly interpreting the teaching of a moderate civil religion as an attempt to suppress their voices, evangelicals in particular reacted by becoming even more vociferous and sectarian. Culture warriors on the right continue to exploit the ignoring of religious conservative beliefs to convince their more moderate brethren of the hostility of public schools and American culture and to justify their own vitriolic attacks on the left.

Modesto, by contrast, took a more creative approach. Mediators and school administrators understood that democratic values and recognition of strong sectarian views often can be made to operate in a symbiotic, rather than antagonistic, relationship. By including religious conservatives in the process of constructing the school curriculum, many religious conservatives bought into—often enthusiastically—a world religions course intended to advance the major democratic value of tolerance. Modesto's experience suggests that when secure in the understanding that public schools are finally giving their voices a fair and respectful hearing, religious conservatives are more prone to a generous and open-minded consideration of alternative political views than many secularists give them credit for.

To be fair, Modesto incorporated religious conservatives into the process of constructing the curriculum, rather than including a robust discussion of religious conservative views in the compulsory or elective curriculum. Moreover, Modesto is only one instance; it does not provide conclusive evidence that a dialectical approach of strengthening commitment to the principles of good faith by simultaneously recognizing sectarian beliefs would work. Public schools historically have excluded discussion of religion, taught sectarian beliefs uncoupled from democratic guidance about their use, and encouraged a civil religion to counter sectarian beliefs. Conclusive evidence about the dialectical approach must wait until public schools teach recognition of sectarian views alongside good-faith guidance. But the powerful imperative of staying true to America's twin commitments to political and religious democracy compels us to try the dialectical approach, and Modesto's experience and Christian Smith's and Alan Wolfe's research about evangelicals suggest that it might work.

Besides, secularists have little to lose in the process of experimenting. Recognition puts the truce proposals of religious conservatives to the test. If religious conservatives are not satisfied by robust recognition of their beliefs, secularists can use this as evidence of bad faith and battle for greater secularization as an antidote. If religious conservatives are content, as the example of Modesto suggests they are likely to be, the results are even happier for not only secularists but American democracy. Understanding that their fear of a Christian nation has been exaggerated, secularists will realize that religious conservatives can be reasoned with rather than just shouted at.

An even more important, if less obvious, way in which the teaching about Judaism and Christianity recommended here can challenge the idea of a Christian nation stands to benefit not only secularists but evangelicals. An ascending approach can reshape students' conceptions about the proper relationship between religion and the state in a way that can enhance civil political dialogue and attachment to the principle of good faith.

The ability of religions to transform politics, culture, and society depends on an attitude toward the state that is at once attached and detached. Too much of an ascetic distance from politics defeats religion's prophetic function (Mathewes 2007b). Retreating too far into the wilderness of dissidence only ensures that one's preaching will not be heard. Besides, the compassion that many religions preach for the victims of injustice compels not only political participation but, at times of great injustice, the willingness to assume political power. Taking pride in the special potential destiny of one's nation, its people, and its political form can serve as a powerful inspiration to bring heavenly ideals to bear on earthly affairs. Still, an excessive compatibility between a religion and the state is the recipe for religious and political disaster. Such familiarity most obviously breeds contempt among those of different faiths and no faith at all who are excluded from the alliance. But the religions who make this Faustian bargain also often gain the world at the expense of their souls. Pride and self-interest too often blind powerful religions to the ills of the body politic and mute criticism even of recognized ills.

Even when American religions recognize the need for this balance in spirit, worldly temptations can tip them toward the rewards of state identification. Christian Smith (2000) has shown that the idea of Christian America may not mean to evangelicals what secularists think it means, but many evangelicals too often sanction unquestioning patriotism and see the state as the partner of the church. Mann and the civil religionists of the 1950s made the opposite mistake by appointing religion the junior partner of the state and attempting to create a religion hospitable to democratic ends.

Communicating the at least occasional tension between the demands of democratic citizenship and of one's religion is inherent in the structure of an ascending approach to teaching about Judaism and Christianity. On the one hand, recognizing the political and social concerns of each religion suggests the legitimacy of students bringing their religion to bear on politics. Religious freedom, schools should imply and express, allows citizens to strive for the realization of the vision of the good society their faith endorses. On the other hand, exploring a plurality of views about the interaction of religion and politics also reminds students that they live in a society where other traditions, even within their very own religion, hold often dramatically different interpretations about this relationship. Democracy is unique, schools ought to remind students, in requiring citizens to recognize obligations of fairness to others. Successful democratic politics requires consensus building with those who hold very different religious and political views and understandings of the relationship between church and state. Sectarian appeals may be counterproductive in light of these differences.

Secularists are rightly concerned with the glib assumption of many evangelicals that God can only be invoked on one side of political debates like those about gay marriage and capital punishment. Good faith cannot coexist with such naive faith. When schools challenge students to consider that their conclusions about the particular version they hold of the relationship between politics and religion are wrong, they trample on the rights of parents and religious communities. But schools can remind students simply that others who hold different views about capital punishment and gay marriage may also believe that their views are grounded in faith and the Bible. By challenging politically naive faith, schools can start students down the path of good faith.

By reminding students of the occasional tension between democratic and religious demands, the ascending approach can also play a role in helping religions to reclaim their critical, countercultural function. The central message of the ascending approach is that American democracy currently has no religious center. The more that each faith, whether evangelical or centrist, realizes that American democracy is currently the possession of no one faith, the more they will realize that a major function of their faith is not to legitimize but to criticize the status quo. This does not, of course, mean that each religion cannot aspire to make their visions central. But students will realize that these visions are aspirations to be contended for by navigating pluralistic interests in a democracy, rather than facts reflecting the status quo.

## HUMILITY AND DEMOCRATIC FAITH

For the final word on how public schools can help reconcile civil politics and uncivil religion, we must return to and end with the period with which this chapter began and with the thought of its most notable prophet, Reinhold Niebuhr. To be sure, Niebuhr hardly constituted a still small voice in the wilderness amid the triumphalism of the vital center and the blaring trumpets of public piety. He was a frequent contributor to the quintessential midcentury American magazine, Henry Luce's *Life*. His support for maintaining prayer in the schools and castigation of the young Billy Graham's revivals suggest that Niebuhr was not immune from serving as the mouthpiece of moderation. Despite these occasional lapses, Niebuhr had both the prophetic vision to realize and the courage to reveal to Americans that their parading of a moderate Christianity compatible with democracy lacked perhaps the most central of all Christian virtues—humility.

Humility takes several forms in Niebuhr's thought, and not all its forms are appropriate for transmission in a public education. In Niebuhr's view, the root of humility lies, of course, in the Christian concept of original sin. Though a Niebuhrian Christian may be right that human nature is flawed and fallible, public schools must refrain from encouraging any particular conception of human nature. Similarly, to preach that students should maintain some skeptical distance from their own religious and moral beliefs would intrude on students' free conscience.

But the *implications* that Niebuhr drew from the doctrine of original sin for the relationship between religion and democratic politics are relevant and sufficiently nonsectarian for schools to transmit to students. Against the overly simplistic identification of religion and democracy prevalent in the 1950s, Niebuhr largely resisted the temptation to declare the United States an expression of God's will on earth. Niebuhr's insight was not limited, of course, to the United States. Like Augustine, he held the central political belief that no form of government, state, or nation can be considered the complete incarnation of divine will and justice, that the contingent can never embody the absolute (Silk 1988, 47). In this view, any religion that associates itself with the state succumbs to pride, and any state that attempts to capture religion surrenders prophecy. With the expansion of religious diversity and the breakdown of the consensus religion and politics of the 1950s, Niebuhr's position is particularly relevant today. That recognizing evangelicals' contribution to the status quo against centrist attempts at a normalizing Christianity is essential to this humility is an irony that Niebuhr unfortunately did not appreciate, though, as a supreme ironist himself, he should have (ibid., 102).

If Niebuhr's position serves as a rebuke to those who would too easily entangle religion and the state, it should not be mistaken for secularism. For liberals like John Rawls (1993), recognizing the burdens of judgment based on human fallibility requires the exclusion of religion from politics. Pluralism means we cannot hope to convince others of our religious vision of the good life. We may pray for a better world in private, but we must abstain from publicly basing our working for a better world on our religious vision.

Niebuhr's brand of humility is more inclusive and optimistic. Religions are the source of ultimate moral and social commitments. We may never be able to realize heaven on earth, but the conclusion to Niebuhr's *The Irony of American History* reminds us that we owe it to God and our fellow citizens to strive for justice. Invoking Abraham Lincoln's second inaugural address, Niebuhr cautions us to be humble by reminding us that we only know the right "as God gives us to see the right." But this awareness Niebuhr stresses only qualifies and does not defeat our obligation to act "with firmness in the right." We cannot assume the easy assimilation of our views by others, but rather than surrendering their public import, we must tailor them to account for our limitations and fallibility. Democracy, with its emphasis on voluntarism and consensus, places strong emphasis on humility, and by its very nature it constantly reminds us of the difficulty, but not impossibility, of translating heavenly ideals into earthly realities. This message of humble activism is the one that public schools can implicitly communicate to students when they simultaneously recognize sectarian beliefs and teach the principles of good faith. They should also teach it explicitly in required world religions courses and elective courses about the Bible.

If democracy requires humility on the part of believers when they attempt to bring their beliefs to bear on politics, it also requires trust and faith in the future, grounded in humility, when the state deals with religious beliefs. This does not mean that, as John Dewey thought, democracy should encourage each religion to take a progressive or Hegelian view of the changing nature of religious truth. A belief in the static nature of God's word, James Davison Hunter (1991) reminds us, is a sine qua non of religious conservative thought. Those Hunter describes as "orthodox" believers could never accept Dewey's vision as the guiding philosophy of public schools, nor should they, because it would entail a severe violation of religious freedom. Moreover, encouraging such progressivism would homogenize American religion and make obsolete the criticism that faith in the future is intended to promote. The faith at issue here is not a promiscuous arrogance that the latest developments in religion are necessarily the greatest.

The faith in the future on which public school treatment of religion must be based concerns whether the state has the right to guide, however gently, the nature of American religious beliefs. Mann, the public pietists of the 1950s, and Prothero all—albeit in very different ways—look to the past in trying to recapture aspects or trends in religion that they find beneficial. Honoring the choices that individuals and communities make and the religious consensus or dissensus that results, by contrast, allows not only for religions best tailored to the American's needs and interests as they develop over time but also for religions that challenge mainstream practices. Contrary to Deweyan progressivism, this form of dynamism can appeal to evangelicals and secularists, who have too often been left on the outside looking in when the state engages in the business of tutoring religion. Most evangelicals are simply asking for a public education that gives them an equal chance to compete on fair terms in the marketplace of religion—a marketplace where they have fared quite very well over the last fifty years.

A public school curriculum about religion will have the best chance to reconcile civil politics and uncivil religion if it encourages humble activism and embodies a faith in the future. The stress on humble activism ensures a civil dialogue and the tempering of strong sectarian religious claims brought into the public square. Faith in the future ensures a space for an occasionally countercultural religion that is never content with the political, social, or cultural status quo. When taught together, emphasis on civil politics and on allowing for uncivil religion can temper each others' excesses.

Critical religion can prevent civil politics from becoming bland and overly agreeable; the rules of civil politics can prevent critical religion from being too offensive. This path may not lead to the Edenic peace that the 1950s civil religionists desired or to the religious redemption that Prothero hopes for, but it can produce the type of peace and religious consensus that is most faithful to the basic principles of American political and religious democracy.

# Conclusion

Chapter 5 addresses how the proposals in this book would respond to and avoid the problems with the curricular treatment of religion in public schools in the past. But recent developments in national politics present unique opportunities and perils for the future of American religion and democracy. This conclusion contends that the curricular changes this book recommends would help America to take advantage of these opportunities and avoid the perils. To understand why this is the case, we need to begin with an analysis of which aspects of the relationship between religion and politics are changing and which are not.

## EVIDENCE OF THE COMING CONSENSUS

Forty is a number associated in the Bible with narratives of trial and redemption. The Genesis flood lasted for 40 days, Moses spent 40 days on Mt. Sinai, Jesus spent 40 days fasting in the desert, and the Israelites spent 40 years in the desert. Numerology is not ordinarily among the foremost concerns or inspirations of political analysts. But during and after the 2008 election cycle, several esteemed analysts (Sullivan 2007; Beinart 2009; Saletan 2009a; Rich 2009) have speculated about whether America may now be completing its own 40-year cycle of trial and redemption. Andrew Sullivan provided perhaps the most prominent and prescient of these arguments in a December 2007 *Atlantic Monthly* piece provocatively entitled "Goodbye to All That."

> At its best, the Obama candidacy is about ending a war . . . within America that has prevailed since Vietnam and that shows dangerous signs of inten-

sifying, a nonviolent civil war that has crippled America at the very time
the world needs it most. It is a war about war—and about culture and about
religion and about race. And in that war, Obama—and Obama alone—offers the possibility of a truce.

Barack Obama's nonideological approach to politics and his accompanying emphases on bipartisanship and civility, Sullivan contended, contrasted sharply with the divisive politics of the previous two presidents.
Karl Rove's political strategy for the 2000 and 2004 elections, Sullivan argued, relied heavily on the exploitation of religious and cultural conflicts,
such as homosexual marriage, to mobilize conservative Christians to vote
for Republican candidates. President Clinton was not above manipulating
America's religious and cultural divides to his political advantage, but Sullivan argues that it was Clinton's history and behavior that proved most divisive. His failure to participate in the Vietnam War, however justified it
might have been, rendered him unable to be a neutral arbiter in culture war
disputes, "and his personal foibles only re-ignited his generation's anxiety
over sex and love and marriage" (Sullivan 2007).

Obama himself—all of seven years old in 1968—recognized the political value of stressing his postboomer biography. In *The Audacity of Hope*
(2006), Obama argued for moving beyond "the psychodrama of the Baby
Boom—a tale rooted in old grudges and revenge plots hatched on a handful of college campuses long ago—played out on the national stage" (36).
He also attempted to stake out centrist positions on controversial cultural
issues. Government, Obama argued, should take measures to reduce the
number of abortions. While arguing that gay couples deserve equal hospi-
tal visitation rights and joint health insurance, he also explained in *Audacity* that "society can choose to carve out a special place" for traditional marriage (222). Obama's campaign turned this conciliatory attitude toward
cultural and religious differences into action through its outreach to white
evangelical voters. Recent Democratic presidential candidates had not
completely ignored these voters, but the Obama campaign's appeals were
both more visible and more frequent. His appearance at the Civil Forum on
the Presidency at Rick Warren's Saddleback Church and his campaign's co-
ordination with the Matthew 25 Network, a political action committee devoted to establishing support for Obama among moderate evangelical voters, were only the most notable examples of these appeals (Luo 2008).

Judged strictly by his overall performance among white evangelical voters, Obama's outreach efforts appear to have failed. Employing John Green's (2009) distinction between evangelicals, Obama did not improve at all on John Kerry's performance among modernist, centrist, or traditionalist white evangelicals. Moreover, the contentious battle over the repeal of gay marriage in California served as a reminder that the culture war on this issue was far from over, and the intense allegiance Sarah Palin inspired in some Republican quarters suggested the continued vitality of culture war politics.

But even if the 2008 election does not provide abundant evidence of the imminent end of American conflicts over religion and culture, a broader look at the evidence suggests that they might be in the process of abating more gradually.[1] For instance, in swing states his campaign focused on, such as Virginia, Indiana, and North Carolina, Obama did significantly better than Kerry among white evangelical voters. Older white evangelicals may have voted for McCain in even greater numbers than they did for George W. Bush in 2004, but younger white evangelicals in the age-groups of 18–29 and 30–44 voted in significantly greater numbers for Obama than they did for Kerry (Goodstein 2008). This shift appears to be part of a broader trend among young voters. Perhaps turned off by Karl Rove's attempt to divide and conquer, many younger voters, unmoved by cultural and religious issues that occupied the baby boom generation's political consciousness, did not respond to attempts to drive a wedge between the "real" America and the other America.

Focusing solely on white evangelicals ignores the significant gains that the Obama campaign made among other religious voters. For instance, Obama outperformed Kerry among traditionalist Catholics by 17 points. The reasons for this shift, as John Green (2009) explains, are complex and not perfectly clear, but it is possible that Obama's civil and conciliatory approach was able to convince these voters that he was more sympathetic to religious conservative concerns than previous Democrats. Obama also performed significantly better than Kerry among Hispanic Catholics and Protestants, many of whom are culturally conservative. Obama's conciliatory religious and cultural attitude was certainly not the most important factor in his victory. The economic crisis and his sizable organizational and funding advantages weighed more heavily. Still, the approach Obama voiced in his speech at the 2004 Democratic Convention—that we are less blue states and red states than one United States of America—paid distinct electoral dividends, and similar claims may pay even more handsomely in the future as the electorate continues to change.

In the early days of his presidency, Obama offered signs that he intended to act on his message of greater religious inclusion. His selection of Rev. Rick Warren to provide the invocation at the presidential inauguration sent a powerful message to and received plaudits from many religious conservatives. While some secularists and liberals objected to this choice, he won praise from the left for his selection of gay Episcopal bishop Eugene Robinson to provide the invocation at the inaugural concert and, even more, for reminding Americans through a statement in his inaugural address that "we are a nation" of Hindus, Muslims, and nonbelievers as well as Christians and Jews.

In February 2009, Obama announced the formation of a White House Office of Faith-based and Neighborhood Partnerships, composed of clerical leaders from various backgrounds, to advise him and seek out common ground on a wide range of issues, including abortion, poverty, and promoting fatherhood. The council included several prominent evangelicals who oppose crucial aspects of Obama's agenda. Even decisions that rankled cultural conservatives received some praise for the conciliatory way they were made. When Obama overturned the "gag rule" preventing international organizations performing or counseling abortions from receiving U.S. funds, Rev. Jim Wallis praised him for accompanying the reversal with a statement urging the reduction of abortions and for waiting to sign the executive order until a day after a major pro-life march in Washington, D.C. (Stein and Scheer 2009).

## SHOULD OUR INTENSE CONFLICTS OVER RELIGION END?

Before rushing to celebrate the end of our intense conflicts over religion and culture or at least getting comfortable with the idea that they are gradually abating, two related fundamental issues are worth examining. First, we must dig underneath the emerging conventional wisdom about the end of our religious and cultural conflicts to examine what it would really mean for them to end. Second, we must examine whether we should want these intense conflicts to end and whether their end would be consistent with fundamental democratic norms.

The most obvious way for these intense conflicts to end would be for Americans on both sides of the religious and cultural divide to find common ground on controversial religious and cultural issues. Clearly, it is unrealistic to expect *all* Americans to unite around solutions on these controversial issues. Many prognosticators of an emerging religious and cultural consensus hope that a *growing majority* of Americans will come to agree on previously controversial religious and cultural issues. In a thoughtful article, Damon Linker (2009) distinguishes between "conquest" and "conversion" scenarios for ending the culture wars.

> One option is to demoralize the other side to such an extent that they effectively give up and go home. This is pretty much what fundamentalists did after the humiliation of the Scopes Trial in 1925. For the next five decades, conservative evangelical Protestants stayed out of American public life . . . But in the age of blast faxes, talk radio, and Internet-based political organization, I frankly doubt this would be successful. More likely the provocation would radicalize the religious right more than anything since 1973. The other way in which one could imagine a culture war coming to an end is through conversion: the slow migration of right-wing culture warriors away from extremism and toward the political and cultural center. Obama clearly hopes to motivate such conversions.

An alternative way to achieve a cultural détente—albeit one compatible with Linker's "conversion" scenario—is for religious issues and the cultural issues related to them to largely disappear from the national political discourse. After claiming that Obama's goal is to "remove culture from the political debate," Peter Beinart (2009) offers that "culture wars do end." "In the 1920s, immigration, Darwinism, and the Ku Klux Klan dominated political debate," Beinart explains, "but in the 1930s, they receded as Washington turned its attention to the Depression and the specter of war." The shift in the youth vote noted in the previous section provides some support for both Linker's "conversion" thesis and Beinart's thesis of "fading significance."

An essential point to realize about all three scenarios, however, is that they would at best involve a *political* end to our intense conflicts over religion and culture, rather than an elimination of their roots in religion and culture themselves or a true reconciliation, at least in the short term. Beinart and Linker (2009) openly acknowledge that the major issues at the heart of our religious and cultural conflicts do not allow for genuine compromises that will equally satisfy and accommodate both sides of the religious divide. Among efforts to establish a majority coalition on controversial issues, there are, to be sure, significant differences between more civil approaches that make some attempt at genuine compromise and more extreme approaches that do not, as Linker's distinction between the "conquest" and "conversion" scenarios suggests. Still, as Beinart (2009) concedes, Obama "is not offering to split the difference with cultural conservatives, only to make his cultural liberalism less conspicuous."

Resolving policy disputes on these controversies thus inevitably boils down to a zero-sum game in which one side wins and the other loses. Liberal groups may have tolerated, to an extent, the symbolic selection of Warren to provide the inaugural invocation, but they are unlikely to allow Obama similar leeway on religious and cultural *policy* matters dear to them. Obama, for instance, may have postponed his decision to reverse the gag rule and accompanied it with a call for reduction in abortion, but liberal groups would not have been patient much longer. As Ross Douthat noted (2009b), Obama's concessions to the pro-life community could not obscure that his decision was fundamentally at odds with their convictions.

> So waiting a day to reverse the ban on overseas funding for groups that provide abortions, for instance, isn't a compromise in the culture wars, or an act of moderation—it's a way of making a victory for the left *seem* like an act of moderation to people who aren't that invested in the issue.[2]

Douthat and more liberal observers, like Beinart, agree about the inevitable zero-sum nature of policy conflicts about religious and cultural issues. They disagree about whether this means that conflicts related to religion and culture will continue to motivate as many voters as they have in the recent past and to command significant attention in national politics. Douthat may well be right that the status quo will persist. But let us put his claim aside for the moment and imagine that American politics returns to its pre-1968 form because of "conversion," "fading significance," or both. In this scenario, consensual *politics* will prevail on religious and cultural matters, and, as a result, American politics will focus on economic and international policy rather than religious and cultural issues. Would this really put an end to our intense religious and cultural conflicts once and for all?

Chapter 5's discussion of the roots of our present intense conflicts over religion provides reason to doubt that it would. Although it is fashionable to mark 1968 or at least the 1960s as the beginning of our present conflicts, locating the roots of the conflicts in the Eisenhower era, with its strong emphasis on consensus and moderation, is equally plausible. To be sure, given genuine and robust differences of opinions, real conflicts over controversial social and cultural issues were inevitable in the late 1960s and early 1970s, but they need not have been as angry and filled with mistrust as they were. The bland civil religion and the vital center politics of the 1950s helped ensure the latter by ignoring key cultural concerns of those outside of the mainstream, on the right and the left. Atheists and evangelical Christians alike, whose views were so different, were left on the outside looking in. Civil religion was too religious for most secularists and not sincerely religious enough for many evangelicals.

Had these groups and their concerns been recognized, the groups might have expressed their concerns in more reasonable terms and offered them in the spirit of compromise. Instead, the rush to consensus and shunting aside of the concerns of both groups led to a mistrust of the moderate establishment, an inflexible and often shrill expression of opinions, and a reluctance to compromise. The politics of the Eisenhower era only produced the short-term appearance that intense religious and cultural conflicts did not exist, while it was busy planting the seeds of deeply divisive conflicts that the future would reap. The period's shortcomings are a reminder that instead of extremism creating a need for exclusion, exclusion is often the parent of extremism. When the center too easily dismisses the margins, the margins are likely to become more vocal and extremist to call attention to themselves.

More specifically, previous attempts to push aside religious and cultural concerns only reinforce that religion and culture matter deeply to many Americans. Even at their most optimistic, Linker, Beinart, and Sullivan only imagine a removal of cultural conflicts from center stage in American *politics.* Their hope seems to be that as the political significance of these issues fades, the roots of these disagreements in Americans' opinions will fade as well. But, if anything, American history suggests that the exclusion of religious and cultural issues from national politics and their relegation to the private sphere only increases the concern for their importance among large portions of the population.

The more serious problem with such exclusion, however, is that it would be contrary to democracy.[3] If cultural issues related to religion matter to a significant portion of the American public, the core democratic principles of inclusiveness and participation demand that these concerns be reflected in our politics. For all its faults—and there were indeed many—the intense religious and cultural conflicts of the last forty years have given a voice to many groups on the left and the right who previously felt excluded. Extremist spokespersons too often captured the spotlight and exaggerated the extremism of their followers for political benefits, but this does not change the fact that the political landscape of the last forty years was more broadly inclusive than the landscape that preceded it. Moreover, the cultural politics of the last forty years gave public attention to prophetic religious voices that were absent from the bland civil religion prevailing during the 1950s. Just because some of these previously marginalized prophetic views were extreme does not mean that they were necessarily wrong or that their views were socially harmful.

To be sure, the error of American democracy during the Eisenhower era lay not in its striving for consensus itself. Excessive polarization is the enemy of social trust, and democratic deliberation requires calm deliberation. Too much inclusion of marginal yet intolerant voices can lead to the alienation of the vulnerable minorities they target. This was clearly the case, for instance, with Southern evangelicals who used the Bible to justify Jim Crow laws during the 1950s. But if an emphasis on consensus is legitimate in a democracy, an exclusive concern with it is not—especially in the case of religion. Democracy works best when it preserves the precarious balance between a republican emphasis on consensus, civility, and moderation, on the one hand, and a populist emphasis on conflict-driven participation and inclusiveness, on the other.

Putting an end to a significant focus on religious and cultural conflicts in national politics is thus no more realistic or desirable than attempting to end debate over American's economic differences. This does not mean that the same cultural conflicts related to religion that Americans have clashed over for the last forty years must continue to be front and center. Each generation has its own set of cultural concerns related to religion, and democratic politics should reflect these shifts. Conservative Christians today, for instance, are scarcely concerned with the prohibitionist legislation that many focused on 80 years ago. The priority given to cultural concerns should also not always be the same; international threats and economic crises may justly direct our attention away from them at times. Still, cultural concerns related to religion have been a persistent concern of a large number of Americans, and it would be foolish to think that this will cease to be the case in the future. As long as this continues to be the case, it would be antidemocratic to banish cultural concerns from national politics for an extended period.

## PUBLIC SCHOOLS AND OUR CONFLICTS OVER RELIGION AND CULTURE

That predictions and hopes for the end of our intense conflicts over religion and culture are neither realistic nor desirable does not mean that the status quo is acceptable[4] or that Obama's challenges to it are not meaningful. The divisive cultural politics that reached their crescendo in the 2004 election cycle offer a poor model for how democracy should work. By exaggerating the differences between Americans on cultural issues related to religion, they did serious damage to civil discourse. Obama's conciliatory outreach to those with different religious and cultural values than his own and most of his supporters constitutes a welcome change that politicians on both sides of the aisle should seek to emulate. Still, the zero-sum nature of legislating about controversial cultural issues seems to provide a hard and fast limit to how much progress can be made on civilizing our too-often-unruly religious and cultural conflicts, confining attempts at conciliation to merely symbolic gestures.

If this book's claims are correct, however, this conclusion is overly pessimistic. Changing how public schools address religion will not eliminate religious conflicts—nor should it attempt to do so—but it goes beyond the realm of the merely symbolic and provides a realistic and substantive way to improve how Americans navigate their religious conflicts. Indeed, it provides the best hope available for creating a more civil society regarding religion.

The crucial difference between disputes about the public school curriculum and other cultural disputes relating to religion is that while the latter are zero-sum, the former need not be. Whether the dispute is about abortion, gay marriage, or stem cells, the disagreements between Americans are so sharp that government has no choice but to endorse one side. The partisans on both sides expect no less. But most Americans on both sides of the religious and cultural divide understand that the purpose of public schools is not to choose sides on controversial issues and that public schools disregard their public character when they do so. They agree that public schools serve democracy best when they secure students' acknowledgment of views other than their own and the rights of others to express those views.[5] This understanding of the distinctive nature of public schools makes it possible to resolve disputes over the curriculum in a neutral and mutually beneficial way—an option unavailable in the battles over abortion and gay marriage.

Possible is not, however, the same as easy. It would be a serious mistake, for instance, to confuse—as many liberals do—a neutral treatment of religion in public schools with a cosmopolitan treatment that teaches consensus but not conflict. A cosmopolitan approach to teaching religion involves not only addressing the differences between people's religious views but encouraging students to look beyond surface differences and seek out the underlying similarities between beliefs. Cosmopolitans are surely right that the world is getting smaller (especially for a hegemonic power like the United States) and that knowing the difference between, for example, what Sunnis and Shi'ites believe is essential knowledge for competent democratic citizenship. The growth of religious diversity at home makes it all the more essential for today's students to learn that religious freedom in a democracy requires citizens not only to refrain from discrimination but to go out of their way to protest religious discrimination that does occur. *These concerns are so important, this book argues, that not only should public schools follow Modesto's lead and require world religions courses, but these courses should last at least one full semester.*

But while a world religions course's strong encouragement to be open and more respectful of other points of view may be necessary for democracy, it is also a burden on those conservative Christians who view religious truth as mutually exclusive. When schools promote consensus, openness, and cosmopolitanism too exclusively, they violate the religious liberty that belongs equally to open and mutually exclusive religious beliefs, and they risk undermining their own intent in practice by opening themselves up to charges of liberal bias. Some conservative Christians have reacted to an excessive and exclusive concern with openness by seeking out educational options besides public schools, while many more who choose to have their children remain may simply encourage them to ignore what is being taught.[6] As Aristotle recognized, justice often requires treating unequals unequally. A truly neutral and mutually beneficial public school curriculum would pay more attention to those religions imperiled by an emphasis on openness.

This does not, of course, mean that public schools should accommodate every conservative Christian claim simply because it is justified by references to neutrality and fairness. Schools must not allow participation and inclusion of religious conservative voices to come at the cost of excessive conflict, alienation, or incivility. If having world religions courses as the only robust discussion of religion in the curriculum overall is too cosmopolitan, privileging conservative Christian beliefs or Christian beliefs in general in the required curriculum is too parochial. Intelligent design is more than a statement of sectarian beliefs, but it is sufficiently sectarian that discussing it in a required biology course would send a message of exclusion to non-Christian religious minorities and nonbelievers alike. Fairness and neutrality to both these groups and conservative Christians is best served by placing privileged robust discussions of crucial conservative Christian views in elective courses and ensuring that these courses contain significant, if not always equal, discussions of alternatives to these views. *To this end, schools should offer (1) a one-semester elective course on intelligent design theory and its critics and (2) a one-semester elective course on Judaism, Christianity, and the Bible.* Following the discussion in chapter 5, the latter course should be bottom-up rather than hierarchical and should focus mainly on the different ways that major Jewish and Christian groups in the United States today interpret the Bible and on the extent to which their religious views rely on the Bible.

A fair resolution to the curriculum wars would eliminate a considerable source of controversy and ill will among religious and cultural combatants. Freed from the perception that attention in the public school curriculum is a scarce resource that groups must compete over, secularists, conservative Christians, and non-Christian religious minorities are more likely to acknowledge the legitimacy of each others' major concerns. To this point, we have considered the potent role that public schools can play in the present. Resolving the curriculum wars can create a more civil society right now by sending an important message to parents and communities at large about what views society includes and recognizes and by guiding how students who hold different religious views relate to each other. But the discussion of our historical moment in this chapter suggests the crucial role that resolving the curriculum wars can have in transforming the future as well.

Public schools can play a role in shaping the future by encouraging students to develop more civil attitudes toward religious and political conflict resolution, which they will engage in as adults. Increasing active tolerance for religious minority views is one obvious virtue schools should help to inculcate, but schools also have a role to play in improving the quality of political discussions on issues related to religion. *In particular, required world religions courses and elective Bible courses should encourage students to adhere to the principle of good faith and should expose students to arguments consistent with this principle.* Good faith does not require religious believers to forgo the use of religious arguments in political debates, but it does require them to balance sectarian claims with secular and logical claims to a very significant extent. In return, schools should urge secularist students to take arguments made in good faith seriously and to abstain from crude and mistaken caricatures of conservative Christian positions as extremist and unsophisticated.

The changing religious landscape in America makes this a particularly favorable time for schools to advocate the principle of good faith. While previous generations of conservative Christians concentrated on exclusively sectarian and scriptural arguments for their preferred political and cultural positions, many conservative Christians today increasingly rely on hybrid arguments that combine the sectarian with the secular. Not only does this shift make the teaching of good faith possible, but teaching good faith can reinforce and broaden the commitment to this valuable development among conservative Christians by ensuring respect for such arguments among all American citizens. By doing so, schools can also help to undercut the excessive power that the media's culture wars narrative gives to unrepresentative extremists on both sides of the religious divide. While the media gives the greatest prominence to conservative extremists who use offensive sectarian arguments and to liberal extremists who deny religion any place in public life, the majority of conservative Christians and secularists hold more tempered views. Teaching good faith will help ensure that these more moderate and representative views have a voice proportionate to their numbers.

Changing the way that Americans talk about their religious views in the public square can help American culture escape the vicious cycle it has been trapped in for most of the past century. Attempting to temper disagreements as divisive and alienating as many of those on cultural issues related to religion have been over the last 40 years is a worthy democratic goal. This book may disagree with Sullivan and Beinart about the need to end our intense and unruly conflicts over religion and culture altogether, but it does agree with them that they need not be waged as viciously as it has been in recent years. The zero-sum nature of policy disputes about cultural issues related to religion means there will inevitably be winners and losers in our cultural conflicts. But greater civility can ensure that losing will not create so much bitterness that it forecloses the possibility of any goodwill and cooperation. We should still strive for and can achieve some degree of consensus in the midst of conflict.

History shows, however, that attempts by government to create consensus are often too crude. Excluding cultural disputes related to religion from national politics and relegating religion to a largely formal role are contrary to the democratic principle of inclusion and likely to create a backlash. The Eisenhower era's emphasis on civil religion only achieved a temporary cessation of political clashes over culture, at the extravagant price of sowing the seeds of disruptive culture wars in the future. Adopting Beinart's recommended approach of focusing exclusively on economic and foreign policy issues rather than cultural matters would likely produce similar results. These attempts at consensus underestimate the likelihood that our religious differences relating to politics will persist, as well as the democratic and moral imperative that they should be allowed to persist.

Contrary to the spirit of these previous attempts at consensus, the recommendations in this book do not presume that civility and inclusion are mutually exclusive democratic values. Their goal is to help create a democratic society where robust disagreements about religion are reflected in our politics but where the expression of those disagreements does not degenerate into mindless and hostile attacks. Promoting active tolerance will ensure civility for the most religiously vulnerable among us, and the good-faith requirement that religious arguments in politics temper the sectarian with the secular checks the power of divisive extremists. But recognizing conservative Christian beliefs in the curriculum not only accepts but promotes respect for major religious differences, and the principle of good faith ensures respect for properly framed religious arguments in politics.

These steps will not help put an end to our intense conflicts over religion and culture in the way that Sullivan, Beinart, and others hope for. But they can help to establish ours as the generation where liberals, religious minorities, and religious conservatives learned to treat their inevitably strong disagreements with respect and without simply setting the stage for another set of unruly religious and cultural conflicts in generations to come. Respecting religious liberty in a democracy means balancing respect for consensus and conflict. Striking the right balance between consensus and conflict over religion in public schools is crucial to striking the right balance in America, both today and tomorrow.

# Notes

## Introduction

1. Here and elsewhere in the book, the term *secularist* refers to a person who believes in a strict division between church and state and who supports a political discourse largely free of theological and scriptural references and justifications. Secularists believe that public schools must be particularly careful in teaching about religion, to avoid influencing students' views about religion and alienating religious minorities, humanists, atheists, and agnostics. While almost all humanists, atheists, and agnostics are secularists, many secularists hold strong allegiances to particular religious communities. For instance, Rev. Barry Lynn, who heads Americans United for the Separation of Church and State, is among America's most well-known secularists and is an ordained minister in the United Church of Christ.

2. While teaching of religion that favors one religion is clearly unconstitutional, the Supreme Court has made it equally clear that teaching students about religion in a nondenominational way is consistent with the First Amendment's establishment clause. In his majority opinion in *Abingdon School District v. Schempp*, which struck down sectarian Bible reading, Justice Tom Clark was careful to qualify the ruling by noting that "it might well be said that one's education is not complete without a study of comparative religion and its relation to the advance of civilization" (*Abingdon* 1963, 226).

3. Although not familiar with his work when I wrote this book's passages about zero-sum games, the logic of zero-sum and non-zero-sum games and their relation to religion receives powerful expression in the recent work of Robert Wright (2000, 2009).

4. This book confines its attention to the high school curriculum. Elementary and middle schools certainly play a role in inculcating students' commitments to democratic values. But while sectarian religious and democratic commitments do not contradict each other, an understanding of how to reconcile them is often subtle. The recommendations in this book are thus targeted at high school students because, to a far greater extent than younger students, they have the intellectual sophistication necessary to appreciate fully the relationship between teaching about religion and the fulfillment of America's central democratic values.

5. Nord 1995, Nord and Haynes 1998, Wexler 2002, and Prothero 2007 offer pio-

neering discussions of the civic benefits of teaching about religion in an American context. This book takes particular inspiration from the common-ground approach advocated by Nord and Haynes. Although written too recently to allow for extended treatment in this book, Warren Nord's (2010) *Does God Make a Difference?* is yet another profound meditation from a consummate expert on the subject of religion and public education. Other excellent contributions to this topic include Tomasi 2001, Owens 2007 and 2008, and Viteritti 2007. Jackson 1997, 2003, and 2004 and Jackson and McKenna 2005 provide enlightening examinations of the civic effects of teaching about religion in European contexts. Greenawalt 2005, McConnell 2002, Yerby 1989, Wexler 1997 and 2003, George 2001, and Beckwith 2003 offer distinguished recent discussions of the legal and constitutional validity of teaching more about religion.

6. The more frequent treatment of religion in European schools has produced much valuable empirical research. See, for instance, Jackson 1997, 2003, 2004; Jackson and McKenna 2005.

7. This book does not focus primarily on the legal and institutional history regarding treatment of religion in the public schools. In part, this is in deference to other accomplished works in this particular field, such as Fraser 1999, Nord 1995, and McMillan 1985. More crucially, this is a consequence of the lack of a usable past that provides appropriate guidance for today's public schools. Indeed, the longest-lasting legally approved practices and most dominant educational philosophies in American history regarding the treatment of religion in public schools favored a sectarian treatment of religion unsuitable for American society today. Daily school prayer and Bible reading favoring Protestant Christian beliefs were widely used and constitutionally accepted until the Supreme Court struck down both practices in the early 1960s. Horace Mann—the most influential thinker in the history of the American common school—supported required Bible reading and recital of prayers and hymns in public schools partly as a way to encourage recent Catholic immigrants to adopt the moral and political values mainstream Protestants favored. Since the bulk of legal tradition and the history of American educational philosophy cannot offer effective guidance for the treatment of religion in public schools today, such guidance must be sought by examining what type of education is consistent with fundamental American democratic values and can receive the support of a wide variety of today's Americans.

*Chapter 1*

This chapter is based on an article Patrick Roberts and I cowrote (Lester and Roberts 2006a). I am deeply indebted to Patrick for suggestions about content and style that were invaluable in converting the article into this chapter. Another important intellectual debt of this chapter deserves mention. Although he does not use the term *active tolerance* itself, Charles Haynes emphasizes, in his mediation of cultural disputes, that public schools should not only discourage students from expressing intolerance but encourage students to welcome those of different faiths. His emphasis is the inspiration for this chapter's discussion of active tolerance. My goal is to provide a more elaborate definition of the concept and a theoretical justification that shows how our core democratic commitments require its practice.

1. Thus, the principle of active tolerance is intended to benefit atheists and agnostics. Of all the views about religion Americans hold, perhaps the one least respected is that which holds allegiance to no religion. Gallup polls remind us quadrennially that more Americans are unwilling to vote for an atheist for president than for members of any other view on religion (Edgell, Gerteis, and Hartmann 2006, 215). But a 2006 University of Minnesota study found that reluctance to associate with atheists extended beyond the political sphere. The study's authors found that "out of a long list of ethnic and cultural minorities, Americans are less willing to accept intermarriage with atheists than with any other group, and less likely to imagine that atheists share their vision of American society" (ibid., 216).

2. I use the term *conservative Christian* in this book to refer to those evangelical and fundamentalist Protestants, Catholics, Russian and Greek Orthodox, and other Christians who believe in a transcendent God, and that the basic religious and moral precepts of their religions do not change significantly over time and draw fairly sharp distinctions between faiths. Conservative Christians emphasize, to a greater degree than other Christians, the mutual exclusivity of truth claims made by different faiths and that eternal salvation can only be found through Christ. Those believers I describe as conservative Christians are thus very similar to those believers James Davison Hunter (1991) describes as "orthodox" Christians. Just as Hunter emphasizes orientation over denomination, my classification suggests that on matters of religion and education, conservative believers belonging to different denominations and forms of Christianity often share more in common than conservative and religiously progressive or liberal believers of the same denomination. Occasionally, I refer to subsets of conservative Christians, such as evangelical Protestants, when such a distinction is relevant to the point I am making or specified by the research I am discussing. Conversely, I sometimes use the more inclusive term *religious conservatives* when I am discussing a topic where conservative believers of other faiths, such as Judaism and Islam, hold religious or political views similar to conservative Christians.

I use the term *conservative* to qualify the term *Christian,* rather than the other way around, to emphasize that the group I am concerned with is more united by religious than political concerns and is not confined to members of the religious or Christian right. A growing number of religiously conservative Christians, like Jim Wallis, hold political views at odds with conservative Republican Christians. But the shared religious concern of these politically disparate groups means that they would likely, for instance, have a common objection to a public school education about religion if it promoted a relativistic belief in the equal truth of all faiths.

3. Gallup poll, May 2–4, 2004 ($N = 1,000$, MoE ± 3).

4. Agnostics or nonbelievers who steer clear of religious inquiry make a stronger case for not being defined in opposition to a deity, but even in their case, the terms that define their stance suggest a negation of religion, not a positive identity.

5. There are, of course, other, more mundane reasons that people change their religion, and it is unlikely that people who convert for these reasons hold their religious identity to be immutable. Proving the importance of religious tolerance only requires showing that many people, not all, feel their religion to be immutable.

6. The exceptions are members of esoteric sects, such as the Eleusinians in ancient Greece or Freemasons, who pride themselves on holding their religious beliefs in secret.

7. "In the United States today," contends Yoshino (2006, 170), "Muslims are the most visible targets of the religious covering demand." He proceeds to identify examples of such covering, including Muslim private schools encouraging students to conceal religious emblems, as well as the increased reluctance of Muslims from the Middle East to speak Arabic in public and to display flags from their families' native Middle Eastern countries outside their residences.

8. In general, intolerance is not simply a function of individual characteristics; the level of intolerance in a society can rise or fall according to social changes. Increases in immigration and economic dislocation, for example, can cause an increase in hostility toward immigrants (Coenders and Scheepers 1998). Similarly, perceived threat or negative affect toward out-groups can lead to intolerance (Tajfel 1981).

9. ABC News poll, September 4–7, 2003 ($N = 1,004$, MoE ± 3).

10. The same poll found that the percentage of Americans who believed "that mainstream Islam promotes violence against non-believers" had risen from 14 to 32 percent since 2002 (*Washington Post*–ABC News poll, March 2–5, 2006 [$N = 1,000$, MoE ± 3]).

11. Evangelical and fundamentalist Christians are much more likely than other Americans to hold intolerant and critical views of Muslims. A 2006 *Washington Post*–ABC News poll (March 2–5 [$N = 1,000$, MoE ± 3]) found white, evangelical Protestants 15 percent more likely than other Americans to hold unfavorable opinions of Islam. A fall 2002 Ethics and Public Policy Center survey of 350 fundamentalist and evangelical leaders found that 77 percent held unfavorable views of Islam and that 70 percent saw Islam as "a religion of violence" (EPPC Online 2003). Franklin Graham has publicly characterized Islam as "an evil and wicked religion" (Goodstein 2002). Jerry Falwell (2002) described Muhammad as a "terrorist," while Pat Robertson claimed that Islam's prophet was a "wild-eyed fanatic" (Wazwaz 2002).

While some scholars, like Michael McConnell (2002), have wondered whether the exodus of conservative Christians to sectarian schools and homeschooling is really a problem after all, these numbers suggest why public schools should strive to improve their inclusiveness to ensure that they retain conservative Christians. Students attending conservative Christian religious schools often not only lack classroom or curricular encouragement to develop religiously tolerant attitudes but are deprived of the opportunity to form friendships or at least acquaintances with students from different religious backgrounds. See, for instance, Dwyer 1998, 2002; and Peshkin 1986. Public schools serve as meeting places for students with different points of view, so they can better learn to negotiate and deliberate about these differences as future citizens. Schooling segregated by religion erases this opportunity to interact and makes it likely that the conflicts over religion of the future will be as intense as those of the present.

12. This increasing hostility comes at exactly the wrong moment in American history. Religious diversity in the United States is burgeoning like never before, because of the recent influx of immigrants from Asia and Africa who belong to neither the Jewish nor the Christian tradition (Wuthnow 2004; Eck 2002; Kohut and Green 2000, 128). Increased globalization and the war on terror have produced increased contact and tension with Muslim nations around the world. "This is a time," wrote conservative Republican ex-congressman Bob Barr in a coauthored editorial about the Guantánamo prison scandal (Abrams, Barr, and Pickering 2005), "when we should be making extra efforts to reach out to Muslims and ask them to work with us in the war against terrorism." Instead, fear of a repeat of the 9/11 attacks has led many Americans to support policies that endanger the rights of Muslims at home and abroad. Strenuous vigilance is appropriate, because terrorism inspired by extreme Islam is a real and menacing threat. But politicians have too often exaggerated fears and played on citizens' vulnerability to support aggressive and counterproductive policies that have only increased alienation from America in the Muslim world. Even politicians professing more tolerant views in general have been reluctant to come to the defense of or reach out to Muslims. Concerned by politically perilous rumors about his Muslim background, Barack Obama spurned the support of Keith Ellison, the only Muslim U.S. congressman, during the 2008 presidential campaign, and his campaign did not include a single visit to a mosque, although his itinerary included numerous visits to churches and synagogues (Elliott 2008). *Washington Post* columnist Richard Cohen (2010) has condemned President Obama's defense of the Islamic center near Ground Zero as overly circumspect and equivocating. Meanwhile, Senate Majority leader Harry Reid's spokesman said that the senator believes the Islamic center "should be built some place else" (Beutler 2010).

13. For excellent discussions of the long history of negative portrayals of Arabs in American movies, see Shaheen 1997 and 2001.

14. The only objection to the belief that students should all stand for the pledge was expressed by a foreign exchange student who identified herself as a Buddhist.

15. Although this chapter has previously focused on intolerance toward the most recent immigrants to America, this should not obscure continued intolerance toward those who arrived or originated in America before. Members of groups with far longer histories still too often stand on the outside of the mainstream looking in. Despite Will Herberg's (1960) famous declaration almost a half century ago that America more or less equally accommodated Catholicism, Protestantism, and Judaism, old prejudices sometimes truly die hard. Phillip Jenkins (2003), for instance, has made a compelling case for the rise of a "new anti-Catholicism," and my travels to Modesto provided a vivid reminder of his argument. Not only many students but several parents I spoke with explained that the three major religions in Modesto were Judaism, Christianity, and Catholicism, suggesting a belief that Catholicism was an inferior or even illegitimate form of Christianity. "For many American Jews, the question has shifted," claims Yoshino (2006, 169), "from whether they should convert or pass to whether they are 'Too Jewish?'" But my Modesto experience sug-

254 NOTES TO PAGES 26–31

gests that even this may be too optimistic, as the local rabbi told me that students in his congregation sometimes hid their religious background to avoid alienating their friends. The 2008 presidential candidacy of Mitt Romney revealed widespread ignorance in American mainstream culture about and more than occasional hostility toward Mormonism (Feldman 2008). The required world religions course that this chapter and chapter 3 argue for would serve the vital function of increasing religious understanding and respect not only for the most recent immigrants to America but for these more well-established religious groups as well.

16. The fact that conservative Protestantism has a strong hold on American religion should not be mistaken for immunity from religious misunderstanding. Right-wing fears of a secularist humanist plot against conservative Protestants are exaggerated, but frequent caricaturing by the mainstream media and inflated secularist fears of an aggressive Christian nation have left their mark. In the aforementioned 2004 American National Election Study that ranked Muslims so low on favorability scores, the average rating for "fundamentalist Christians" (58.5) was not much better and was well below the ratings for Catholics (69.2) and Jews (66.7) (Bartels 2008, 136).

17. Some studies do include feeling thermometers toward different groups, but these do not exactly measure tolerance. Instead, they measure homophobia or racist attitudes. See Sniderman, Brody, and Tetlock 1991.

18. Too much encouragement of the robust expression of identity may at times be contrary to the preferences of the minorities tolerance is intended to protect. Yoshino (2006, 23) refers to such encouragement as "reverse-covering demands—demands that individuals act according to the stereotypes associated with their group." There are some members of minority groups that would prefer just to fit in and assimilate. Others may prefer to see their religious identity as part of who they are but do not wish others to view them solely in terms of this identity. These concerns are analogous to Michel Foucault's concern that gay liberation movements of his time often attempted to construct standards of behavior for those who engaged in homosexual behavior (J. Miller 1993, 254). Avoiding such an exaggeration of the importance of religious identity, especially for those who see their religion as an important but limited part of who they are, is a legitimate concern, but Yoshino is right to be more concerned with covering than reverse-covering. The major problem for most religious minorities in America today is that their beliefs are provided not too much but too little public recognition. Still, if American society succeeds in providing enough space for robust expression of religious identity, the problem of too much encouragement to self-identify as a member of one's religious group may need to be addressed down the road.

19. This example also suggests the way in which knowledge of other religions might practically benefit Americans, who now work in increasingly diverse workplaces. Religious tolerance creates a better workplace environment, enables businesses to reach out to more customers, and enables all to get ahead equally within companies. Several Modesto school board officials and administrators stressed this logic as a primary justification for the world religions course.

20. Despite their numerous differences, James Davison Hunter and Alan Wolfe

(2006) agree that elites today tend to take even more extreme positions than ordinary citizens. According to Wolfe, "In the 1950s and 1960s, political scientists argued that one of the main functions of political leadership was to moderate the more extremist views of ordinary Americans in order to make consensus possible. In the 1990s by contrast . . . ordinary Americans had become more moderate than their leaders" (ibid., 49).

21. See Galeotti 2002 for another excellent discussion of tolerance as recognition.

22. In the fall of 2005, Philadelphia became the first major city to require that all students take a course in African American history for graduation (Janofsky 2006).

23. Relativism is defined here as the belief that ultimate, metaphysical truth cannot be known, either because it does not exist or because the differences between individuals and cultures are too great to allow for a clear knowledge of such truth. While relativism poses the greatest and clearest threat to the beliefs of most religious conservatives, such as conservative Christians, two distinct but related beliefs often conflict with religious conservative points of view as well. Ecumenism is defined here as the belief that religious groups should strive to cooperate and understand each other's theological beliefs to a far greater extent than they currently do. Often, but certainly not always, this practical desire is based on a belief in syncretism. Syncretism is defined here as the belief that despite differences in their forms, institutions, and rituals, what most, if not all, religions share in common outweighs what separates them. Syncretists support incorporating elements of other religious belief systems into their own views about religion.

24. Opponents of the curriculum for racial tolerance might invoke John Stuart Mill's argument in *On Liberty* that valuable and true beliefs can only flourish when contrasted with evil or worthless beliefs. This chapter is arguing not that racist views should be censored or banned but only that schools should discourage these beliefs. Using critical reading and discussion of racist texts, such as *Mein Kampf*, in order to reinforce racial tolerance is consistent with the racial tolerance curriculum outlined in this chapter. Mill recognized that state toleration of worthless or evil views could and should be coupled with state and social discouragement of these views.

25. The views of the Christian fundamentalist parents in the federal court case of *Mozert v. Hawkins County Board of Education,* which involved a dispute over students' exposure to a variety of religious beliefs in the public school curriculum, illustrate this point. One parent said, "We cannot be tolerant in that we accept other religious views on an equal basis with ours." The school board stipulated that an education that exposed students to alternative religions and aimed to convince students that "all religions are merely different roads to God" would be unconstitutional (*Mozert v. Hawkins* 1987, 1069).

26. The state, of course, also has an obligation to avoid promoting theological aversion where it does not already exist. Where citizens have tepid commitments to their religious beliefs, it is not the job of the state to encourage them to have more robust beliefs.

27. Similarly, although all religions, to some extent, require their adherents to deny the truth claims of other religions, no religion requires its adherents to engage

in willful misperceptions about other religions. Indeed, some religions command learning about the true nature of other beliefs. Many Christians and particularly evangelicals follow Paul in believing they have an obligation to learn about other beliefs in order to proselytize more effectively. In Acts 17:28, Paul demonstrates his familiarity with Greek pagan and philosophical thought and attempts to convert adherents of these perspectives by showing that these beliefs are actually consistent with Christian beliefs. In 1 Corinthians 9:19–22, Paul writes,

> For though I am free with respect to all, I have made myself a slave to all, so that I might win more of them. To the Jews I became as a Jew, in order to win Jews. To those under the law I became as one under the law . . . so that I might win those under the law. To those outside the law I became as one outside the law . . . so that I might win those outside the law.

28. The recent debate over the proposed Islamic Center near Ground Zero suggests that many Americans still confuse the vast majority of Muslims with Muslim extremists, and that this confusion can lead to an unfair treatment of Muslims. See, for instance, Young 2010 and Greenwald 2010.

29. In practice, avoiding the promotion of empathy would mean, for instance, that public schools are strictly forbidden from using role playing in teaching about religion. An excellent example of what not to do occurred in 2001 when a history teacher in Contra Costa, California, told students to take on roles as Muslims for three weeks to help them understand what Muslims believe (Egelko 2005). Students used Muslim names, recited prayers in class, and tried fasting; the instructional guide the teacher used notes that "in many Islamic countries a husband usually walks several paces ahead of his wife and family." I am grateful to Patrick Roberts for bringing this example to my attention.

30. Most of the activists and scholars who have promoted this "natural inclusion" also argue that the treatment of religion especially as an independent subject in the curriculum remains insufficiently robust. Modesto's school district is the only district in the entire nation requiring all students to take an independent and extended course on world religions at the high school level. The treatment of religion in the elective curriculum is only slightly greater. Only 8 percent of public high school students have access to elective Bible courses (Prothero 2007, 127).

31. Lack of short-term effect on students' beliefs is no guarantee that the course does not promote syncretism and ecumenism in the long run. Modesto's school superintendent, James Enochs, spoke of the course as sowing an "unseen harvest." He was thinking primarily of the course's benefits that are undetected in the present, but his metaphor could also be applied to the course's harms.

32. The offense here is not only to conservative Christian students themselves but to their parents. An essential part of religious freedom, after all, is the right to pass along religious beliefs to one's children. For a more elaborate and technical discussion of the justifications of and issues surrounding parental rights regarding religious upbringing, see Lester 2004 and 2006.

33. "There is not one text reference to marriage as the foundation of the family," writes Vitz (1986, 84). He continues, "Not one of the many families described in

these books features a homemaker—that is, a wife and mother as a model. The words 'housewife' and 'homemaker' never occur in these books. Yet there are countless references to mothers and other women working outside of the home in occupations such as medicine, law, transportation, and politics." Vitz argues that by portraying the role of religion in Native American and European cultures but failing to discuss their role in contemporary American society, the textbooks implicitly suggest that religion once played an important role in human life and culture but no longer does so. "There is not one story or article in all these books in which the central motivation or major content is connected to Judeo-Christian religion," he writes (81), adding, "No character has a primary religious motivation . . . In contrast to the treatment of Christianity and Judaism, there was a minor spiritual or occult emphasis in a number of stories about American Indians."

34. Ten years after Vitz's research, Paul Boyer (1996, 197) ventured that Vitz's findings most likely remained relevant. In chapter 5 (section "Not Redemption, but Ascension"), I argue that the most widely used resource in Bible elective courses, *The Bible and Its Influence,* emphasizes social, theological, and political themes more favorable to liberal religious believers.

35. See, for instance, the exaggerated claims in Noebel, Baldwin, and Bywater 1995.

36. See the problematic claims in Tobin and Ybarra 2008.

37. See chapter 3 section "Similarity of Religions: A Careful Balance."

38. Nord (1995, 257) claims that conservative religious believers would accept a world religions course because most want their views not privileged but, rather, given a fair place in the curriculum. As the evidence from chapter 2 suggests, Nord's description of religious conservatives is accurate but does not prove that most conservative Christians would accept the educational approach to teaching world religions. His educational approach would provide conservative Christian views a place in the curriculum but would also promote openness to other religions, which many conservative Christians might find problematic.

39. Countering the biases of a required world religions course is one strong reason for recognition of conservative Christian beliefs, but is not the only reason. Chapter 4 suggests, for instance, that such recognition is also necessary to counter the current teaching of beliefs directly at odds with conservative Christian viewpoints.

## Chapter 2

1. In a Virginia Commonwealth University poll, respondents were asked to describe the extent to which they relied on their religious beliefs in deciding how they felt about abortion and government assistance to the poor. On both issues, 33 percent of respondents said they had relied a lot on their religious beliefs in formulating their opinions. On the poverty issue, religion was more important to those taking a liberal position (Kohut and Green 2000, 61).

2. Secularists might object that they would prefer that public schools actively encourage students to leave religion out of politics rather than ignoring the issue of

religion's involvement in politics. But even if this advice was politically feasible, telling students not to mix religion and politics will do nothing to discourage the millions who believe it justified. Indeed, by confirming their sense of secular and liberal hostility to their views, it will more likely persuade many religious believers to assert their religious beliefs in politics more strenuously.

3. This chapter focuses on evangelicals, rather than all religious conservatives as a whole, largely because the literature expressing doubt about whether American political discourse and public schools can and should accommodate religious conservatives focuses on evangelicals. It also focuses on evangelicals because they are the most widely and comprehensively researched religious conservative group. The relative moderation of most evangelicals does not, of course, automatically prove the moderation of most nonevangelical Christian and religious conservatives. But this is a reasonable assumption. Wolfe (2003, 263), for instance, suggests that conservative Catholics share many political characteristics with evangelicals.

4. Christian Smith (1998, 38) also found that 69 percent of evangelicals thought it was very important that Christians "work for political reform," compared to 53 percent of mainline and 49 percent of liberal Christians.

5. For a good summary of empirical research connecting conservative forms of religion with intolerance and intellectual rigidity, see Klosko 2000, 82–104.

6. Pew Forum on Religion and Public Life poll, July 7–17, 2005 ($N = 1,000$, MoE ± 2.5).

7. For instance, an in-depth study of public opinion about evolution and creationism across the nation and in North Carolina identified an "evangelical center" position held by the majority of evangelicals, distinct from hard-line creationism (Toumey 1994, 62–67). The evangelical center shares an appreciation of the religious basis of creationism with hard-liners, and their socially conservative views trigger concern about the moral effects of belief in evolution. But concerned primarily with conversion, evangelical centrists are pragmatic and keen to avoid a divisively partisan position that would interfere with this mission.

8. "Evangelicals are often seen as people who try to censor beliefs and views that they consider threatening," writes Christian Smith (2000, 41), "but in our interviews we continually heard evangelicals affirm everyone's freedom to think and speak as they believe."

9. Smith adds, "The meaning that evangelicals most frequently gave to the idea that America was once a Christian nation was that it was *founded by people who sought religious liberty and worked to establish religious freedom*" (C. Smith 2000, 37). Kohut and Green (2000, 101) qualify their claims about evangelical political participation by noting that "overall, most Americans—even among the religiously committed—support both religious pluralism and action in its defense."

10. Some evangelicals in Christian Smith's interviews (2000, 69) viewed pluralism "as good because of the positive impact they think it has on the nation," while "many" others "emphasized how personally enriching and stimulating American pluralism is."

11. Smith maintains elsewhere (2000, 68), "Some evangelicals are hard-line exclusivists, and others are virtual universalists. Most fall somewhere in the middle,

working to retain both their belief that Christianity is the true religion and their belief in mutual respect and religious freedom of choice."

12. The media, as this book's introduction notes, plays an essential role in exaggerating extremism among conservative Christians. An example from Modesto has to do with a Catholic, rather than an evangelical, cleric, but it is far from being a unique reflection of how the media misconstrues conservative Christian beliefs and actions in general. In December 2008, Father Joseph Illo of St. Joseph's Catholic Church in Modesto preached a sermon and wrote a pastoral letter to his parishioners urging them to confess before taking communion if they had voted for Barack Obama, due to the candidate's views on abortion. First reported in the *Modesto Bee* (Nowicki 2008), Father Illo's actions received mention in newspapers around the country and were the subject of stories on network affiliate newscasts as far away as Pittsburgh and Chicago. His actions earned particular attention from the liberal blogosphere. In his widely read blog on the *Atlantic*'s Web site, for instance, Andrew Sullivan called Illo out as a representative of the extreme "Christianist" element of the religious right (Sullivan 2008). I interviewed Father Illo for about an hour, and we never touched on the topic of abortion. But he did serve as the Catholic representative on the religious advisory council that approved the implementation of Modesto's world religions course, and in our conversation, he stressed both the importance of teaching for religious tolerance in public schools and the need for schools to avoid the proselytizing of any one religious tradition. The Father Illo I met with and knew from his acquaintances in Modesto was, to say the least, far more multidimensional than the Father Illo caricatured in the media.

Although the thirst for profit surely plays a role in these distortions, many in the mainstream media also buy into the culture war narrative out of ignorance. Too many journalists simply do not know much about religion and, in particular, do not have much contact with evangelical Protestants. A 2002 study by Weaver et al. (2006, 15) found that 44 percent of journalists for news magazines and wire services practice no religion—a far higher percentage than the American public at large—and that only 5 percent describe themselves as evangelical Protestants.

13. The process works both ways of course. Religious conservative stereotypes about the alleged relativism and godlessness of liberals and secularists encourage liberals and secularists to stake out more extreme opinions, thus confirming the suspicions of religious conservatives. While secularists must avoid caricaturing most evangelicals as intolerant extremists, evangelicals and others have an equal obligation to avoid caricaturing secularists. Some secularists, such as Michael Newdow, fit the media stereotype of aggressive atheists who wish to banish God completely from the public square by striking "In God we trust" from coins and removing "under God" from the Pledge of Allegiance. Most secularists, however, hold more tempered views. The secularists I talked with in Modesto, for instance, all thought that having students learn more about religion was essential to a well-rounded education. A social studies teacher who described herself as an atheist told me about how much she looked forward to communicating knowledge about world religions to new students each semester.

14. Providing a comprehensive review of competing models of democratic the-

ory and their views on democratic deliberation is beyond the scope of my argument here. For excellent overviews of democratic theory, see Gutmann and Thompson 1996; Benhabib 1996; Barber 1984. Given my particular concern with restrictions on religious reasoning, my classifications of various theorists may be at odds with conventional classification systems. William Galston, for instance, has expressed sympathy with deliberative democracy in general, but his writings on religion and civic education indicate that he is closer to the proceduralist position regarding restrictions on religious reasoning.

15. "The idea," observes Jeff Spinner-Halev (2000, 101), "that we must be empathic with arguments we oppose, that we must imaginatively enter into the moral perspective of people who we think are wrong is sometimes burdensome if not impossible."

16. The transformation in evangelical political argumentation bears a resemblance to the transformation away from sectarian political argumentation that has already taken place among Catholics. John Coleman (2003, 243) explains that after World War II, the Catholic Church began to use more "universal appeals" and reliance on its natural-law tradition to justify its political positions.

17. Reardon, Cougle, and Coleman's work on postabortion syndrome, while highly contested by other social scientists, has been published in a variety of peer-reviewed journals. See, for instance, Cougle, Reardon, and Coleman 2003.

18. Sometimes the caricature of religious conservative positions comes from the media itself instead of from secularist critics. Several important evangelical leaders, for instance, took exception to a December 2008 *Newsweek* cover story that portrayed the evangelical case against gay marriage as consisting solely of biblical arguments. Richard Land, the president of the Southern Baptists' Ethics and Religious Liberty Commission, responded to the article by emphasizing that the arguments evangelicals use against gay marriage are "often not biblical arguments" but "secular arguments, arguing about marriage as being a civic and a social institution" (Burns 2008).

19. For a discussion of the liberal educational approach, see chapter 1 at the section "Required World Religions: The Civic and Liberal Educational Approaches Compared."

20. "If texts and teachers are to take religion seriously," writes Nord (1995, 50), "they must let the advocates of that religion speak for themselves, using the cultural and conceptual resources of their own traditions. The point is not to strain their world through our conceptual nets, but to hear what they say and see what they do in the context of their own beliefs, experiences, motives, and worldview—from the *inside*, as it were."

21. This does not mean, however, that sectarian views should have no place in the curriculum at all. Chapter 5 argues that students should be exposed to these sectarian views in elective Bible courses that students can opt into.

22. Schools need not wait for the adoption of a required course about religion to provide this discussion. Social studies courses that touch on contemporary church-state controversies are a natural home for such a discussion. Indeed, discussion of

good faith need not stop in these courses even if a required course about religion is adopted. A little repetition and overemphasis in the pursuit of civility is no vice.

23. Greater participation and a greater sense of inclusion in the political process can lead to greater moderation for more practical reasons. For instance, Clyde Wilcox's research (1996, 110) found that "the more conservative Evangelical activists participate in politics, the more willing they are to compromise with others in the Republican party to advance common electoral interests."

## Chapter 3

This chapter is based on research I conducted with Patrick Roberts of Virginia Tech. The results of our research were published by the First Amendment Center (Lester and Roberts 2006b). Patrick's advice was both generous and invaluable in converting the research report into this chapter.

1. Previous research on religion in schools has focused on examining references to religion in textbooks. See, for instance, Vitz 1986. While this research is invaluable in helping us to understand what students are supposed to be learning, a more direct way of measuring what students are actually learning about religion from textbooks and the curriculum is to survey students themselves.

2. A significant part of the increased Catholic presence is attributable to the influx of Hispanic immigrants.

3. Jim Ridenour, Modesto's mayor since 2003, is a Republican. The 1990 census split Stanislaus County into two congressional districts. The representative from the Eighteenth District, which contains Modesto, has been Dennis Cardoza since 2004. Cardoza is a member of the Blue Dog Coalition in the House of Representatives, which consists of moderate and conservative Democrats.

4. Superintendent Enochs (2004) stressed the intrinsic value of knowing about major world religions, by noting that this knowledge is necessary for "a person to be considered truly civilized." School board president Gary Lopez (2005) stressed the more practical goal of "prepar[ing] kids" to tolerate diversity in "the workplace" and providing them with whatever knowledge about religion is essential for making informed political decisions.

5. We surveyed 426 students in October 2004, 392 in January 2005, and 308 in May 2005. The numbers for each survey vary because some students dropped out or produced unreadable surveys. Approximately 3,000 students took the course that year. We administered the surveys ourselves during the May 2004, October 2004, and January 2005 iterations. We were able to survey approximately 40 students each during nine course periods. We chose the classes surveyed, in consultation with school officials and teachers, primarily because they suited our interview schedule.

We also first administered a survey in May 2004 to 168 students who had then almost completed the course, in order to refine our survey and test our questions. The students surveyed were selected because their classes suited our travel schedule to Modesto. We refined the survey to suit a high school audience. For instance, a small minority of students in this survey iteration had trouble understanding a political tolerance question concerning their "least-liked group." The question asked students to choose their "least-liked group" in their mind (the district did not allow us to ask students to write the groups on the survey) before answering questions about whether that group was entitled to four basic First Amendment rights (see note 12 and fig. 2). These students did not realize that the four questions referred to their least-liked group. For future iterations of the survey, we asked teachers to explain the question carefully before students began work on the survey.

Finally, although 29 percent of our respondents (see table 1) reported speaking a language other than English at home, we do not believe that this led to a significant measurement error. The students we surveyed were proficient enough in English that they were not in ESL (English as a Second Language) or SDAIE (Specially Designed Academic Instruction in English) classes. None of the administrators or teachers we spoke with mentioned that language would be or was a barrier to students reading and answering the questions effectively.

6. Polls for political races are considered valid when they have a response rate between 20 and 40 percent (Keeter 2000; Deane 2003). The validity of our survey is further enhanced by the serious manner in which students approached the survey. Unlike adults in most surveys, the students had authority figures—teachers—who repeatedly stressed the survey's importance.

7. Every question on the first survey was used on the second survey, and wording was identical. The only difference between the two surveys was that the second survey included four questions on students' evaluation of the course, which obviously would have been irrelevant before students took the course. Discussion and wording of particularly notable questions are examined in this chapter's sections on the surveys' results.

8. In many instances, we coded "tolerant" responses as 1 and "intolerant" or "less tolerant" responses as 0, in order to distinguish between these poles. We were not certain that scaled responses were always useful, since we did not know how to interpret the difference between "agree" and "somewhat agree" and because the intervals between respondents do not always regard intervals on a five- or seven-point scale as equidistant (Babbie 2004, 174). We were able to distinguish, however, between "tolerant" and "less tolerant" responses, or between varieties of "agree" or "disagree."

9. Although school regulations required that an administrator be present for the interviews, the students' teachers were not present. Teachers selected the students. We asked teachers not to select only students with the highest grades or the greatest interest in the course material but to choose a representative sampling of their overall classes.

10. The major drawback of our survey questions was the inability to ask students about their specific religious identifications and their religious practices, such as how often they personally prayed or went to church. California state regulations did not allow us to ask several of these questions, while our desire to avoid alienating students and parents with overly personal questions prevented us from asking the others.

However, the unique benefits of surveying Modesto's students outweighed the disadvantages. Although numerous school districts around the nation provide various elective courses on religion, the self-selection bias resulting from the fact that students must opt into these courses poses a significant obstacle for external and internal validity. If students in these courses demonstrated an increase in tolerance, we could not be sure how much of the increase was attributable to students' idiosyncratic characteristics or the course itself and if the results could be repeated among a wider, more representative swath of public school students. In addition, the number of students taking electives on religion in individual high schools or even school districts constitutes relatively small samples. Modesto is the only school district in the nation to require all students to take an independent and extended course on religion. Modesto's students constitute a relatively large and more random sample than students in elective courses, and thus research on them confers significant advantages for internal and external validity.

11. See chapter 1 for a more elaborate definition of passive tolerance.

12. We introduced the question with this preface: "Here's a list of political groups that some people have problems with: Racists; Feminists; Nazis; members of Al Qaeda; Communists; skinheads; Ku Klux Klan; members of groups that support rights for gays and lesbians. In your head, choose the group that you dislike the most. (You don't need to write down the name of the group)."

13. For these questions, $t$-tests indicated a significant difference between the pretest and posttest ($P > |t| = 0.01$). Though the mean in agreement with the statement "Religious views don't exclude a candidate from running for office" increased by three points, the change did not reach an acceptable level of statistical significance. (For each of three questions, we coded "agree" or "strongly agree" as 1 and "disagree" or "strongly disagree" as 0.)

14. Julia Ipgrave's (2005) empirical research on religious education in British schools found that making religious minority students "collaborators in teaching and learning" increases their self-esteem.

15. The differences between the scores were statistically significant according to $t$-tests ($P > t = 0.000$).

16. "The Arab serves as the ultimate outsider, the other," according to Jack Shaheen, "who doesn't pray to the same God, and who can be made less human" (Booth 2007). Shaheen stresses that negative stereotypical portrayals of Arabs in movies predate 9/11. See also Shaheen 2001.

17. Forty-seven percent said they found the course "interesting," and 26 percent said they found the course "very interesting."

18. This result is statistically significant at $p < 0.002$.

19. For instance, in a 2000 survey, the University of Connecticut's Center for Survey Research and Analysis polled more than 500 seniors at 55 of the nation's best colleges and found that 65 percent of these students failed to pass an American history test written for the high school level (*Education World* 2000).

20. See note 23 in chapter 1 for definitions of ecumenism, relativism, and syncretism and for a discussion of why these beliefs are at odds with those of religious conservatives and particularly conservative Christians.

21. In fact, the number of students who agreed or strongly agreed with this state-

ment in May (27 percent) was slightly higher than the percentage who agreed or strongly agreed with it in January (23 percent).

22. Coupled with the fact that Modesto's course provided some, but not overwhelming, evidence of an increase in active tolerance, this means that a longer course aimed much more directly at increasing active tolerance may produce a greater dilution of some students' faith than Modesto's course did.

23. This raises the possibility that reduction of threat is actually an intervening variable of an increase in knowledge and not a truly independent variable. It is also possible that an increase in the civic skills of conversing about other religions and with members of other religions in civil terms is responsible for the reduction of threat.

24. We lack a control group for this period, so we cannot determine whether students' sense of threat decreased because of the effects of the course or simply because of the passage of time since the terrorist attacks of 2001. We suspect, however, that the course produced the measurable change during the almost four months between pretest and posttest.

25. The dependent variable question asks, "Imagine that you lived in a place where most people disrespect members of a small religious group. How likely would you be to . . . defend the small religious group when talking to friends?" The answers "definitely would" and "probably would" are coded as 1, and "probably would not" and "definitely would not" are coded as 0.

26. The belief that all religions share the same moral values was correlated with religious knowledge, however.

27. The results of the mediation process that led to the course's creation reflect the value of similar civil deliberation among adults. Among our interviewees, the differences between the views of those who had and had not participated in the mediation process were stark. Unlike those most likely to indulge in stereotypes, the evangelicals and secularists in Modesto who were least likely to indulge in caricatures knew and had engaged those with opposing views. For instance, Modesto evangelicals I met with expressed moderate concerns about students having to read books with sexual themes. But some liberal clerics and teachers who had not participated in the mediation process characterized many evangelicals in Modesto as extremists out to take over the school system, including an evangelical Christian school board member who turned out to be an ardent supporter of the course and who had worked closely with members of religious minorities in the Modesto community. I met with secularist-leaning school board members and members of vulnerable religious minorities who expressed moderate concern about Christian clubs and proselytizing on campus, but some evangelicals who had not participated in the mediation process portrayed them as wishing to banish any form of religion from school campuses.

28. Readers may wonder if there are enough First Amendment Center consultants like Beauchamp to go around. The First Amendment Center has established a network of teachers knowledgeable about and sympathetic to its goals in various states around the nation and provides various resource books on how to teach about religion in a civil manner.

29. The one exception among the teachers we interviewed was a first-year teacher who admitted feeling stifled by the guidelines. Given his lack of experience in handling difficult classroom situations, this may have been just as well.

30. The examples of critical thinking that Modesto's teachers described to us in interviews focused on moral practices related to religious tradition and on church-state issues. The teachers did not mention a single instance where they encouraged students to engage in comparative or critical thinking about the truth of central theological claims that various religions made.

31. Conover and Searing (2000, 119) write, "Our study suggests the importance of narratives in helping students to translate shared understandings about citizenship into concrete terms they can relate to their own lives. Many students mention English classes as having influenced their understanding of citizenship, because it is in those classes that they read narratives in which fictional characters confront real-life dilemmas."

32. The religious backgrounds of the interviewed teachers were varied. Three teachers identified themselves as Protestant, one as Catholic, one as Greek Orthodox, and three as atheists.

33. Asked whether they "feel that each religion has been treated fairly in the world religion course," 12 percent of students responded "maybe no," and 16 percent responded "no." It is unfortunate that California state educational regulations prevented us from asking about students' religious identities in the surveys. As opposed to the interviews, the surveys do not allow us to determine if students from minority religions felt differently about the fairness of the course than did students in general.

34. The small number of parents who have opted out of the course are equally divided, according to a Modesto administrator, between atheists and "hard-core Christian fundamentalists."

35. The first section of the course, on religious liberty, does stress to students the need to respect the nonreligious as well as members of other religions.

36. It is reasonable to conclude that the *particular civic approach* Modesto took, which focused on only describing faiths and avoiding comparisons and critiques of them, is responsible for the lack of robust representation of atheist and agnostic viewpoints. But concluding that the civic approach must inevitably produce these oversights would go too far. The particular civic approach this book advocates differs from Modesto's and emphasizes active tolerance for all, including humanists and those critical of religion. If this requires an occasional departure from an exclusively descriptive approach to religion, public schools' commitment to active tolerance allows this.

The fact that the civic approach allows for views critical of religion and the presenting of humanist points of view by no means ensures that they will be welcome, especially to conservative Christians. In one prominent example, fundamentalist Christian parents brought suit against a high school English class that assigned Gordon Parks's *The Learning Tree*, because of passages critical of religion and Christianity (see *Grove v. Mead* 1985). But the civic approach advocated by the present study would most likely preempt these complaints. One reason conservative Christians are particularly concerned about having discussion of views critical of religion in the curriculum is because they hold—quite reasonably—that religious views in general and their own views in particular are ignored and given no opportunity to respond. The civic approach of this book endorses a robust presentation of conservative Christian views in the elective curriculum. Confident that their own views are given a fair hearing, many conservative Christians are likely to accept some discussion of views critical of religion, as long as schools and teachers stress that these views are not the schools' own but, rather, held by humanists themselves.

37. Schools must respect the subtle but crucial distinction between teaching about atheism and teaching about humanism. The term *atheism* connotes that people who do not hold deistic views should be defined negatively, or by what they reject. The term *humanism* defines these believers positively, by stressing the robust "human-centered" moral code they stand for. In teaching about these religious alternatives, schools must stress what these believers affirm at least as much as what they deny. For this point, I am grateful to the discussion group I participated in at the leadership conference on religion and education in Nashville, Tennessee, in March 2006.

38. Moreover, the greater attention public schools have paid in recent years to the importance of teaching about religion has led to a proliferation of resources available for high school teachers. For instance, high school teachers interested in teaching about world religions can make use of, among many other resources, a CD-ROM entitled *On Common Ground: World Religions in America*, developed by Harvard University's Pluralism Project, and a multivolume series entitled *Religion in American Life*, published by Oxford University Press.

39. This conclusion receives support from a 1994 Gallup poll (May 10–June 8 [$N$ = 1,326, MoE ± 3]). Asked if they favored "nondevotional instruction about various world religions in the public schools in [their] community," 66 percent of those surveyed agreed. Various other polls have indicated widespread dissatisfaction with the current treatment—and particularly the lack thereof—of religion in public schools. A 2001 Gallup poll (February 9–11 [$N$ = 1,016, MoE ± 3]) found that 62 percent of respondents felt that the influence of religion in public schools was too little, 30 percent felt that it was the right amount, and only 8 percent felt that it was too much. A 2005 Gallup poll (August 8–11 [$N$ = 1,001, MoE ± 3]) produced virtually the same results, with 60 percent of respondents believing that the presence of religion in public schools was too little, 27 percent thinking that it was the right amount, and 11 percent thinking that it was too much. Finally, a 2005 poll by the Pew Research Center for the People and the Press (July 7–12 [$N$ = 2000, MoE ± 2.5]) found that 67 percent of respondents felt that "liberals have gone too far in trying to keep religion out of the schools and the government." This result is of particular interest because it suggests that dissatisfaction with treatment of religion in schools is not confined to conservative Christians and that implementing world religions courses—which liberals tend to view favorably—might help correct conservative caricatures about liberal views on religion, as was the case in Modesto.

40. Agreement about the need for greater teaching of religion, apparent on the lo-

cal level in Modesto, has been evident on the national level as well. For instance, a 1995 document entitled *Religious Liberty, Public Education, and the Future of American Democracy: A Statement of Principles* affirmed that "schools demonstrate fairness when they ensure that the curriculum includes study *about* religion" (Nord and Haynes 1998, 17). The 21 groups that sponsored the document spanned the religious and ideological spectrum and included People for the American Way, the Christian Coalition, and the American Center for Law and Justice (18).

## Chapter 4

1. Gallup poll, May 8–11, 2006 (*N* = 1,002, MoE ± 3).

2. A 1999 Gallup poll (August 24–26 [*N* = 1,000, MoE ± 3]) found that 47 percent of Americans believed that God created human beings "in their present form in the last 10,000 years or so." A 1991 Gallup poll found that 47 percent believed that God created humankind within the last 10,000 years, while 40 percent believed that God directs evolution (Nord and Haynes 1998, 143).

3. See also Plantinga 2003.

4. For an excellent discussion of the history of the YE creation science movement, see Larson 2003.

5. Warren Nord (1995, 152), who is not a proponent of ID himself, found evidence in his survey of North Carolina public school textbooks that "biology textbooks do not teach *generic* evolution, but a neo-Darwinian view according to which change is inescapably *purposeless*, the result of natural selection working on random genetic mutations and recombinations."

6. A survey by Edward Larson, drawn from a directory of American scientists and reported in the journal *Nature,* found that 40 percent of biologists, physicists, and mathematicians said they believed in God. But when the same survey was given to "leading scientists," defined as members of the National Academy of Sciences, "fewer than 10 percent professed belief in a personal God or human immortality" (Dean 2005a). Creationist opponents of evolution might want to use this survey to suggest that a belief in evolution causes the abandonment of religious beliefs, but the causal connection is not clear, and the alleged effect may actually be the cause. People could go into scientific fields because they are irreligious and believe in evolution. More likely, belief in evolution, commitment to science, and lack of religious beliefs are all effects of shared causes. Growing up in a secular household, a practical orientation to the world, and skepticism of traditional forms of authority are likely causal candidates.

7. A related mistake to be avoided is the assumption that all or most supporters of creationism are fundamentalists. A 2005 *New York Times* series on the evolution controversy, for instance, claimed mistakenly that "most of the Discovery Institute's science fellows are self-described fundamentalist Christians." The newspaper subsequently corrected its claims and explained that "most [of the fellows] are conservative Christians, including Roman Catholics and evangelical Protestants—not fundamentalist Christians" (Chang 2005). During the historical controversy over

268   NOTES TO PAGES 168-72

evolution, supporters of evolution have consistently indulged in this caricature to suggest that creationist views are only held by an extremist minority but not by the majority of mainstream religious believers (Larson 2003, 162).

8. Most public schools do not require all students to take biology courses teaching evolution to graduate. But this does not mean the evolution controversy can be resolved by noting that students do not have to take these specific courses. Biology courses teaching only evolution are required in the sense that students who wish to take biology to complete their science credit for graduation must take these courses. Students who wish to learn about biology in schools where biology courses that teach evolution are one of the few courses available to fulfill their science credits do not have much choice about whether to take these courses.

9. For insightful discussions of the various moral and political positions compatible with evolutionary biology, see Ruse 2001 and Hofstadter 1955.

10. Dennett explains that "creationists who oppose Darwin so bitterly are right about one thing. Darwin's dangerous idea cuts much deeper into the fabric of our fundamental beliefs than many of its sophisticated apologists have yet admitted" (Larson 2003, 192).

11. Edward Larson's 1997 Pulitzer Prize–winning account of the Scopes trial concludes, "More than anything else, the crusaders opposed evolutionary teaching because it harmed the spiritual and moral development of students" (36). See also Wills 1990.

12. Many of the early major antievolutionary leaders, such as Bryan and John Roach Straton, connected their activism against evolution to their support of progressive positions on various social issues, including income redistribution, work, housing, and prison reform. By contrast, H. L. Mencken, whose merciless caricature defined Bryan for many in later generations, held openly social Darwinist views on various moral and political issues.

13. John Angus Campbell (2003, 22), a prominent ID supporter, follows Alexis de Tocqueville in arguing that the health of our democracy depends on robust participation in religious associations, and he has expressed concern that teaching evolution might interfere with this participation.

14. See also Wexler 1997, 454.

15. The official position of the Catholic Church on evolution, expressed by Pope Pius XII in the 1950 papal encyclical *Humani Generis,* is that regardless of human origins, God infuses the soul into the body at some point, and thus God's existence or goodness and basic spiritual truths are not dependent on evolution. In a *New York Times* op-ed from July 7, 2005, apparently sanctioned by Pope Benedict XVI, Vienna archbishop Christopher Schonborn (2005) ignited controversy among Catholics by asserting that "evolution in the neo-Darwinian sense—an unguided, unplanned process of random variation and natural selection—is not [true.]" But the same op-ed recognized the possible truth of common ancestry. Just six months prior to the op-ed, the official Vatican newspaper approved of Judge Jones's decision not to permit the teaching of ID in Dover schools.

16. A 2005 Pew Research Center poll (July 7–17 [$N = 2,000$, MoE ± 3.5]) found that 70 percent of white evangelicals say that "living things have always existed in their

present form," while only 32 percent and 31 percent of mainline Protestants and Catholics, respectively, accept the creationist account.

17. The "Wedge Document," a recent five-page outline of a five-year plan for the Discovery Institute's science center, claims, "Design theory promises to reverse the stifling dominance of the materialist worldview, and to replace it with a science consonant with Christian and theistic convictions." Philip Gold, a former fellow who left the Discovery Institute in 2002, complained that the institute "evolved from a policy institute that had a religious focus to an organization whose primary mission is Christian conservatism" (Wilogren 2005).

18. The school board in Dover, Pennsylvania, encouraged students to read *Of Pandas and People* if they were interested in learning about ID. Jay Wexler (1997, 456) explains that the book refers implicitly to a sectarian concept of God: "But who or what is this intelligent agent and what are his, her, or its characteristics? Although the authors claim that the specifics of intelligent design theory are open to various interpretations and further research, the book presents an agent who looks very much like the God of the Bible. He, she, or it is a designer who devised a blueprint or plan, created organisms, made fully formed creatures, designed and formed life on earth, 'coordinated the design requirements of multifunctional adaptational packages,' shaped matter, ordered pieces into a coherent whole, and may be assumed to have had good reasons for making decisions and to have used a variety of design approaches. The designer is supernatural, 'a master intellect and consummate engineer.' Moreover, the designer acts in ways that humans do not understand."

19. Robert Eshbach, a science teacher in Dover, observed about his students' likely reaction to teachings about ID, "Kids are smart enough to understand what Intelligent Design means. The first question they will ask is, 'Well, who's the designer? Do you mean God?'" (Bannerjee 2005).

20. The hypothetical disclaimer suggested by Kent Greenawalt (2005, 114) provides a good model.

21. "To achieve these goals," writes Wexler (2003, 788), "schools should teach not just about Christian views on origins but also about the views on origins held by religious traditions from all parts of the globe . . . Such instruction would include not only a 'full-blown literalist version of the Genesis creation and flood,' but also a variety of other views on origins, both ancient and modern, including, for example, 'the Babylonian Gilgamesh epic, the Hindu cycles of creation, different Native American creation stories as well as the evolutionary story of the modern secularist.' This makes good sense. Schools should teach about these varied perspectives, as well as others. Particular emphasis might be placed on the similarities and differences among Native American creation stories, such as the stories told by the Cherokees, the Sioux, and the Navajo. On the one hand, teaching these stories would inform students of their own nation's history, which, of course, began long before European settlers landed on our shores. On the other hand, students would learn about the differences between minority religious views on origins and views of majority traditions such as Christianity, while at the same time learning to appreciate the diversity among minority religions on the subject." For additional arguments

supporting the teaching of the controversy in nonscience classes, see N. Miller 2001 and Ruse 2003.

22. Several additional suggestions Wexler makes highlight the problems with presenting ID in a nonscientific way. He argues (2003, 789) that "at least for older students, schools should consider teaching a systemized approach to religious views on origins, perhaps classifying them according to their similarities and differences." Noting that "creation stories often contain common elements across cultures," he suggests that "schools might illustrate these relationships among creation beliefs to teach students that people around the world and across history have thought about these fundamental concerns in similar ways." Not only do these suggestions ignore the claim of ID's supporters that it is a unique creationist view because of its scientific validity, but they violate the rights of religious conservatives by encouraging syncretism and ecumenism.

23. The bias in the course was also obvious in a description that was sent to parents: "The class will take a close look at evolution as a theory and will discuss the scientific, biological and biblical aspects that suggest why Darwin's philosophy is not rock solid. The class will discuss intelligent design as an alternative response to evolution. Physical and chemical evidence will be presented suggesting the earth is thousands of years old, not billions" (Barbassa 2006).

24. World religions courses should provide a substantial discussion of religious accounts of creation that do not rely on scientific evidence or make claims to scientific legitimacy.

25. "The world of the 20th century," note Nord and Haynes (1998, 139), "appears to be more hospitable to religion than the classical scientific world of atoms and determinism." In particular, Nord and Haynes discuss three significant views that indicate a possible reconciliation between religion and science and are worthy of examination in the proposed elective course: (1) the belief held by several important astronomers, including Robert Jastrow, that the big bang theory and developments in cosmology are consistent with religious design arguments (145), (2) the official view of the Catholic Church that "evolution *is* purposeful, though God has chosen to work through the secondary causes of nature" (143), and (3) the views of liberal and process theologians that "God is *immanent*, a creative and purposeful force working *within* us and all of nature, moving us to higher moral and spiritual plans of existence through evolution" (143). The course should also expose students to views about the limitations of scientific points of view. For more discussion of this issue, see chapter 4 at the section "Going Beyond the Current Evolution Controversy?"

26. The selection of teachers poses a significant challenge to an effective implementation of this elective proposal. The course's primary emphasis on science suggests that biology teachers are the best fit, but since the material treated in the course consists of natural and social science components, its teachers must, to a certain extent, be jacks of two trades. Yet teacher choice and training need not be insuperable obstacles to a successful course. At the least, the problem of needing versatile teachers applies as much to proposals like Wexler's that *social* science courses teach ID as it does to the proposal here that they be taught in *natural* science courses. "If history

or literature teachers are likely to have a better feel for religion than science teachers," explains Nord (1995, 291), "they are still not likely to possess any great sophistication about current religious accounts of nature and creation." The success of training teachers for Modesto's world religions course suggests the possibility of training teachers about other religiously controversial material. Moreover, teaching controversial material that teachers themselves might disagree with would not be unique to this elective. Teachers frequently teach about material they disagree with and handle this challenge professionally.

27. Pew Research Center poll, July 7–17, 2005 ($N$ = 2,000, MoE ± 2.5). This poll also found that 64 percent of respondents favored "teaching creationism along with evolution in public schools." Of those who were familiar with intelligent design, more than two out of every three respondents in a 2005 Gallup poll (March 21–23 [$N$ = 1,001, MoE ± 3]) supported its teaching in public school science classes. Perhaps of most interest is that when offered a choice concerning how creationist theories should be addressed in the public school curriculum, only 28 percent of respondents in a 1999 Gallup poll (August 24–26 [$N$ = 1,000, MoE ± 3]) supported discussion of these theories in required courses, while 49 percent believed they were more appropriately handled in elective courses.

28. Several important advocates of teaching ID agree. See, for instance, Beckwith 2003, 49–78.

29. See "The Good-Faith Approach" in chapter 2.

30. This argument does not contradict the previous observation that there are no *compelling* secular purposes for teaching ID. That observation came in the context of discussing inclusion of ID in required courses. A compelling purpose was required because required courses might violate the constitutional rights of religious minorities and atheists. But examining ID in an elective course does not entail this violation, and thus a *legitimate* secular purpose is sufficient to pass the *Lemon* test.

31. Placing discussion of the controversy mostly in an elective, which many or most students would not take, may seem contradictory to this book's overall emphasis on using the curriculum to promote democratic discussion. Discussion of the controversy in the required curriculum, by contrast, would seem to promote thought and discussion by all students. But not all discussion is created equal. The goal of an education about religion is not to promote a greater overall discussion about religion but to promote a greater amount of civil discussion about religion, consistent with democratic principles.

Examining the evolution controversy in the required curriculum may generate a greater amount of discussion, but much of it would not be civil. The greater focus on ID would breed insecurity among religious minorities and secularists and triumphalism among conservative Christians. Focusing on the controversy in an elective is much less likely to have these effects. Even though the elective will not provoke discussion among all students, it will spark more discussion than the current approach, which banishes creationism from the curriculum altogether. Examining the scientific merits of ID, the moral concerns surrounding evolution, and alternative ways to conceive not only of creation accounts but of religious truth can make the conservatives, fundamentalists, atheists, and liberals who take the course more informed, thoughtful, and willing to listen to alternative opinions than they were before.

32. Apocalyptic separatists such as Jehovah's Witnesses make critiques similar to Toumey's and Armstrong's, though they draw very different results. They accuse creationists of being "too scientific" and believe that the Bible does not need scientific corroboration to confirm its own authenticity. "The genius of this denunciation," explains Toumey (1994, 53), "is that the separatists are doing to the scientific creationists just what the creationists are doing to the evolutionists: namely, accusing them of being so seduced by the values of the secular world that they refuse to accept simple biblical truth."

33. Armstrong (2000, xvi) argues that there is compelling historical evidence that the account in Genesis was intended to be not scientifically verifiable but a meaningful myth: "To ask whether the Exodus from Egypt took place exactly as recounted in the Bible or demand historical and scientific evidence to prove that it is factually true is to mistake the nature and purpose of the story." No less an early Christian authority than St. Augustine held that Moses wrote in a metaphorical or allegorical form, rather than describing the literal truth, because ancient Jews were untutored in science (Ruse 2001, 51). Armstrong (1993, 395) similarly explains that creation is a central teaching in the Qur'an but that "like all [the Qur'an's] utterances about God, this is said to be a 'parable' or a 'sign' (*aya*) of an ineffable truth. Muslim rationalists found it a difficult and problematic doctrine . . . In any case, cosmology was not a scientific description of the origins of the world but was originally a symbolic expression of spiritual and psychological truth [in Islam]."

34. Several influential thinkers associated with conservative religious views have held similar positions. Karl Barth's "neo-orthodox" Christianity, which, like American evangelical Protestantism, emphasizes the centrality of sin to Christianity, encourages Christians to think about God in a nonempirical and nonliteral way (Ruse 2001, 47).

35. For good general criticisms of Armstrong's work, see Douthat 2009a and McCulloch 2009.

36. Warren Nord points out this association in his review of a 1984 National Academy of Sciences statement on evolution that supports the independence approach. "For the fundamentalist," notes Nord (1995, 284), "science and religion are not separate and exclusive realms; they make competing claims about the same territory." Kent Greenawalt (2005, 96) makes a similar point in critiquing Gould's view of religion and science as "nonoverlapping magisteria."

## Chapter 5

1. Assuming too much consensus among those who supported consensus about religion would be a mistake. Support for centrist politics did not automatically imply support for civil religion. Moderate Republicans like Dwight D. Eisenhower were far more comfortable with public displays of piety than were liberals like Schlesinger (Ledewitz 2007, 101).

But it would also be a mistake to exaggerate the differences between those on the

moderate left and right over religion. Centrist liberals were not aggressive secularists but at least tolerated, in the case of Schlesinger, or supported, in the case of the
sociologist Will Herberg (1958), relatively nonsectarian forms of public piety. Thus,
a letter published by the center-left National Council of Churches protested a growing secularization of public schools and American society and suggested that "a
'reverent reading' of biblical passages in the public schools would go a long way to
deepening the awareness of God in the public schools" (Boles 1965, 245). Centrists
on the right, like Eisenhower, were uncomfortable with the extreme patriotism and
occasional racism of fundamentalist versions of Christianity.

There were dissenters to the use of religion for the purposes of consensus among
the vital center's proponents. Reinhold Niebuhr, whose views on the exploitation of
religion by democracy receive treatment later in the chapter, was perhaps the most
notable critic. But even these critics were often ambivalent. Niebuhr, for instance,
sharply criticized the Supreme Court decisions removing devotional prayer and
Bible reading from public schools (Brown 1992, 229). For more comprehensive accounts of the relationship between religion and politics during the 1950s, see Marty
1996; Silk 1988; W. L. Miller 1964.

2. The Eisenhower administration issued a red, white, and blue postage stamp
emblazoned with "In God We Trust" (W. L. Miller 1964, 41).

3. According to a colorful description by Charles Mathewes (2007a), theorists
promoting the vital center "marginalized all those who opposed liberalism as reactions or relics of the past, a crotchety old lunatic fringe of back-country wackos who
should be ignored or, better, put on cognitive reservations until they die off." In a recent issue of the *Atlantic,* Ross Douthat (2008) makes a similar point while describing the recent increase of a more aggressive form of secularism and atheism. "The
new mass-market atheism," he writes, "is following the same pattern as the Christian Right before it, which likewise drew strength from a sense of embattlement and
persecution. These mirror-image movements can be seen as backlashes against the
genteel secularism of mid-century, with its faintly condescending respect for the
idea of Religion, and its studious indifference toward actual belief. This backlash
has made debates over religion more polarizing than they used to be—and also
more interesting."

While these views are persuasive, several qualifications are necessary. The 1950s
and early 1960s did not involve a complete exclusion of evangelical cultural views
from politics. These views influenced local and state politics, even as they were
largely ignored in national politics. Moreover, the exclusion from national politics
was not completely unjustified. For instance, 1950s white Southern evangelicalism's
frequent alliance with segregation and hyperpatriotism meant it posed a greater
challenge to basic democratic values than does evangelicalism today.

4. William Lee Miller's balanced assessment of the 1950s suggests that the time's
greatest virtue was also its most dire fault. "Somewhere in between there was a brief
happy moment, when a combination of prosperity, Eisenhower, peace, religiosity,
moral language, nostalgic patriotism, and public relations brought a precarious
plateau of repose to many characteristic Americans," writes Miller (1964, xiv), who
continues, "But these higher yearnings had no critical edge. They did not unsettle

conventional opinions. They required little significant new effort either of thought or of action." Miller elsewhere suggests that religion during the period "appears as a wholesale endorsement of the aims and purposes of America, 'the mightiest power which God has yet seen fit to put upon his footstool'" (34).

5. "In moments of candor public educators," writes Neuhaus (1984, 23), "had recognized that the common denominator was somewhat artificial and contrived; too much of what people really believed most deeply had to be swept under the carpet in order to maintain the putative consensus. At the same time, there were new and aggressive forces in American cultural and political life that did not go along with the minimal belief system." Neuhaus describes the arrival of the religious right on the national scene in the following terms: "Millions of Americans have half marched, half stumbled, into the public space we mistakenly thought was ours. They make no apologies for breaking down the door, since they think it should not have been locked in the first place. To put it differently, at the family reunion of American religion, the disreputable side of the family has for the first time shown up in force . . . The mainliners boast of being ecumenical, but do not want to carry ecumenism too far" (57).

6. *Religious Literacy* has received a Quill Award and has been the subject of a *Time* magazine cover article.

7. Jay Wexler (2002, 1242) suggests that classes about the Bible "cannot provide the best context for teaching mutual respect and toleration, as they focus on the most prominent religions instead of those that might more broadly be met with ignorance and suspicion." The Society for Biblical Literature (2009, 8), one of the two most prominent organizations advocating expanded academic treatment of the Bible in public schools, cautions in its 2009 guidelines that "many considerations weigh against requiring students to take a Bible course." "Most importantly, students may believe that the very act of approaching the Bible from a critical or academic (rather than a religious perspective)," the guidelines continue, "violates their religious beliefs and practices."

8. Georgia, for instance, has decided to focus on implementing elective courses on the Bible in all its public schools without a similar requirement for world religions courses, and the Alabama legislature has recently debated taking the same course of action (Jonsson 2006).

9. A hundred years is a long time, and significant changes in education about the Bible took place during this time. The local control of schools meant that Mann's approach was not, of course, followed uniformly at any one period in time (Fraser 1999, 95–98; Boles 1965, 9; Del Fattore 2004). Skepticism is always appropriate about claims of historical influence when the span of years between alleged cause and effect is large. But Mann's vision did, on all accounts, have a large influence on how the Bible was treated in many places around the country for a very long period of time, and the devotional Bible reading in place during the heyday of 1950s civil religion still reflected Mann's innovations in important ways.

10. Donald Boles (1965, 11) emphasizes that sectarian instruction did, in fact, disappear for a time in many schools in the early nineteenth century, due to the proliferation of Protestant sects. In many cases, the adoption of Mann's innovations in-

volved not a revision of the existing treatment of the Bible but a reintroduction of Bible teaching.

11. Mann's civic education proposals, according to Christopher Lasch (1995, 153), emphasized "only those articles in the creed of republicanism, which are accepted by all, believed in by all, and which form the common basis of our political faith."

12. "Mann's goal," explains Joseph Viteritti (2007, 71), "was to produce good republicans who could vote for wise and decent political leaders. He did not embrace pluralism."

13. The solutions that Catholic thinkers of a slightly later generation proposed for the problem of religion in schools attempted to reconcile assimilation and diversity in a more thoughtful and complex way. Archbishop John Ireland's "Poughkeepsie Plan," introduced in 1890, is of particular interest. The plan proposed that the state rent parochial schools and pay their teachers from 9:00 a.m. to 3:00 p.m., during which time students would only learn secular subjects. After 3:00 p.m., teachers could turn their attention to the teaching of the Catholic faith (Fraser 1999, 62).

14. Prothero (2007, 99) notes that by the late nineteenth century, public schools became dominated by "largely vestigial civic rites—hymn singing, praying, Bible readings—that under the newly nonsectarian public school regime had the trappings of religious significance with little actual piety."

15. Readers may reasonably question this chapter's primary focus on attempts to teach the Bible in a mainstream or centrist way. After all, most proposals and curricula for teaching elective Bible courses over the last 50 years have come from conservative Christian groups. Still, these courses have little chance of being implemented outside of southeastern Bible Belt communities, because of their obvious sectarian biases. Even if implemented, they stand no chance of passing First Amendment scrutiny and court review. This chapter focuses on more mainstream and centrist approaches to Bible electives because they enjoy broader support and are more likely to be implemented and receive court approval in a wider range of school districts. As I argue later in this chapter, however, these approaches that lack the obvious biases of conservative Christian courses are not necessarily free of significant bias.

16. "And plainly the way" to teach about religion, adds Prothero (2007, 132), "is to steer clear of both advocating religion and impugning it while at the same time communicating the individual religious convictions are to be treated, as a matter of both law and civility, with respect."

17. In his *New York Times* review of Prothero's book, Mark Oppenheimer (2007) asks, "Would wider knowledge of the Baltimore Catechism or New Testament stories really advance debates on, say, stem-cell research? Or would people find new reasons to cling to their old opinions?"

18. "Today it is a rare American," writes Prothero (2007, 9), "who can follow with any degree of confidence biblically inflected debates about abortion or gay marriage."

19. Alan Wolfe (2000) calls attention to this surprising intellectual kinship. Despite their divergent views, evangelicals and postmodernists are united by a suspicion of liberal political theories that claim to be based on universal agreement.

20. Space limitations require a basic summary of Prothero's argument, even if this fails to do full justice to the provocative, scrupulously researched, nuanced, and always engaging nature of Prothero's achievement.

21. Even if the counternarratives to Prothero's account that are discussed shortly are correct, this does not necessarily invalidate it. Historical changes often occur for many reasons, and it is, of course, not unprecedented for bad and good reasons for change to coexist.

22. Evangelicals, of course, are not alone in lamenting these changes. Christopher Lasch (1995, 208–12), for instance, complains notably, in his *The Revolt of the Elites,* that American mainstream culture has attempted to abolish shame over the body and sexual relationships.

23. Public opinion polls have consistently shown strong public support for teaching about the Bible in the public school curriculum. A 1999 Gallup poll (June 25–27 [$N$ = 1,016, MoE ± 3]) found that 71 percent of respondents favored "using the Bible in literature, history, and social studies classes." A 2006 CBS News poll (April 6–9 [$N$ = 899, MoE ± 3]) found that 64 percent of respondents believed that public schools "should . . . be allowed to teach the Bible as a piece of literature, in classes like English or Social Studies."

24. As Randall Balmer (2007) notes in his *Washington Monthly* review of Prothero's book, the evangelical desire for intellectual understanding of the text and belief in doctrinal precisionism fueled the modernist-fundamentalist splits of the early twentieth century. His point contradicts Prothero's emphasis on evangelical anti-intellectualism. But just because many evangelicals share Prothero's concern about increases in biblical illiteracy does not mean they would accept his claim that the current ethical focus of evangelicals is misplaced. Many evangelicals whose overall biblical literacy could be better are often able to offer textual support for the particular moral positions they are most concerned with. Balmer claims that the emphasis on theology and doctrine is as strong as the emphasis in mainline Protestantism but that there are legitimate differences between mainline and evangelical Protestants about what parts of theology and doctrine should be emphasized most. Thus, despite their agreement on biblical illiteracy as a problem, many evangelicals would still reject the form of Bible education Prothero advocates.

25. While views like Prothero's that Jews and Christians should strive to incorporate a more broad-based knowledge of the Bible into their religious beliefs have a place in such an education, they should not have a privileged one. Such arguments would be pleas from some faiths to others and are not messages schools should communicate to students.

26. The ascending approach to teaching about the Bible that is advocated for the high school curriculum here has several key affinities with the pluralistic approach that John Courtney Murray (1960, 135) advocated for teaching about religion at the university level.

The assertion I chiefly wish to venture is that the university is committed to its students and to their freedom to learn. Its students are not abstractions . . . Or to put it even more concretely, they are Protestants, Catholics, Jews. The university as such has no right to judge the validity of any of these commitments. Similarly, it has no right to ignore the fact of these commitments . . . Whatever the concrete formula may be, it must reckon with the factual pluralism of American society, insofar as this pluralism is real and not illusory. There can be no question of any bogus irenicism or of the submergence of religious differences in a vague haze of "fellowship."

27. See also Bible Literacy Project and First Amendment Center 1999. This document, entitled *The Bible and Public Schools: A First Amendment Guide* and endorsed by a diverse array of Jewish and Christian organizations, advocates teaching about the Bible to promote knowledge of biblical stories and concepts and their applicability to literature and history (5). It supports teaching about the Bible in required literature and history classes and is also supportive of an independent Bible elective course that treats the Bible as literature and in literature (12).

28. A paragraph on BLP's Web site devoted to making the case for Bible literacy reads as follows: "There are many important rationales for bringing high-quality, academic instruction about the Bible to all American schoolchildren. Students of all faiths (and none) need to know about the Bible to engage their American heritage in key areas of language, arts, and literature, as well as history, law, and politics. Why should any student, regardless of faith tradition, be denied the tools to understand some of the most inspiring rhetoric in American history? Or contemplate just a few of the achievements of Western culture that have been inspired, in part, by Biblical language and narratives: Milton's *Paradise Lost*, Handel's *Messiah*, Michelangelo's David" (Bible Literacy Project 2008).

29. See Bible Literacy Project and First Amendment Center 1999, 8–9.

30. The creation of the NCBCPS curriculum predates the creation and use of *BI* in public schools. But the use of *BI* has galvanized support for NCBCPS implementation among some conservative Christians. Given the omissions of *BI*, its further implementation is likely to only increase and widen calls for an alternative curriculum among hard-line evangelicals and fundamentalists.

31. Former *BI* supporter and noted conservative Paul Weyrich (2008) claims in a recent article that *BI* "demeans God" and "denies the moral value of Old Testament illustrations."

32. In comparing the older and revised version of NCBCPS's text, Mark Chancey (2008) of Southern Methodist University effectively summarizes the major flaws of the NCBCPS curriculum.

Most troubling is the fact that the new curriculum still clearly reflects a political agenda. Like the old version, it seems to Christianize America and Americanize the Bible. It continues to recommend the resources of WallBuilders, an organization devoted to the opposition of church-state separation, and it still advocates showing that group's video, *Foundations of American Government*, at the beginning of the course. This video, narrated by the founder of WallBuilders, David Barton, argues that the Founding Fathers never intended for church and state to be separated and that America has descended into social chaos since devotional Bible reading and prayer were removed from public schools . . .

Unit 17, "The Bible in History," . . . goes well beyond a discussion of the Bible's influence on American society to make a broader argument for an increased role of religion in public and civic life. There is simply no other explanation for the new content on pages 237–240 entitled "Observations of the Supreme Court," which discusses the legality of civic nativity scenes, congressional prayers, Thanksgiving holiday, the motto "In God We Trust," and the phrase "One Nation Under God." The following pages (241–250) duplicate material from the previous edition of the curriculum, with numerous quotations—some of them spurious— on the importance of the Bible and Christianity set against the backdrop of images of the American flag and soldiers. Both this unit and Unit 6 ("Hebrew Law") include out-of-context quotations from the Founding Fathers that imply that the idea of separation of church and state is misguided. Since no quotations from famous figures supporting church-state separation are included, the curriculum's own position is quite clear—and it is the position of the NCBCPS's endorsers and advisors, the belief that America was founded as a distinctively Christian nation and should remain so.

For these reasons, among others, the NCBCPS curriculum clearly runs afoul of the establishment clause. When a school district in Odessa, Texas, attempted to base a Bible elective course on the NCBCPS curriculum, eight parents sued, and the district dropped the use of the curriculum as part of the lawsuit's settlement (Associated Press 2008).

33. The report was published prior to the publication of *BI*, so the teachers interviewed were not using the text. But they were taking the same academic and literary approach to the Bible that is used in *BI*.

34. *The Bible and Public Schools: A First Amendment Guide* (Bible Literacy Project and First Amendment Center 1999, 7) wisely suggests that devotional texts and instructional materials of the types used in Sunday schools should not be used in class, and public schools in the course that this chapter recommends should discourage religions from using these texts. Besides their alienating effect, there is a basic educational and practical problem with the use of these texts. Promoting understanding of and securing respect for their religious beliefs among those who hold different beliefs is a primary purpose of the course, but texts written and aimed at those who already adhere to these faiths are ill-fitted for this purpose. Each group included in the course should write descriptions of their religions or use texts that are more accessible to those who hold other beliefs about religion.

35. The Central Conference of American Rabbis, the United Synagogue of Conservative Judaism, and the Union of Orthodox Jewish Congregations of America could prepare statements about Judaism. Statements about Christianity could be solicited from the Catholic Church, the National Council of Churches, the National Association of Evangelicals, the Church of Jesus Christ of Latter-Day Saints, the Greek Orthodox Archdiocese of America, the Orthodox Church in America, the Unitarian Universalist Association of Congregations, the Pentecostal/Charismatic Churches of North America, and the Southern Baptist Convention. This list is not intended to be exhaustive or definitive. These organizations should also be encouraged to ad-

dress the distinctive concerns of racial and ethnic minorities. The statement by the National Council of Churches that students read, for instance, should discuss the distinctive views of African American denominations belonging to the council.

36. The SBL guidelines and the BLP do emphasize the importance of introducing students to various interpretations of the Bible. Still, the ascending approach is more favorable to diversity and countercultural beliefs because it allows religious groups to discuss the degree to which their religious beliefs depend on the Bible, as well as the other elements that influence their perspectives.

37. There are, of course, limits to how far the state should carry a bottom-up, democratic approach to teaching about Judaism and Christianity. A fully democratic approach allowing each religious denomination and different groups within denominations to prepare statements and texts for students is a possible alternative to allowing only multidenominational councils, like the National Council of Churches (NCC) and National Association of Evangelicals (NAE), to address students. The more democratic approach would avoid giving students the impression that the positions taken by groups like the NCC and NAE are normative for all mainline and evangelical Protestants, respectively. But the sheer impracticality of accommodating the astounding number of denominations in America's religious landscape in a single semester must trump this concern. Schools may want to reserve some time during the semester to allow students who feel that the course does not adequately address their form of Judaism and Christianity to provide a statement of their religious views if they wish. The statements of these students could be written by their local religious leader.

A purely bottom-up approach would also fail to accommodate the requirements of a liberal education. Biblical illiteracy may not be the civic problem Prothero contends it is, but he and the BLP convincingly claim that it impedes a proper understanding of art, literature, and world history. The artistic and historical influences of the Bible should not be the sole purpose of a course about Judaism and Christianity, but neither should such a public school course neglect them. Since religious groups might be more interested in discussing their central religious and social concerns, the curriculum they construct might omit important artistic and historical concerns. Besides, if the course jumps right into what each group believes about the Bible while students are largely unfamiliar with the Bible, they may be unable to understand the concerns of each group.

Public schools should consider dividing a course on Judaism and Christianity into two parts. In the first and shorter part of the course, students would read parts of *BI* to familiarize them with key biblical concepts and stories and with the Bible's literary and historical influence. To avoid the limitations of using a single text, *BI* would simply be one among the many sources that students read for the course. The second and longer part of the course would focus on statements and texts prepared by major religious groups. To counter the selectivity of *BI*'s presentation of the Bible, religious groups would be free to critique the textbook and, more important, to provide students with crucial information they believe that *BI* omits.

38. Appropriate teacher training is obviously crucial to the success of this approach. The SBL guidelines and *The Bible and Public Schools: A First Amendment Guide*

both provide excellent advice about teacher selection and training that are relevant to the course this chapter recommends. Both advise that outside organizations or committees should not hire or supervise teachers, and *The Bible and Public Schools* stresses that teachers should not be selected according to their religious beliefs or lack thereof (Society for Biblical Literacy 2009, 7; Bible Literacy Project and First Amendment Center 1999, 6).

Having teachers consult with or learn from religious leaders in preparing for the course is acceptable *as long as* they seek similar training from each faith the course teaches. As previously discussed in chapter 3, Modesto teachers visited religious ceremonies and met with religious leaders from each of the faiths their required world religions course covered; this training enhanced instruction and did not lead to controversy. *The Bible and Public Schools* also advocates the creation of in-service workshops and summer institutes (Bible Literacy Project and First Amendment Center 1999, 9).

39. Legitimate educational reasons for exposing students to biblical passages critical of one or more religious perspectives may occasionally override concerns of alienation. The SBL guidelines raise the case of passages in the New Testament gospels and epistles critical of Judaism (Society for Biblical Literacy 2009, 18). Some Christian religious groups may find these passages to be useful in helping other religious groups understand their differences with Judaism.

At the same time, the SBL guidelines provide useful advice for limiting the alienating impact of exposure to these statements. In examining these passages, public schools should note the historical context and polemical purpose of these New Testament statements and should direct students to secondary literature that discusses these matters in depth. In the bottom-up approach I recommend, Jewish groups can counteract these passages, for instance, by noting Jesus's Jewish background and emphasizing what they believe to be early Christianity's intellectual and theological debts to Judaism.

40. In many communities around the nation, of course, support for a more open view of marriage and civil unions is a countercultural view. Providing conservative Christians with the ability to express their views on these issues in ascending, elective courses would benefit more liberal religious groups by enabling them to express views that the current curriculum ignores. By contrast, *BI* ignores gay marriage and fails to acquaint conservative students with defenses of gay marriage by more liberal forms of Judaism and Christianity.

41. The consistency of the elective Bible course recommended here with the First Amendment's establishment clause seems clear from the fact that courses using *BI* and relying on the BLP's nonsectarian Bible-as-literature approach have not been the subject of any successful constitutional challenges. This is not surprising given that the Supreme Court has affirmed several times the constitutional legitimacy of teaching about the Bible as long as it is "presented objectively as part of a secular program of education" (*Abingdon* 1963, 225; see also *Stone* 1980, 42). Still, as noted by *The Bible and Public Schools: A First Amendment Guide* (Bible Literacy Project and First Amendment Center 1999, 5), various federal court cases have specified crucial features that Bible courses must possess in order to survive constitutional scrutiny

(*Hall* 1981; *Gibson* 1998; *Chandler* 1997; *Herdahl* 1996; *Doe* 1989; *Crockett* 1983; *Wiley* 1979; *Vaughn* 1970). The course recommended here is clearly consistent with the major criteria courts have established. For instance, the course neither promotes nor disparages religion, nor does it promote a particular sectarian point of view (*Wiley* 1979, 394; *Gibson* 1998, 1433; *Herdahl* 1996, 595). It does not select teachers based on their religious beliefs (*Herdahl* 1996, 593–94; *Wiley* 1979, 152). The civic approach, like the Bible-as-literature approach, has the legitimate academic goal of providing students with an appreciation of the Bible's contribution to history and culture (*Abingdon* 1963, 225; *Stone* 1980, 42; *Hall* 1981,1002; *Gibson* 1998, 1432; *Chandler* 1997, 1063; *Herdahl* 1996, 592; *Doe* 1989, 1508; *Crockett* 1983, 1427; *Wiley* 1979, 392; *Vaughn* 1970, 433).

The fundamental difference between the BLP and the civic approach concerns the means used to achieve this end. The civic approach prefers a more pluralistic, bottom-up approach to providing students with a robust understanding of the Bible's influence, which has the added academic and secular benefit of promoting greater understanding between Jews and Christians. That the civic approach, unlike the BLP approach, has this added secular benefit only strengthens its claim to constitutional legitimacy.

## Conclusion

1. Sullivan's claim that greater support for Obama is evidence that our conflicts over religion and culture are abating assumes that Obama's campaign was in fact more civil and conciliatory than McCain's campaign. This is obviously a contestable claim, but Obama's outreach to religious voters, the selection of Sarah Palin as McCain's running mate, and the prominent attempts by the McCain campaign to contrast those who are "pro-American" or live in the "real" part of Virginia with more urban and cosmopolitan liberals suggest that Sullivan's claims are not unreasonable.

2. The same zero-sum dynamic was evident in the Obama administration's decision within its first 50 days to reverse President George W. Bush's restrictions on stem cell research (Saletan 2009b) and President Bush's executive order allowing health care workers to refuse to participate in providing services violating their moral and religious beliefs (Dionne 2009). Furthermore, inaction is just as unlikely as careful action to change the zero-sum dynamic of culture war policy disputes. Thus, the Obama administration's postponement of a change in the military's "Don't Ask, Don't Tell" policy has only fed hostility toward the policy among gay rights' groups. In other words, a neutral policy course is simply not an option in most disputes at the heart of the culture wars.

3. The same problems would apply if Linker's conversion or conquest scenarios came to fruition, since both scenarios assume that a significant, albeit diminished, number of Americans would still care deeply about prevailing cultural norms and policies.

4. The divisive debate over the proposed Islamic center near Ground Zero in August 2010 and contemporaneous opposition to other mosques and Islamic centers

around the country (Gowen 2010; Loller 2010) suggest both how far American discourse over religion still often is from being truly civil, and the costs of incivility for vulnerable religious minorities.

5. For evidence that most evangelicals support a public school curriculum that gives "equal time" to different views rather than priority to one view, see "The Moderate Majority" in chapter 2.

6. The status quo policy of ignoring religion in public schools has already helped to fuel a recent enrollment boom in conservative Protestant schools and a dramatic increase in the number of students homeschooled for religious reasons (Prothero 2007, 130; Lines 2000; Associated Press 2006). Given that conservative Christians are more likely than other Americans to hold intolerant views toward groups like Muslims and atheists, a public school policy that drove conservative Christians away from public schools by teaching only required world religions courses without any recognition of conservative Christian beliefs would be profoundly counterproductive. See also note 11 in chapter 1.

# References

Abdrabboh, F. 2005. Letter to the editor. *New York Times,* June 24.

Abernethy, B. 2007. Religious literacy. *Religion and Ethics Newsweekly,* May 18.

*Abingdon School District v. Schempp.* 1963. 374 U.S. 203.

Abrams, F., B. Barr, and T. Pickering. 2005. Justice before politics. *Washington Post,* June 7.

Allport, G. 1950. *The individual and his religion.* New York: MacMillan.

Altmeyer, B., and B. Hunsberger. 1992. Authoritarianism, religious fundamentalism, quest, and prejudice. *International Journal for the Psychology of Religion 2.*

Antenore, J. 2009. Interview by Emile Lester. December 18.

Armstrong, K. 1993. *A history of God.* New York: Ballantine.

Armstrong, K. 2000. *The battle for God: A history of fundamentalism.* New York: Ballantine.

Associated Press. 2006. Evangelicals intensify calls for public-school pullout. September 6.

Associated Press. 2008. Texas school district, parents settle lawsuit over Bible course. March 7.

Association for Supervision and Curriculum Development. 1987. *Religion in the curriculum.* Alexandria, VA: ASCD.

Audi, R. 1993. The place of religious argument in a free and democratic society. *San Diego Law Review 30.*

Audi, R., and N. Wolterstorff. 1997. *Religion in the public square: The place of religious convictions in political debates.* Lanham, MD: Rowman and Littlefield.

Babbie, E. 2004. *The basics of social research.* Belmont, CA: Thomson Wadsworth.

Balmer, R. 2007. Joan of Arc, wife of Noah? *Washington Monthly,* April.

Bannerjee, N. 2005. An alternative to evolution splits a Pennsylvania town. *New York Times,* January 16.

Barbassa, J. 2006. California school system calls off class on intelligent design. Associated Press, January 18.

Barber, B. 1984. *Strong democracy: Participatory politics for a new age.* Berkeley: University of California Press.

Bartels, L. 2008. *Unequal democracy: The political economy of the new gilded age.* Princeton: Princeton University Press.

Bazelon, E. 2007. Is there a post-abortion syndrome? *New York Times,* January 21.

Beauchamp, M. 2007. Interview by Emile Lester. June 15.

Beckwith, F. 2003. *Law, Darwinism, and public education: The establishment clause and the challenge of intelligent design.* Lanham, MD: Rowman and Littlefield.

Behe, M. 1996. *Darwin's black box: The biochemical challenge to evolution.* New York: Simon and Schuster.

Beinart, P. 2009. The end of the culture wars. *Daily Beast,* January 26. http://www.thedailybeast.com/blogs-and-stories/2009-01-26/the-end-of-the-culture-wars/.

Bellah, R. 1986. *Habits of the heart: Individualism and commitment in American life.* New York: Harper and Row.

Bellah, R., and P. Hammond. 1980. *Varieties of civil religion.* San Francisco: Harper and Row.

Benhabib, S. 1996. *Democracy and difference: Contesting boundaries of the political.* Princeton: Princeton University Press.

Berra, T. 1990. *Evolution and the myth of creationism.* Stanford: Stanford University Press.

Beutler, B. 2010. Reid's opposition to the "Ground Zero mosque" surprises Dems—and leaves them vulnerable. *Talking Points Memo,* August 16. http://tpmdc.talkingpointsmemo.com/2010/08/reids-mosque-position-leaves-dems-raw.php.

Bible Literacy Project. 2008. The case for Bible literacy in secondary schools. http://www.bibleliteracy.org/site/PressRoom/thecase.htm.

Bible Literacy Project and First Amendment Center. 1999. *The Bible and public schools: A First Amendment Center guide.* New York: Bible Literacy Project.

Bird, A. 1998. Trustees heed advice of safe-schools panel. *Modesto Bee,* January 21.

Bishop, B. 2008. *The big sort: Why the clustering of like-minded Americans is tearing us apart.* New York: Houghton Mifflin.

Blankenhorn, D. 1995. *Fatherless America.* New York: Basic Books.

Blankenhorn, D. 2007. Defining marriage down. *National Review,* April 2.

Boles, D. 1965. *The Bible, religion, and public schools.* Ames: Iowa State University Press.

Booth, W. 2007. Cast of villains: "Reel bad Arabs" takes on Hollywood stereotyping. *Washington Post,* June 23.

Bowers, I. 2005. Interview by Emile Lester. January 12.

Boyer, P. 1996. In search of the fourth "R": The treatment of religion in American history textbooks and survey courses. *History Teacher* 2.

Brown, C. C. 1992. *Niebuhr and his age.* Philadelphia: Trinity.

Buckley, M. 1987. *At the origins of modern atheism.* New Haven: Yale University Press.

Burns, A. 2008. Newsweek draws fire on gay marriage. *Politico,* December 8.

Callan, E. 1997. *Creating citizens: Political education and liberal democracy.* Oxford: Clarendon.

Campbell, J. 2003. Intelligent design, Darwinism, and the philosophy of public education. In *Darwinism, design, and public education,* ed. J. Campbell and S. Meyer. East Lansing: Michigan State University Press.

Carey, G. 2000. Tolerating the intolerable. In *The politics of toleration in modern life*, ed. S. Mendus. Durham, NC: Duke University Press.

Chait, J. 2010. Say it ain't so. *The New Republic*, August 3. http://www.tnr.com/blog/jonathan-chait/76755/say-it-aint-so.

Chancey, M. 2008. The revised curriculum of the National Council on Bible Curriculum in Public Schools. http://www.bibleinterp.com/articles/Chancey_Bible _Curr_Revised.htm.

*Chandler v. James.* 1997. 985 F. Supp. 1062.

Chang, K. 2005. A debate over Darwin: Evolution or design? *New York Times*, August 22.

Citrin, J., D. Sears, C. Muste, and C. Wong. 2001. Multiculturalism in American public opinion. *British Journal of Political Science* 31.

Coenders, M., and P. Scheepers. 1998. Support for ethnic discrimination in the Netherlands, 1979–1993: Effects of period, cohort, and individual characteristics. *European Sociological Review* 14.

Cohen, R. 2010. Obama muddles his mosque message. *Washington Post*, August 17.

Coleman, J. 1998. Civic pedagogies and liberal-democratic curricula. *Ethics* 108.

Coleman, J. 2003. American Catholicism, Catholic Charities USA, and welfare reform. In *Religion returns to the public square: Faith and policy in America*, ed. H. Heclo and W. McClay. Washington, DC: Woodrow Wilson Center Press.

Conover, P. J., and D. D. Searing. 2000. A political socialization perspective. In *Rediscovering the democratic purposes of education*, ed. L. M. McDonnell, P. M. Timpane, and R. Benjamin. Lawrence: University Press of Kansas.

Couchman, J. 2004. Interview by Emile Lester. May 13.

Cougle, J., D. Reardon, and P. Coleman. 2003. Depression associated with abortion and childbirth: A long-term analysis of the NLSY cohort. *Medical Science Monitor* 9.

Council on American-Islamic Relations. 2004. *The status of Muslim civil rights in the United States: Guilt by association, 2003.* Washington, DC: Council on American-Islamic Relations.

*County of Allegheny v. American Civil Liberties Union, Greater Pittsburgh Chapter.* 1989. 491 U.S. 573.

Crapanzano, V. 2000. *Serving the word: Literalism in America from the pulpit to the bench.* New York: New Press.

*Crockett v. Sorenson.* 1983. 568 F. Supp. 1422.

Dahl, R. 1982. *Dilemmas of pluralist democracy: Authority versus control.* New Haven: Yale University Press.

Dawkins, R. 1995. *River out of Eden: A Darwinian view of life.* New York: Basic Books.

Dean, C. 2005a. A debate over Darwin: Squaring God and evolution. *New York Times*, August 23.

Dean, C. 2005b. Evolution takes a back seat in U.S. classes. *New York Times*, February 1.

Deane, C. 2003. About *Washington Post* response rates. *Washington Post*, July 7.

Del Fattore, J. 2004. *The fourth R: Conflicts over religion in America's public schools.* New Haven: Yale University Press.

Dembski, W. 1998. *The design inference: Eliminating chance through small probabilities.* Cambridge: Cambridge University Press.

Dembski, W. 2002. *No free lunch: Why specified complexity cannot be purchased without intelligence.* Lanham, MD: Rowman and Littlefield.

Deveaux, M. 2003. A deliberative approach to conflicts of culture. *Political Theory* 31.

Devlin, P. 1968. *The enforcement of morals.* London: Oxford University Press.

Dewey, J. 1991. *A common faith.* New Haven: Yale University Press.

Dewolf, D., S. C. Meyer, and M. E. Deforrest. 2003. Teaching the controversy: Is it science, religion or speech? In *Darwinism, design, and public education,* ed. J. Campbell and S. Meyer. East Lansing: Michigan State University Press.

Diament, N. 2008. Works, not words. *New Republic,* December 29.

Dionne, E. J. 2009. All's fair: Has Obama ruined his chances of ending the culture wars? *New Republic,* March 5. http://www.tnr.com/article/politics/alls-fair.

*Doe v. Human.* 1989. 725 F. Supp. 1503.

Douglass, S. 2000. *Teaching about religion in national and state standards.* Arlington, VA: Council on Islamic Education and First Amendment Center.

Douthat, R. 2008. Mass-market atheism. *Atlantic,* July–August.

Douthat, R. 2009a. The case for God. *New York Times Book Review,* October 4.

Douthat, R. 2009b. Ending or winning? *Atlantic,* January 28. http://rossdouthat.the atlantic.com/archives/2009/01/ending_or_winning.php.

D'Souza, D. 2002. *What's so great about America.* Washington, DC: Regnery.

DuBois, W. E. B. 2004. *The souls of black folk.* Boulder, CO: Paradigm.

Duckitt, J., and K. Fisher. 2003. The impact of social threat on worldview and ideological attitudes. *Political Psychology* 24.

Dwyer, J. 1998. *Religious schools v. children's rights.* Ithaca: Cornell University Press.

Dwyer, J. 2002. *Vouchers within reason: A child-centered approach to educational reform.* Ithaca: Cornell University Press.

Eck, D. 2002. *A new religious America.* San Francisco: HarperCollins.

Edgell, P., J. Gerteis, and D. Hartmann. 2006. Atheists as "other": Moral boundaries and cultural membership in American society. *American Sociological Review* 71.

*Education World.* 2000. Students flunk U.S. history test. July 7. http://www.educa tion-world.com/a_issues/issues100.shtml#editor%20note.

*Edwards v. Aguillard.* 1987. 482 U.S. 593.

Egelko, B. 2005. Court clears school of pushing religion with lesson on Islam. *San Francisco Chronicle,* November 18.

Elliott, A. 2008. Muslim voters detect a snub from Obama. *New York Times,* June 24.

Enochs, J. 2004. Interview by Emile Lester. October 11.

EPPC Online. 2003. Most evangelical leaders favor "evangelizing Muslims abroad." *Ethics and Public Policy Center,* April 7. http://www.eppc.org/news/newsID.8/news_detail.asp.

*Epperson v. Arkansas.* 1968. 393 U.S. 97.

Falwell, J. 2002. Interview on CBS's *60 Minutes.* October 3.

Family Research Council. 2009. Homosexual parenting: Placing children at risk. http://shakinandshinin.org/HomosexualParenting.html.

Feldman, N. 2005. *Divided by God: America's church-state problem—and what we should do about it.* New York: Farrar, Straus and Giroux.

Feldman, N. 2008. What is it about Mormonism? *New York Times,* January 6.

Feldman, S., and K. Stenner. 1997. Perceived threat and authoritarianism. *Political Psychology* 18, no. 4:741–70.

Fitzgerald, F. 2006. The evangelical surprise. *New York Review of Books,* April 26.

Focus on the Family. 2009. Focus on the Family's position statement on same-sex "marriage" and civil unions. http://www.citizenlink.org/FOSI/marriage/ssuap/A000000985.cfm.

Fowler, R. B. 1989. *Unconventional partners: Religion and liberal culture in the United States.* Boulder, CO: Westview.

Fraser, J. W. 1999. *Between church and state.* New York: St. Martin's.

Friedman, B. 2006. *The moral consequences of economic growth.* New York: Vintage.

Galeotti, A. 2002. *Toleration as recognition.* Cambridge: Cambridge University Press.

Galston, W. 2002. *Liberal pluralism: The implications of value pluralism for political theory and practice.* Cambridge: Cambridge University Press.

George, M. 2001. And then God created Kansas? The evolution/creationism debate in public schools. *University of Pennsylvania Law Review* 149.

Ghazala, A. J. 1993. The children of homosexual and heterosexual single mothers. *Child Psychiatry and Human Development* 23.

Gibson, J. L. 1988. Political intolerance and political repression during the McCarthy red scare. *American Political Science Review* 82.

*Gibson v. Lee County School Board.* 1998. 1 F.2d 1426.

*Gonzalez v. Carhart.* 2007. 550 U.S. 124.

Goodstein, L. 2002. A nation challenged: The religious right. *New York Times,* February 23.

Goodstein, L. 2008. Obama made gains among younger evangelical voters. *New York Times,* November 7.

Gordon, P. 2004. Interview by Emile Lester. May.

Gould, S. J. 1999. *Rock of ages: Science and religion in the fullness of life.* New York: Ballantine.

Gowen, A. 2010. Far from Ground Zero, other plans for mosques run into vehement opposition. *Washington Post,* August 23.

Green, J. 2009. What happened to the values voter? *First Things,* March.

Greenawalt, K. 2005. *Does God belong in the public schools?* Princeton: Princeton University Press.

Greenwald, G. 2010. The "mosque" debate is not a "distraction." *Salon,* August 23. http://www.salon.com/news/opinion/glenn_greenwald/2010/08/23/park51/index.html.

*Grove v. Mead.* 1985. 753 F.2d 1528.

Gutmann, A., and D. Thompson. 1996. *Democracy and disagreement.* Cambridge, MA: Belknap.

Gutmann, A., and D. Thompson. 2004. *Why deliberative democracy?* Princeton: Princeton University Press.

Hagerty, B. 2008. Understanding the Gospel according to Huckabee. National Public Radio transcript, February 8.

*Hall v. Board of Commissioners of Conecuh County.* 1981. 656 F.2d 999.

Harris, S. 2004. *The end of faith.* New York: Norton.

Hauerwas, S., and W. Willimon. 1996. *Where resident aliens live: Exercises for Christian practice.* Nashville, TN: Abingdon.

Haynes, C. 2004. Darwin under fire (again): Intelligent design vs. evolution. *First Amendment Center,* December 5. http://www.firstamendmentcenter.org/com mentary.aspx?id=14476.

Haynes, C. 2006. Interview by Emile Lester and Patrick Roberts. May 8.

Herberg, W. 1958. Religion, democracy, and public education. In *Religion in America,* ed. J. Cogley. New York: Meridian.

Herberg, W. 1960. *Protestant, Catholic, and Jew: An essay in religious sociology.* New York: Anchor Books.

Herbert, B. 2005. From "gook" to "raghead." *New York Times,* May 2.

*Herdahl v. Pontotoc County School District.* 1996. 933 F. Supp. 582.

Herendeen, S. 2002. Study of religions sets Modesto schools apart. *Modesto Bee,* December 22.

Hofstadter, R. 1955. *Social Darwinism in American thought.* Boston: Beacon.

Hunter, J. C. 2008. *A new kind of conservative.* Ventura, CA: Regal.

Hunter, J. D. 1991. *Culture wars: The struggle to define America.* New York: Basic Books.

Hunter, J. D., and A. Wolfe. 2006. *Is there a culture war?* Washington, DC: Pew Research Center.

Illo, J. 2005. Interview by Emile Lester. January 14.

Ipgrave, J. 2005. Pupil-to-pupil dialogue as a tool for religious education in the primary classroom. In *Intercultural education and religious plurality,* ed. R. Jackson and U. McKenna. Oslo: Oslo Coalition on Freedom of Religion or Belief.

Jackson, R. 1997. *Religious education: An interpretive approach.* London: Hodder and Stoughton.

Jackson, R. 2003. *International perspectives on citizenship, education, and religious diversity.* London: RoutledgeFalmer.

Jackson, R. 2004. *Rethinking religious education and plurality: Issues in diversity and pedagogy.* London: RoutledgeFalmer.

Jackson, R., and U. McKenna, eds. 2005. *Intercultural education and religious plurality.* Oslo: Oslo Coalition on Freedom of Religion or Belief.

Janofsky, M. 2006. Philadelphia mandates black history for graduation. *New York Times,* June 25.

Jefferson, T. 1993. *The life and selected writings of Thomas Jefferson.* New York: Random House.

Jenkins, P. 2003. *The new anti-Catholicism.* Oxford: Oxford University Press.

John S. and James L. Knight Foundation's High School Initiative. 2004. http://first amendmentcenter.jideas.org/professionals/news_release.php.

Jonsson, P. 2006. Georgia may OK Bible as textbook. *Christian Science Monitor,* May 26.

Keeter, S. 2000. Consequences of reducing nonresponse in a large national telephone survey. *Public Opinion Quarterly* 64.

Kinder, D., and L. Sanders. 1997. *Divided by color: Racial politics and democratic ideals.* Chicago: University of Chicago Press.

Kinder, D., and D. Sears. 1981. Prejudice and politics: Symbolic racism versus racial threats to the good life. *Journal of Personality and Social Psychology* 40.

Kirkpatrick, D. 2007. The evangelical crackup. *New York Times,* October 28.

*Kitzmiller, et al. v. Dover Area School District, et al.* 2005. 400 F. Supp. 2d 707.

Klosko, G. 2000. *Democratic procedures and liberal consensus.* New York: Oxford University Press.

Kohut, A., and J. Green. 2000. *The diminishing divide.* Washington, DC: Brookings Institution.

Krauss, L. 2006. How to make sure children are scientifically illiterate. *New York Times,* August 15.

Kristof, N. 2008. The push to "otherize" Obama. *New York Times,* September 20.

Kurtz, S. 2007. The end of marriage in Scandinavia. *National Review,* February 2.

Larson, E. 1997. *Summer for the gods.* New York: Basic Books.

Larson, E. 2003. *Trial and error: The American controversy over creation and evolution.* Oxford: Oxford University Press.

Lasch, C. 1995. *The revolt of the elites and the betrayal of democracy.* New York: Norton.

Laudan, L. 1996a. The demise of the demarcation problem. In *But is it science? The philosophical question in the creation/evolution controversy,* ed. M. Ruse. Amherst, NY: Prometheus Books.

Laudan, L. 1996b. Science at the bar—causes for concern. In *But is it science? The philosophical question in the creation/evolution controversy,* ed. M. Ruse. Amherst, NY: Prometheus Books.

Lawrence, L., and R. E. Lee. 1955. *Inherit the wind.* New York: Random House.

Ledewitz, B. 2007. *American religious democracy: Coming to terms with the end of secular politics.* Westport, CT: Praeger.

*Lee v. Weisman.* 1992. 505 U.S. 577.

*Lemon v. Kurtzman.* 1971. 403 U.S. 602.

Lester, E. 2004. Gratitude and parents' rights over their children's religious upbringing. *Journal of Beliefs and Values* 25.

Lester, E. 2006. The right to reasonable exit and a religious education for moderate autonomy. *Review of Politics,* 68.

Lester, E., and P. Roberts. 2006a. The distinctive paradox of religious tolerance: Active tolerance as a mean between passive tolerance and recognition. *Public Affairs Quarterly* 20.

Lester, E., and P. Roberts. 2006b. *Learning about world religions in public schools: The impact on student attitudes and community acceptance in Modesto, Calif.* Nashville, TN: First Amendment Center.

Lines, P. 2000. Homeschooling comes of age. *Public Interest* 140.

Linker, D. 2009. How to end the culture war. *New Republic,* January 29. http://www.tnr.com/blog/damon-linker/how-end-the-culture-war.

Loller, T. 2010. Far from Ground Zero, opponents fight new mosques. Associated Press, August 8.

Lopez, G. 2005. Interview by Emile Lester. January 11.

Luo, M. 2008. New PAC seeks to court Christians for Obama. *New York Times,* June 10.

Lynn, B. 2006. *Piety and politics: The right-wing assault on religious freedom.* New York: Harmony.

Macedo, S. 1995. Liberal civic education and religious fundamentalism: The case of God v. John Rawls? *Ethics* 105.

Macedo, S. 2003. *Diversity and distrust.* Cambridge, MA: Harvard University Press.

Magoulias, J. 2004. Interview by Emile Lester. May 12.

Marcus, G. E. 1995. *With malice toward some: How people make civil liberties judgments.* Cambridge: Cambridge University Press.

Marks, C. 2004. Interview by Emile Lester. May 14.

Marty, M. 1996. *Modern American religion.* Vol. 3, *Under God, indivisible, 1941–1960.* Chicago: University of Chicago Press.

Marty, M., and S. Appleby. 1991. *The fundamentalism project.* Vol. 1, *Fundamentalisms observed.* Chicago: University of Chicago Press.

Mathewes, C. 2007a. Romney and the Eisenhower approach. *Religion and Ethics Newsweekly,* December 6.

Mathewes, C. 2007b. *A theology of public life.* New York: Cambridge University Press.

Matteson, R. 2004. Interview by Emile Lester. October 12.

McClosky, H., and A. Brill. 1983. *Dimensions of tolerance.* New York: Russell Sage Foundation.

McConnell, M. 2002. Educational disestablishment: Why democratic values are ill-served by democratic control of schooling. In *Moral and political education 101,* ed. Stephen Macedo and Yael Tamir. New York: New York University Press.

McCormick Tribune Freedom Museum. 2006. Characters from "The Simpsons" more well known to Americans than their First Amendment freedoms, survey finds. March 1. http://www.freedomproject.us/files/pdf/museum.survey_release.pdf.

McCulloch, D. 2009. The greatest story or the trickiest? *Economist,* September 19.

McFarland, S. 1989. Religious orientations and the targets of discrimination. *Journal for the Scientific Study of Religion* 28.

McKibben, B. 2008. Taking the Gospels seriously. *New York Review of Books,* January 17.

*McLean v. Arkansas Board of Education.* 1981. 663 F.2d, 47, 48 (8th Cir.).

McMillan, R. 1985. *Religion in the public schools: An introduction.* Atlanta: Mercer University Press.

Miller, J. 1993. *The passion of Michel Foucault.* New York: Anchor Books.

Miller, N. 2001. Life, the universe, and everything constitutional: Origins in the public schools. *Journal of Church and State* 43.

Miller, W. L. 1964. *Piety along the Potomac.* New York: Houghton Mifflin.

*Mozert v. Hawkins County Board of Education.* 1987. 827 F.2d 1058.

Murray, J. C. 1960. *We hold these truths: Catholic reflections on the American proposition.* New York: Sheed and Ward.

Nesbitt, E. 2005. Ethnography, religion, and intercultural education: Some possibilities for Europe. In *Intercultural education and religious plurality,* ed. R. Jackson and U. McKenna. Oslo: Oslo Coalition on Freedom of Religion or Belief.

Neuhaus, R. J. 1984. *The naked public square: Religion and democracy in America.* Grand Rapids, MI: Eerdmans.

Newman, J. 1982. *Foundations of religious tolerance.* Toronto: University of Toronto Press.

Niebuhr, R. 1962. *The irony of American history.* New York: Scribner.

Noebel, D., J. F. Baldwin, and K. Bywater. 1995. *Clergy in the classroom: The religion of secular humanism.* Manitou Springs, CO: Summit.

Nord, W. 1995. *Religion and American education: Rethinking a national dilemma.* Chapel Hill: University of North Carolina Press.

Nord, W. 2010. *Does God make a difference?* Oxford: Oxford University Press.

Nord, W., and C. Haynes. 1998. *Taking religion seriously across the curriculum.* Nashville, TN: First Amendment Center.

Nowicki, S. 2008. Modesto pastor: Consider confession if you voted for Obama. *Modesto Bee,* November 29.

Nunn, C. A., H. J. Crockett Jr., and J. A. Williams Jr. 1978. *Tolerance for nonconformity,* San Francisco: Jossey-Bass.

Nussbaum, M. 2008. *Liberty of conscience: In defense of America's tradition of religious equality.* New York: Basic Books.

Obama, B. 2006. *The audacity of hope.* New York: Crown.

Oberdiek, H. 2001. *Tolerance: Between forbearance and acceptance.* Lanham, MD: Rowman and Littlefield.

O'Grady, K. 2005. Pedagogy, dialogue, and truth: Intercultural education in the religious education classroom. In *Intercultural education and religious plurality,* ed. R. Jackson and U. McKenna. Oslo: Oslo Coalition on Freedom of Religion or Belief.

Oppenheim, S. 2005. Interview by Emile Lester. January 12.

Oppenheimer, M. 2007. Knowing not. *New York Times,* June 10.

Ottati, V. C., and L. M. Isbell. 1996. Effects of mood during exposure to target information on subsequently reported judgments. *Journal of Personality and Social Psychology* 71.

Owens, E. 2007. Religion and civic education in American public schools. In *Religion, politics, and policy in the United States and Germany,* vol. 5, ed. K. Johnston. Washington, DC: American Institute for Comparative German Studies.

Owens, E. 2008. Disestablishment as legal *paideia:* Assessing Michael McConnell's educational and religious pluralism. In *Philosophy of education yearbook, 2008.* Urbana: University of Illinois Press.

Patterson, C. J. 1995. Families of the lesbian baby boom: Parent's division of labor and children's adjustment. *Development Psychology* 31.

Perlstein, R. 2008. *Nixonland.* New York: Scribner.

Peshkin, A. 1986. *God's choice: The total world of a fundamentalist Christian school.* Chicago: University of Chicago Press.

Pew Forum on Religion and Public Life. 2006. "Event transcript: Is there a culture war?" Posted May 23. http://pewforum.org/Politics-and-Elections/Is-There-A-Culture-War.aspx.

Plantinga, A. 2003. Creation and evolution: A modest proposal. In *Darwinism, design, and public education,* ed. J. Campbell and S. Meyer. East Lansing: Michigan State University Press.

Popenoe, D. 1996. *Life without father.* Cambridge, MA: Harvard University Press.

Prothero, S. 2007. *Religious literacy: What every American needs to know—and doesn't.* San Francisco: HarperCollins.

Quinn, P. 1996. The philosopher of science as expert witness. In *But is it science? The philosophical question in the creation/evolution controversy,* ed. M. Ruse. Amherst, NY: Prometheus Books.

Rakove, J., ed. 1999. *James Madison: Writings.* New York: Library of America.

Rardin, S. 2006. Eyes wide shut. *Pew Charitable Trust Magazine,* Fall.

Rawls, J. 1993. *Political liberalism.* New York: Columbia University Press.

Reardon, D. 1987. *Aborted women: Silent no more.* Chicago: Loyola University Press.

Rich, F. 2009. The culture warriors get laid off. *New York Times,* March 14.

Riker, W. 1982. *Liberalism against populism.* San Francisco: Freeman.

Robinson, E. 2010. Republicans pander over 'Ground Zero mosque.' *Washington Post,* August 17.

Rousseau, J. 1987. *The basic political writings.* Indianapolis: Hackett.

Rowland, M. 2001. Teen: "Be honest and open." *Modesto Bee,* October 8.

Ruse, M., ed. 1996. *But is it science? The philosophical question in the creation/evolution controversy.* Amherst, NY: Prometheus Books.

Ruse, M. 2001. *Can a Darwinian be a Christian?* Cambridge: Cambridge University Press.

Ruse, M. 2003. On behalf of the fool. In *Darwinism, design, and public education,* ed. J. Campbell and S. Meyer. East Lansing: Michigan State University Press.

Ruse, M. 2005. *The evolution-creation struggle.* Cambridge, MA: Harvard University Press.

Russo, N. 2005. Depression and unwanted first pregnancy: Longitudinal cohort study. *British Medical Journal* 331.

Saletan, W. 2009a. This is the way the culture wars end. *New York Times,* February 21.

Saletan, W. 2009b. Winning smugly. *Slate,* March 9. http://www.slate.com/id/2213287.

Schippe, C., and C. Stetson, eds. 2006. *The Bible and its influence.* New York: BLP Publishing.

Schlesinger, A. 1992. *The disuniting of America.* New York: Norton.

Schonborn, C. 2005. Finding design in nature. *New York Times,* July 7.

Shaheen, J. 1997. *Arab and Muslim stereotyping in American popular culture.* Washington, DC: Center for Muslim-Christian Understanding, Georgetown University.

Shaheen, J. 2001. *Reel bad Arabs: How Hollywood vilifies a people.* New York: Interlink.

Sheppard, S. 2004. Interview by Emile Lester. May 13.

Silk, M. 1988. *Spiritual politics: Religion and America since World War II.* New York: Simon and Schuster.

Skoog, G., and K. Bilica. 2002. The emphasis given to evolution in the state science standards: A lever for change in evolution education? *Science Education* 86.

Smith, C. 1998. *American evangelicalism: Embattled and thriving.* Chicago: University of Chicago Press.

Smith, C. 2000. *Christian America? What evangelicals really want.* Berkeley: University of California Press.

Smith, C., and M. Denton. 2005. *Soul searching: The religious and spiritual lives of American teenagers.* New York: Oxford University Press.

Smith, S. 1991. The rise and fall of religious freedom in constitutional discourse. *University of Pennsylvania Law Review* 140.

*Smith v. Board of School Commissioners of Mobile County.* 1987. 655 F. Supp. 939 (11th Cir.).

Sniderman, P. M., R. A. Brody, and P. Tetlock. 1991. *Reasoning and choice: explorations in political psychology.* Cambridge: Cambridge University Press.

Society for Biblical Literature. 2009. *Bible electives in public schools: A guide.* http://www.sbl-site.org/assets/pdfs/SchoolsGuide.pdf.

Spinner-Halev, J. 2000. *Surviving diversity: Religion and democratic citizenship.* Baltimore: John Hopkins University Press.

Stafford, T. 1997. The making of a revolution. *Christianity Today,* December 8.

Stanislaus County Elections. 2009. Election results. http://stanvote.com/returns.shtm.

Stein, R., and M. Scheer. 2009. Funding restored to groups that perform abortion, other cares. *Washington Post,* January 24.

Stolzenberg, N. M. 1993. "He drew a circle that shut me out": Assimilation, indoctrination, and the paradox of liberal education. *Harvard Law Review* 106.

*Stone v. Graham.* 1980. 449 U.S. 39.

Stotland, N. 1992. The myth of the abortion trauma syndrome. *Journal of the American Medical Association,* October 21.

Sullivan, A. 2007. Goodbye to all that. *Atlantic,* December.

Sullivan, A. 2008. Christianist watch. *Atlantic,* December 1. http://andrewsullivan.theatlantic.com/the_daily_dish/2008/12/christianist-wa.html.

Sullivan., J. L., G. E. Marcus, and J. Piereson. 1982. *Political tolerance and American democracy.* Chicago: University of Chicago Press.

Sullivan, J. L., J. Piereson, and G. E. Marcus. 1979. An alternative conceptualization of political tolerance: Illusory increases, 1950s–1970s. *American Political Science Review* 73:781–94.

Sullivan, J. L., P. Walsh, M. Shamir, D. G. Barnum, and J. L. Gibson. 1993. Why are politicians more tolerant? Selective recruitment and socialization among political elites in New Zealand, Israel, Britain, and the United States. *British Journal of Political Science* 23.

Sunstein, C. 2007. *Republic.com 2.0.* Princeton: Princeton University Press.

Tajfel, H. 1981. *Human groups and social categories: Studies in social psychology.* Cambridge: Cambridge University Press.

Taylor, C. 1992. *Multiculturalism and "the politics of recognition."* Princeton: Princeton University Press.

Taylor, Y. 2006. Interview by Emile Lester and Patrick Roberts. May 8.

Thorp, H. 2006. Evolution's bottom line. *New York Times,* May 12.

Tillich, P. 1958. *Dynamics of faith.* New York: Harper's.

Tiwari, P. 2005. Interview by Emile Lester. December 12.

Tobin, G., and D. Ybarra. 2008. *The trouble with textbooks: Distorting history and religion.* Lanham, MD: Lexington Books.

Tocqueville, A. de. 2000. *Democracy in America.* Ed. H. Mansfield and D. Winthrop. Chicago: University of Chicago Press.

Tomasi, J. 2001. *Liberalism beyond justice: Citizens, society, and the boundaries of political theory.* Princeton: Princeton University Press.

Toumey, C. 1994. *God's own scientists: Creationists in a secular world.* New Brunswick, NJ: Rutgers University Press.

*United States v. Seeger.* 1965. 380 U.S. 163.

*Vaughn v. Reed.* 1970. 313 F. Supp. 431.

Viteritti, J. 2007. *The last freedom: Religion from the public school to the public square.* Princeton: Princeton University Press.

Vitz, P. 1986. Traditional values in public school textbooks. *Public Interest* 84.

Wachlin, M. 2005. *The Bible literacy report.* Fairfax, VA: Bible Literacy Project.

Warner, W. 2004. Interview by Emile Lester. October 12.

Wazwaz, F. 2002. Inexcusable tolerance for religious extremism in America. *Counterpunch,* October 10.

Weaver, D., R. Beam, B. Brownlee, P. Voakes, and C. Wilhoit. 2006. *The American journalist in the 21st century: U.S. news people at the dawn of a new millennium.* London: Routledge.

Weissberg, R. 1998. *Political tolerance: balancing community and diversity.* Thousand Oaks, CA: Sage.

Wexler, J. 1997. Of pandas and people: The constitutionality of teaching intelligent design in the public schools. *Stanford Law Review* 49.

Wexler, J. 2002. Preparing for the clothed public square: Teaching about religion, civic education, and the constitution. *William and Mary Law Review* 43.

Wexler, J. 2003. Darwin, design, and disestablishment: Teaching the evolution controversy in public schools. *Vanderbilt Law Review* 56.

Weyrich, P. 2008. School book demeans God. *Newsmax,* May 29.

White, A. 2004. Interview by Emile Lester. October 10.

Wilcox, C. 1996. *Onward Christian soldiers? The religious right in American politics.* Boulder, CO: Westview.

*Wiley v. Franklin.* 1979. 468 F. Supp. 133.

Williams, B. 1996. Toleration: An impossible virtue. In *Toleration: An elusive virtue,* ed. D. Heyd. Princeton: Princeton University Press.

Wills, G. 1990. *Under God: Religion and American politics.* New York: Simon and Schuster.

Wilogren, J. 2005. Politicized scholars put evolution on the defensive. *New York Times,* August 21.

Wolfe, A. 2000. The opening of the evangelical mind. *Atlantic Monthly,* October.

Wolfe, A. 2003. *The transformation of American religion: How we actually live our faith.* New York: Free Press.

Wright, R. 2000. *Nonzero: The logic of human destiny.* New York: Pantheon Books.

Wright, R. 2009. *The evolution of God.* New York: Little, Brown.

Wuthnow, R. 2004. Presidential address 2003: The challenge of diversity. *Journal for the Scientific Study of Religion* 43.

Wyers, N. L. 1987. Homosexuality in the family: Lesbian and gay spouses. *Social Work* 32.

Yerby, W. 1989. Towards religious neutrality in the public school curriculum. *University of Chicago Law Review* 56.

Yoshino, K. 2006. *Covering.* New York: Random House.

Young, C. 2010. Reality check in the ground zero mosque debate. Real Clear Politics, August 20. http://www.realclearpolitics.com/articles/2010/ 08/20/reality _check_in_the_ground_zero_mosque_debate_106840.html.

Zeek, P. 2004. Interview by Emile Lester. October 13.

# Index

Page numbers in italic indicate tables or figures.

304    INDEX

Miller, William Lee, 194, 209, 273n4
Modesto, California
    as a case study, 106–8
    community support of world religions
        course, 8, 9, 101, 112–13, 228
    covering among religious minorities
        in, 23
    demographics of, 108–10
    harassment of students in, 105, 111, 115
    Hindu community in, 1–2
    political diversity in, 109
    religious diversity in, 108–10
    symbolic intolerance in, 26, 253n15
    See also world religions course,
        Modesto's
moral consensus and democracy, 81
moral development as justification for
    teaching intelligent design, 169–70
moral disagreement, 82, 87
morality
    the Bible and, 200
    evolution and, 169–70
    as outcome of democratic debate,
        81–82
    preservation of, 175
    relativism and, 35
    religion and, 170, 199
    sexual, 210, 212, 214
    similarity among religions, 126, 129–30
Moral Majority, 84
Morris, Henry, 157–58
Mozert v. Hawkins County Board of Educa-
    tion (1987), 255n25
multicultural education, 35, 40–41, 45
Multiculturalism and "the Politics of Recog-
    nition," (Taylor), 32
Murray, John Courtney, 226, 276n26
Muslims
    anti-Muslim sentiment, 25, 31, 252n10,
        253n12
    favorability of Americans toward,
        24–25, 252n11
    fears of elites toward, 31
    in Modesto, 108
    religious covering of, 24, 252n7
mutual exclusivity of religious beliefs,
    37–40, 173, 244–45

National Association of Evangelicals, 80,
    214, 219

National Center for Science Education,
    150, 156
National Council on Bible Curriculum in
    Public Schools (NCBCPS), 219, 222,
    277nn30–32
natural inclusion
    of the Bible, 216, 276n23
    of religion, 49–51
naturalism, methodological, 158–59,
    165–66
Neuhaus, Richard John, 65, 274n5
neutrality
    in Bible courses, 205–6, 208, 215–16,
        217
    in multicultural education for religious
        intolerance, 40
    relativism in curriculum as violation
        of, 34–35
    of teaching religion in elective courses,
        184–86
    of textbooks, 219
Newman, Jay, 36–37
Niebuhr, Reinhold, 231–32, 272n1
Noll, Mark, 216
Nord, Warren, 54–56, 96–97, 98, 159,
    257n38, 260n20, 267n5, 270nn25–26,
    272n36
North Carolina textbooks, 54
Notes on the State of Virginia (Jefferson),
    213
Nussbaum, Martha, 67

Obama, Barack
    and ending of religious and cultural
        conflicts, 15, 239, 243, 281n1
    evangelical voters and, 236–38
    redescription of nonsectarian argu-
        ments, 167
    religious prejudice against, 47, 253n12
    reversal of gag rule, 238, 240, 243
Oberdiek, Hans, 18
objective value
    of cultures, 32
    of religious beliefs, 45–48
O'Connor, Sandra Day, 187
Of Pandas and People (Davis and Kenyon),
    175, 269n18
old earth creationism. See intelligent de-
    sign
Oppenheim, Sam, 110, 123

stigma, religion as, 22
Stolzenberg, Nomi, 59
subjective validity, use of surveys to measure, 48
subjective value vs. objective value of beliefs, 45–48
Sullivan, Andrew, 235–36, 241, 247, 281n1
Sullivan, John, 27
Sunday schools, 208–9
Supreme Court, U.S., 249n2
    citing of research on postabortion syndrome, 84
    compelling interest test, 36, 174
    Compulsory School Act and, 62
    establishment clause cases and, 186–88
    standards for what counts as religion, 152–53, 171
    teaching of creationism, 149, 154, 168–69
    treatment of Bible in schools, 199, 280n41
    young earth creationism and, 158, 168–69
    *See also individual court cases*
surveys
    close-ended, 69–70
    to measure recognition of subjective and objective validity, 48
    on Modesto's world religions course, 51–52, 113–14, 261n5, 262nn6–8, 262n10
    perceptions of Muslims as threat to civil order, 43, 256n28
    on religious intolerance, 25
    *See also* polls
symbolic intolerance. *See under* intolerance, religious
sympathetic imagination vs. empathy, 46–47, 256n29, 260n15
syncretism, 34–35, 52, 126–27, 255n23

*Taking Religion Seriously across the Curriculum* (Nord and Haynes), 55
Taylor, Charles, 41, 42, 60
Taylor, Yvonne, 119, 120, 137, 138, 148
teachers, 138, 141–44, 270n26, 279n38
technology, 73, 156–57
televangelists, 75
Teresa, Mother, 220
textbooks, 53–54, 221–25, 256n33

Thomas, Oliver, 6
Thompson, Dennis, 82–83, 85–90, 91
Thorp, Holden, 156–57
threat perception, 24, 131–32, *132*, 252n10, 264nn23–24
Tillich, Paul, 20
Tiwari, Parmanand, 1, 4, 7, 8, 12–13, 30, 108
Tocqueville, Alexis de, 36, 194, 201, 218, 225
tolerance, religious, 17–18
    definition of, 18, 21
    education and, 130–31
    elites and, 31, 254n20
    factors affecting, 131–35, *133*
    immutability of religious beliefs and, 22
    knowledge of religions and, 42–45, 47–48, 107
    of "least-liked" groups, 116–17, *117*
    vs. lesser sensitivity, 21
    promotion of, 18–19, 51–52, 147, 254n19
    as recognition, 13
    religious minorities and, 7
    school policies of, 33–35
    social interaction and, 134
    synonymous with teaching religious liberty, 10
    *See also* active tolerance; intolerance, religious; passive tolerance
Tomasi, John, 94
Toumey, Christopher, 157, 160, 190, 272n32
tract societies, 209
truth claims, religious
    evolution/intelligent design elective courses and, 188
    as mutually exclusive, 37–40, 244–45
    recognizing legitimacy of, 40
    scientific approach to, 189–91, 272n32

*United States v. Seeger* (1965), 152–53
"Urgent Call to Action" statement (National Association of Evangelicals), 80

vandalism, 1–2, 6, 7, 109–10
vital center, politics of, 193–94, 195, 241, 272n1, 273n3